Black Pro Se

FAITH BARTER

Black Pro Se

Authorship and the Limits of
Law in Nineteenth-Century
African American Literature

The University of North Carolina Press *Chapel Hill*

© 2025 Faith Barter
All rights reserved
Set in Arno Pro by Westchester Publishing Services
Manufactured in the United States of America

Library of Congress Cataloging-in-Publication Data
Names: Barter, Faith Elizabeth, author.
Title: Black pro se : authorship and the limits of law in nineteenth-century African American literature / Faith Barter.
Description: Chapel Hill : The University of North Carolina Press, 2025. | Includes bibliographical references and index.
Identifiers: LCCN 2024044999 | ISBN 9781469685960 (cloth) | ISBN 9781469685977 (paperback) | ISBN 9781469685984 (epub) | ISBN 9781469687711 (pdf)
Subjects: LCSH: American literature—African American authors—History and criticism. | American literature—19th century—History and criticism. | Law and literature—United States—History—19th century. | BISAC: LITERARY CRITICISM / American / African American & Black | LAW / Legal History | LCGFT: Literary criticism.
Classification: LCC PS153.B53 B37 2025 | DDC 810.9/896073—dc23/eng/20240930
LC record available at https://lccn.loc.gov/2024044999

Cover art by E. L. Trouvelot, 1881–82, New York Public Library.

This book will be made open access within three years of publication thanks to Path to Open, a program developed in partnership between JSTOR, the American Council of Learned Societies (ACLS), University of Michigan Press, and The University of North Carolina Press to bring about equitable access and impact for the entire scholarly community, including authors, researchers, libraries, and university presses around the world. Learn more at https://about.jstor.org/path-to-open/.

For James, who always knows just what to say.

Contents

Acknowledgments ix

Introduction 1

CHAPTER ONE
Appeal 39

CHAPTER TWO
Confession 67

CHAPTER THREE
Jurisdiction 105

CHAPTER FOUR
Precedent 136

Coda: African American Literary Futures and Law's Possibilities 167

Notes 179

Bibliography 199

Index 209

Acknowledgments

It is, in equal measures, hard to imagine a time of my life when this book was not in progress, and hard to believe that it has reached a stage of fruition. My difficulty in fixing points of beginning or ending has its counterpart in my sense of deep overwhelm when I try to name the people and institutions to whom this work is indebted. That this book exists as a bound or digital *object* continues to enchant, move, and mystify me, and it represents the culmination of a Big Life Dream. It would not be so at all without the many teachers, colleagues, interlocutors, friends, and humans whose fingerprints and signatures linger in the margins of each page. My various communities have challenged me, held me and held space for me, sharpened my sense of this work, and urged me on from nascent ideas up through final revisions. I hope that my work—and that I personally—have honored your time, labor, care, and generosity. It has been my great privilege to be in conversation, dreams, and imagination with you.

Before proceeding, I must first acknowledge the Black writers, dreamers, and visionaries around whom this book revolves and breathes, as well as their ancestors and their descendants, both literal and otherwise. Their histories are bound up with mine but are not mine to claim as my own. The sense of responsibility that I feel around their histories and actual biographies cannot be overstated; I have endeavored to move through this project with the deepest reverence and respect for the human beings whose creativity, knowledge, labor, and vitality I engage here. That work has been spiritual as well as intellectual, and it has traveled and evolved with me. It is not my place to "do justice" to or for these writers—among others, Harriet Jacobs, Jane Johnson, Nat Turner, David Walker, Mary Ann Shadd Cary, Victor Séjour, Hannah Crafts, John Russwurm, Samuel Cornish, and James Williams/Jim Thornton/Shadrach Wilkins. Rather, in *their* intricate and innovative ways of theorizing and doing justice, themselves, they have challenged, inspired, haunted, and urged me into something like a student's devotion or, perhaps, commitment (if that is a strong enough word).

I know that it is common to reserve some of the more personal and less "formal" acknowledgments until the end of a document like this, but there are several dear friends and colleagues whose "informal" contributions to this project are so outsized as to merit top billing. First, Petal Samuel has been an unparalleled interlocutor, colleague, and friend since we were cohort-mates at Vanderbilt. Over the past few years in particular, her insights, friendship, and engagement in regular writing sessions have been unmatched. I have learned so much from her scholarship and her observations, and while I have tried to document the places in this book that arose in direct conversation with her, it would literally be impossible to fully annotate her presence in these pages. She is the most generous reader—I can scarcely believe that we have been talking about these things since 2011, but that longevity gives some context for the depth of her influence. Likewise, I am so grateful to have crossed paths at Oregon with Shoniqua Roach and V Chaudhry, and even more grateful to remain in ongoing community and dialogue with them— their brilliance, judgment, and friendship have consistently energized and encouraged me. Finally, throughout the height of the pandemic, I regularly met (virtually) with a group of nineteenth-century Americanists—Kristin Allukian, R. J. Boutelle (another fellow Vandy cohort-mate), Monica Mercado, and Alice Rutkowski—whose community and fellowship perpetually elevated my work. I do not think I could have asked for better support, friendship, and insight than I have received from these brilliant souls.

As is already apparent, as this book has evolved, it has traveled through numerous institutions, audiences, and contexts, most recently at the University of North Carolina Press. Without exception, the staff at UNC Press have been kind, professional, and sharp, but Lucas Church deserves special thanks for his enthusiasm and patience. He has been encouraging and communicative at each stage, and with incredible help from Thomas Bedenbaugh and the editorial staff, he deftly shepherded this book through the review and publication process. I have trusted Lucas implicitly from start to finish. He solicited manuscript reviewers who offered sensitive, generous, and rigorous feedback that undeniably elevated the quality of the project in ways large and small—I am deeply grateful to the reviewers for attuning me to areas of strength and opportunity and pressing me to refine the project's stakes and investments. Their feedback helped me find the language and framing for some of the book's trickiest corners and most elusive questions, and it produced a noticeable level-up during the revision stage.

Likewise, I benefited from several stages of manuscript review at different stages in my writing process. Samantha Pinto's manuscript review illuminated many of the project's contributions that begged for deeper attention, and her generosity in reading my work in progress helped me advance the project toward press submission. Thanks to Courtney Thorsson for assisting me in holding this workshop, and for her support as a mentor and friend over these past few years. I am deeply grateful to her for her guidance, advice, and support—her scholarship has been a model, as has her presence as a colleague and mentor at the University of Oregon.

Meanwhile, in 2020, just as a global pandemic shut down the entire world, I was privileged to participate (virtually) in the First Book Institute at Pennsylvania State University, under the incredible leadership of Sean Goudie and Priscilla Wald, and with special thanks to Carrie Hyde, who attended as a respondent for my work, and Justin Smith, who kept us all on track and participated so thoughtfully in our workshops. My experience at the First Book Institute was instrumental for the project and for giving me a sustained community of interlocutors during a time when isolation was at its peak. Thanks to my fellow cohort-mates—Andrew Belton, David Hollingshead, Renee Hudson, Justin Mann, Paul Nadal, Danica Savonick, and Ana Schwartz—whose conversations and friendship gave me confidence and enthusiasm at a crucial stage, and whose suggestions transformed the project and my relationship to it. In subsequent years, I have come to rely in particular on support from Justin, Renee, and Ana—thank you all for the affirmation, joy, and solidarity.

I received crucial research fellowship support from the Oregon Humanities Center, where I especially owe a debt of gratitude to my wonderful departmental colleague Paul Peppis, as well as to Melissa Gustafson, Peg Gearheart, and Jena Turner. Thanks to those who attended my work-in-progress talk at the OHC, and to the other research and teaching fellows there, whose community has been so enriching. Humanities centers have been foundational in the project's evolution, as I also benefited from a dissertation completion fellowship at the Robert Penn Warren Center for the Humanities at Vanderbilt University, where Mona Frederick's leadership was outstanding. In that final year of the dissertation, I was working on early versions of some of the work that eventually became this book, and the fellows in that cohort were incredible peers and colleagues: Michell Chresfield, Jonathan Coley, Alexander Jacobs, Michelle O'Loughlin, Petal Samuel, and Sandy Skene.

Some of that work begun during my PhD eventually became an early version of my chapter on precedent—this work appeared in article form in *MELUS*, where I am grateful for the support of Gary Totten and the editorial staff, the anonymous reviewers whose feedback helped me improve my argument, and for research and copyediting assistance from Rosa Smith and Kate Epstein. The research for that portion of the book was also supported by the

William Nelson Cromwell Foundation and the Association for the Study of Legal History—I am especially grateful to John Gordan, who shared materials from his personal collection and whose generosity on this front was incredible. I am further indebted to Simon Stern at the University of Toronto for his interest in the project, for his help in thinking with me about Mary Ann Shadd Cary, and especially for inviting me to participate in the Law and Literature Works in Progress Webinar, where I received incredible feedback on my jurisdiction research from Jeannine DeLombard (who also thought with me about Mary Ann Shadd Cary and whose work has long been a model for me) and others.

I have truly had an embarrassment of riches in the mentorship and teaching department. My teachers at St. Mary's School and Cony High School in Augusta, Maine nurtured my earliest interest in literature, law, and racial justice. My professors at Dartmouth College—especially William Cook, Ivy Schweitzer, Melissa Zeiger, Donald Pease, and Steven Kangas—helped me appreciate the bigness of the world and were early models for my dream of becoming a college professor. At Washington College of Law, I was privileged to learn from Steven Wermiel, Robert Vaughn, and especially Penny Pether. Penny's mentorship and support as I made the difficult decision to leave my law practice was foundational, and she was my first model for scholarship in law and literature. She was also the first person to make me see myself as a future scholar. She affirmed a decision that others would have written off as chaotic or reckless, and I dearly wish that she were here to see this book reach publication—I hope that she would be proud. Speaking of my legal practice, that period of my life was a crucial stage in my intellectual and professional journey, and I had the good fortune to work with and for some of the sharpest minds I have ever encountered—thanks are due to my mentors Steven Ross and Patricia Millett, and to my very good friends and colleagues but especially Erin Peters, Beth Beacham, Dana Singiser, Gary Heimberg, and Katie Creely, and to all of the staff at Akin Gump, but especially Mary Ellen Moltumyr for her kindness and support.

My mentors at Vanderbilt deserve tremendous credit for taking me from corporate lawyer to scholar of nineteenth-century African American literature. Their knowledge, care, support, and good humor held me during a period of intense personal and intellectual growth. Colin Dayan's brilliance offered a captivating example of what it means to think about law at its limits; her prose has held me in its sway since I first encountered it, and her readerly eye is the one I am still so often addressing. Teresa Goddu's deep integrity and rigor have taught me so much about the ethics of moving through this profession, and I am forever grateful that one of my first graduate school seminars was hers on early African American print culture—my chapter on precedent began as a response paper in that class. I hope to one day approach her talents as a close reader. Mark Schoenfield's generosity and malleability were incredibly formative—I always knew I could trust his reading of my work, his suggestions for revision and future reading, and his judgment. Dan Sharfstein consistently amazed me with his fluency in literary history, and he made me see legal scholarship with new eyes. I will never understand how he has read every book. My outside dissertation reader, Christopher Tomlins, has likewise been a hugely influential scholar and legal historian whose generosity pushed my work in the dissertation and with whom I am thrilled to be in conversation about Nat Turner in my chapter on confession.

There were many other Vanderbilt faculty and staff whose work, support, and example have elevated my work and my person, especially Kathryn Schwarz, Hortense Spillers, Vera Kutzinski, Dana Nelson, Jay Clayton, Mark Wollaeger, Scott Juengel, Jennifer Fay, Rachel Teukolsky, Janis May, and Donna Caplan. The same is true for my classmates and friends there, who shaped this project in countless ways over late-night conversations, beverages, walks, and in seminars. I am especially grateful for the friendship and feedback I have received over the years from Emily August (who continues to dazzle and brainstorm with me), Nikki Spigner, Kat De Guzman, Lucy Mensah, Annie Castro, Dan Fang, Aubrey Porterfield, Tatiana McInnis, and Wietske Smeele. While at Vanderbilt, I participated in two important workshops/institutes: The Futures of American Studies Institute at Dartmouth College, where Soyica Colbert's seminar was a source of incredible conversation, fellowship, and support, and the graduate student workshop at the Association for the Study of Law, Culture, and Humanities, where I felt so fortunate to connect with other graduate students working at intersections of law and the humanities.

More recently, my participation in Derrick Spires's and Carrie Hyde's C19 seminar on citizenship brought me into truly energizing conversation with scholars in citizenship studies and helped me think through some of the questions around belonging and the state that are at the heart of this book. Over the years, I have benefited in countless ways from thoughtful questions and observations when I have presented my work at the American Studies Association, the National Women's Studies Association, the American Literature Association, Law & Society, and the Association for the Study of Law, Culture, & the Humanities. Thank you to everyone who has attended my talks or simply struck up conversation at an event. And thank you to the librarians and archivists everywhere, but especially at the University of Oregon, Howard University Moorland-Spingarn, the University of North Carolina, and the Schomburg Center, all of which I visited at various points and different stages of research and writing of the dissertation and then the book.

Deepest thanks as well to Michelle McKinley and the Center for the Study of Women in Society at University of Oregon. Michelle's organization of a women's work-in-progress group during my first few years at UO gave me the confidence to share my work in other spaces and offered me important community; her friendship and mentorship has likewise been so important. In addition to Michelle, Courtney, and Shoniqua, I am grateful to so many of my colleagues in English at UO, whose support shaped this book in myriad ways. I especially owe thanks to Tara Fickle, Brendan Kelly, Sarah Wald, José Cortez, Brent Dawson, Mattie Burkert, Kara Clevinger, Kirby Brown, Avinnash Tiwari, Stacy Alaimo, Mary Wood, Liz Bohls, Eleanor Wakefield, Lara Bovilsky, Mat Johnson, Quinn Miller, Mark Whalan, and so many others for being friends and colleagues—and for being people I am happy to see on campus. Thank you to Leslie Alexander, whose time overlapping with mine at UO was entirely too short. Thank you to my colleagues in Black Studies, especially Charise Cheney, for building a Black Studies community at UO. Thank you to all of my students but especially to the graduate students I have worked with most closely, because being a mentor to you has consistently pushed me to grow as a scholar and human: Carmel Ohman, Emalydia Flenory, Holly Lowe Jones, Jalen Thompson, Jessie Heine, Jiesha Stephens, Megan Butler, and Rosa Smith. I have learned so much from being in conversation with you during our writing group meetings especially.

Thank you to my family, especially to my parents, Marg and Phil, for standing back and giving me room to try things even when you may have been skeptical; to my sister Hope; and to my irreplaceable Nana who passed away before I completed my PhD. You have shaped me and nurtured me more than you know, and I owe you so much. The same is true for my friend family; some of the realest ones are civilians who have not yet been mentioned: Megan Bastey, who schlepped several hours away to hear me present work from my jurisdiction chapter, and Kymberlie Quong-Charles, with whom I have been talking about racial justice since the 1990s.

Finally, James. I could have mentioned you in so many of the paragraphs above, but I wanted to save you for last. You have been here through Nashville and Oregon and Montreal and many, many nights when I didn't think I could do it. Through coffees and records and vrooms and pomodoros and scratches and our orange cats, through airports and trains, through hours spent hunched over laptops, reading third or fourth revisions. There is no way to measure your influence and brilliance, your presence on every page; no way to sufficiently capture the sharpness of your mind or the generosity of your spirit or the depth of my gratitude for all of the gifts that you share so freely. I love you.

Black Pro Se

Introduction

"We wish to plead our own cause. Too long have others spoken for us." This introduction unfolds in three parts, each of which begins by returning to these two sentences from the inaugural (1827) issue of *Freedom's Journal*, a Black abolitionist newspaper that also holds the distinction as the first newspaper owned and operated by African Americans.[1] We begin this first pass with the testimonial dimensions of the text, to acknowledge the importance of testimony and witnessing in the history of African American literature but also to make visible the ways that other legal and literary features might be obscured by a frame that begins and ends with the testimonial. We then make several additional orbits around these two sentences from *Freedom's Journal*, traveling in concentric circles that establish the context, stakes, and intervention of the book's argument about the centrality of legal form in antebellum Black writing.

In practice, the use of a legal form can take many shapes. Though this book closely examines Black writers' use of four specific legal forms—appeal, confession, jurisdiction, and precedent—legal forms in general are capacious and portable strategies that enable one to reflect on, challenge, negotiate, and reimagine the structures that govern everyday life. By examining their use of legal form in autobiography as well as early fiction, I show how Black writers in the nineteenth century not only documented the violence of law by bearing witness to it; they also used legal form as an alembic in which to transmute their legal realities and imagine alternative legal worlds. While witnessing foregrounds the documentation of "real" events that happened in the past, other legal forms center the future, the speculative possibilities of worlds that do not yet but might one day exist. Other legal forms are surprisingly suitable containers for experimentation in fiction.

That proximity between law and fiction is central to the book's broader claims. The title, *Black Pro Se*, references the practice of pro se advocacy, in which a litigant acts as their own lawyer in judicial proceedings. But the title also plays on the coincidental semantic intimacy between pro se and prose, a lucky correspondence that signals Black writers' use of legal form and pro se advocacy across literary genres and styles, suggesting a deeper affinity between law and literature in general. This book is ultimately about how Black writers use legal form to remake their relationship to (1) place, by theorizing structures of belonging that transcend place- or nation-bound logics of sovereignty, and (2) time, by leveraging law's temporal unfixity in service of counterfactuals and retrospective reviews that practice futurist possibility by reimagining the past.

The First Pass: Witnessing and Testimony

Indeed we begin retrospectively, by approaching John Russwurm and Samuel Cornish through the explosion of Black autobiography and testimonial writing in the decades that followed their 1827 column. With the benefit of that context, it may seem fairly obvious to read this passage through a lens of witnessing and testimony. It is also crucial because it helps demonstrate the fluency and nuance in legal thinking among Black writers. And testimony, as the ostensible container for the freedom narrative literary genre, in many ways acted as a carrier for the other legal forms with which freedom narrative authors experimented. As I suggest in this first pass, however, an overattachment to testimony may cause us to miss the other legal possibilities and literary innovations in this body of literature, particularly in its connection to early African American fiction.

"We wish to plead our own cause. Too long have others spoken for us."[2] Here Russwurm and Cornish appear to call explicitly for Black testimony—for Black thinkers and writers to speak for themselves, about their own experiences, in their own words. The word "our" appears more than sixty times in this relatively brief (approximately 1,500 words) column, an indication of the shared claim of identity that Russwurm and Cornish signal—an "us" that stands in contradistinction to an implied but unnamed "them." The call for Black testimony relies explicitly on that tension and difference, as they write, "Too long has the publick been deceived by misrepresentations in things which concern us dearly."[3] Testimony in this context seeks to document, to supplement an "official" or dominant record in a way that more fully accounts for the experiences of the oppressed—to set the record straight, as it were, in a world of mis- and disinformation.

The specific posture of witnessing or testifying within early African American literature was significant for several reasons. First, legal rules throughout the American South frequently prohibited Black people from testifying in court, or from bringing lawsuits (though I complicate this assertion later in this introduction). To offer testimony in any public space, including print, was therefore a repudiation of the legal regimes then in effect and a claim to fuller legal personhood. But testifying also carries significance as a Black religious practice and feature of Black life. As Rosetta Ross observes, "As moral practice, the significance of witnessing and testifying (like other resources from religious communities) lies in the possibility and hope these practices bring to common civic life.... Witness and testimony carry religious values and practices into the public square, and identify and pass on values that help form other individuals as religious persons."[4] Even in discussing testimony as a spiritual project, Ross relies on the language of personhood to communicate the significance and identity-making capacity inherent in bearing witness. Thus, to offer testimony, to act as a witness—whether of God, or of oneself—is to claim not only legal, but spiritual, being.

Against this backdrop, and even considering the ways that many freedom narratives were mediated by white abolitionist voices, it is impossible to overstate the significance and radical potential of publishing firsthand accounts of slavery by Black writers. Their narration of the everyday violence of enslavement spoke the unspeakable, unearthing and giving air to the ongoing histories embedded in US culture and the bloodied grounds on which false mythologies of equality and democracy were being crafted. As Karla Holloway writes, "When enslaved Africans in America wrote autobiography and memoir and claimed their membership in a human race with narratives that opened with some version of 'I was born,' it was a form of black back talk to the Constitution of the newly formed nation."[5] The freedom narrative's ostensible embrace of realism has proven alluring as a discursive register that could symbolically and materially "give voice" to Black writers, affording them civic access to and in the public square.

Of course, that liberatory potential is not without its limits. We must consider, as one example, the genre's popularity among white readers and its propensity to indulge white attachments to Black pain and suffering. In her reading of Frederick Douglass's description of his aunt Hester's brutal beating, and as part of her theorization of subjection, Saidiya Hartman writes that "the terrible spectacle dramatizes the origin of the subject and demonstrates that to be a slave is to be under the brutal power and authority of another."[6] Hartman's framing of subjection helps bring into view the ways that the genre's spectacular treatment of Black pain reaffirms and recenters structures of white power or, as she puts it, "the ways that the recognition of humanity and individuality acted to tether, bind, and oppress."[7] It also demonstrates why even the study of these autobiographies can feel circumscribed by the spectacular violence that produced them and to which their authors spoke back. Nevertheless, this complicated history of witnessing's relationship to violence is the very thing that Jennifer Nash regards as its superpower; Nash theorizes witnessing as a Black feminist act "of political world-making" by considering that Black women's labor to "name, to make visible, to again and again describe and analyze structures of domination" helps undo forms of violence and oppression that otherwise remain unchallenged.[8]

This broader context for the significance of witnessing frames why speaking in public, but especially in print, was such a radical and dangerous matter of political urgency; it further shows how testimony offered such fertile ground for literary experimentation that Russwurm and Cornish foreground the call to publicness in their inaugural issue. Note how their use of language sets up a tension between publicness and quiet,[9] between registering an awareness of a potentially hostile audience while marking forms of shared Black experience and knowledge: the passive-voiced construction ("Too long has the publick been deceived by misrepresentations") implies an unnamed agent responsible for deceptions about Black life; "misrepresentations" is the subject of the passive verb, abstracting responsibility for the deceptions away from a human agent altogether. The phrasing implies that "the publick" is a white group, as Black readers surely would not be deceived about or misrepresent themselves. But the shiftiness of these terms throughout the column makes it difficult to discern with certainty which groups are inside or outside this hazy sphere of "the publick" at any given time. By hewing to the language of "us" and "our" throughout the piece, Russwurm and Cornish make clear that a Black audience is their primary audience of address, even though they expect to be overheard by white allies as well as antagonists.[10] In this way, their persistent address to Black readers is a performance of Black solidarity that serves multiple purposes for their multiple audiences.

These slippery taxonomies underscore the existence of shared Black knowledge and community—visible in the many unelaborated references to "us" and "our" concerns, as well as references to "our brethren" and "us as a people"—as well as the vexed relationship of both enslaved and free(d) Black people in relation to a white public and, by extension, the state. Their liminal spatial relation to publicness—which, crucially, is introduced through the legal language of "pleading one's own cause"—gestures toward the many ways that law and custom sought to exclude Black people from the protections of public, civic life, as well as the fact that those systems did not succeed at fully effecting these exclusions. Within this context, the call to "plead our own cause" is a call to speak Black life and Black knowledge in public, even if not as a member of "the" public.[11] Russwurm and Cornish exhort their fellow in-group members to bear witness as a corrective measure, to produce a public account of Black life in order to generate a critical reorientation to the history and narrative of legalized slavery.[12]

Reliance on public Black testimony was a fundamental component of both white and Black abolitionism, driving the rise of the freedom narrative[13] in the nineteenth century and much of the scholarly and critical conversation around that genre in the twentieth and twenty-first centuries. The need for Black testimony in abolitionist strategy is straightforward: legalized slavery was a brutal, genocidal culture that deliberately sought to silence enslaved people and depended on a collective regard for them as subhuman in order to maintain the complicity and acquiescence of the greater public in the North and the South. Although Black people have always written about, sung about, and made art about their lives, the structural qualities of legalized slavery included anti-literacy laws that sought to keep enslaved people from learning to read or write, prohibitions on enslaved people bringing lawsuits or testifying in court, and repudiations of citizenship as an available status for African Americans.[14] Families were frequently separated, sold and traded to different places with no way to communicate or even know where their loved ones were. The bureaucracy of legalized slavery persistently sought to dehumanize enslaved people; the business of slavery produced recordkeeping regimes that failed to capture or retain data about individual enslaved people; and through the mechanism of *partus sequitur ventrem*, the heritability of slavery operated such that, as Marisa Fuentes writes, "white women made free humans and enslaved women birthed other slaves."[15] These bureaucratic practices institutionalized the reproduction of slavery and cut off access to family histories for generations of enslaved people's descendants. The archival gaps that reverberate into the present day originated out of a broader network of practices designed to limit Black access to and sharing of information during the eighteenth and nineteenth centuries.

For instance, in her 1861 text *Incidents in the Life of a Slave Girl*, Harriet Jacobs describes the ways that enslavers deliberately misled enslaved people about conditions in the North to discourage their attempts to escape.[16] And in that first issue of *Freedom's Journal* in 1827, Russwurm and Cornish write, "We are aware that there [are] many instances of vice among us, but we avow that it is because no one has taught its subjects to be virtuous: many instances of poverty, because no sufficient efforts accommodated to minds contracted by slavery, and deprived of early education have been made, to teach them how to husband their hard earnings, and to secure themselves comforts."[17] David Walker, who was affiliated with *Freedom's Journal*, would make similar claims several years later in his 1829 *Appeal to the Coloured Citizens of the World*.[18] In exposing the conditions of Black life for a white audience inclined to ignore the full violence of legalized slavery or to believe myths of benevolent slaveholding, disclosures from enslaved, formerly enslaved, and free Black people were necessary to what might be described in more modern terms as a consciousness-raising effort and a campaign to combat widespread misinformation about the nature of slavery and enslaved people. But beyond the need to counter the structural violence and apparatuses of state-sanctioned slavery, as Charles Davis and Henry Louis Gates Jr. have observed, Black testimony—particularly via the genre of the slave narrative—"arose as a response to and refutation of claims that blacks *could* not write."[19] Despite the legal frameworks that actively sought to criminalize Black literacy throughout the South, persistent anti-Black stereotypes stretching back to Thomas Jefferson figured African-descended people as biologically incapable of producing literature.[20]

In their call for Black testimony, Russwurm and Cornish predate and anticipate the rise of the slave narrative, or freedom narrative, a genre that had not yet reached widespread popularity in 1827, though narratives had already been published by Olaudah Equiano, Venture Smith, and Ottobah Cugoano, among others.[21] Mary Prince's narrative would be published four years later, in 1831,[22] but the genre's rise in popularity would not begin in earnest for almost two decades until the 1845 publication of *Narrative of the Life of Frederick Douglass, an American Slave*.[23] Of course, Douglass's *Narrative* also marked a turn toward the mass production of freedom narratives by white antislavery societies. According to Documenting the American South at the Library of the University of North Carolina at Chapel Hill, there were thirty-two North American slave narratives published between the years 1740 and 1839. By contrast, twenty-five such narratives were published between 1840 and 1849, and another thirty-three narratives were published between 1850 and 1859. In other words, in the decade before the Civil War, there were roughly as many narratives published as in the entire century between 1740 and 1840.[24] That steep incline in publication and thus readership coincides with the appropriation of the genre in the 1840s by white abolitionist networks,[25] an appropriation so linked to the genre's critical afterlife that there persists a notion that Douglass originated the freedom narrative genre—despite the fact that his text arrives nearly a century into the genre's history.

The documentary importance of these narratives cannot be overstated for their urgency in a nineteenth-century world where anti-Blackness structured the overt, everyday violence that accompanied, authorized, and sustained legalized slavery. The ideological maneuvers that verify such large-scale violence depend on narratives that obscure, mislead, and misdirect, but also on control over production of narratives in the first place. The rise of the freedom narrative, along with the rise of a fast-growing Black press in the first half of the nineteenth century (see, e.g., Russwurm and Cornish), countered white-controlled narratives that either actively promoted slavery or thought about abolition as a site of potential white largesse for an abject Black population.

In accounting for the history and rise of the freedom narrative, it is useful to think of the genre's several major waves and afterlives: first, in its eighteenth- and nineteenth-century circulation; second, in mid-twentieth-century oral and narrative history projects including those sponsored by the Works Progress Administration; third, in the late twentieth century as part of efforts by Black scholars to develop African American studies curricula and to rewrite canons of American literature; and fourth, in the creation of twentieth- and twenty-first-century neo-slave narratives.[26] A rich body of literary scholarship on the genre emerged in the late twentieth century, including William Andrews's 1986 *To Tell a Free Story: The First Century of Afro-American Autobiography, 1760–1865*; Hazel Carby's 1987 *Reconstructing Womanhood: The Emergence of the Afro-American Woman Novelist*, which links the genre to the rise of the novel; Valerie Smith's 1987 *Self-Discovery and Authority in Afro-American Narrative*; and the 1993 William Andrews–edited volume, *African American Autobiography: A Collection of Critical Essays*, which featured Black feminist interventions by Carby and Deborah McDowell.[27] The genre has thus been central to African American literary traditions during its initial wave and during the establishment and proliferation of African American literary studies and Black studies curricula at universities and K-12 schools.

The genre's central feature, its documentation and depiction in literature of "realistic" everyday life, it is important to note, is a literary practice that did not really take root in American literature more broadly until the end of the Civil War. As Diana Polley observes, this literary and cultural movement emerged out of "a growing distrust of romance" and a need to, in light of the Civil War's aftermath, "face facts."[28] As such, the freedom narrative's investments in realistic documentation of slavery's violence—and Black survival— set it apart, at least theoretically, from the gothic and the romantic, the latter of which in particular is often located in binaristic opposition to realism.[29] At the same time, as Teresa Goddu has demonstrated, antebellum Black autobiography, precisely through its realism, also functions as a lever across which slavery's gothic dimensions haunt dominant national narratives, without resorting to "the gothic's romantic effects."[30] In other words, Black depictions of slavery's horrors leverage the unnaturalness and horror of the institution by calling attention to the ways that white everyday life naturalized and normalized genocide.

In attending to these graphic descriptions, despite acknowledging the realism of testimonial literature, scholars have also theorized depictions of Black pain in appeals and confessions in particular—two of the organizing legal logics in this book, and common containers for freedom narratives—within the frame of sentimentalism. Maria Windell traces "transamerican sentimentalism" in the autobiographies of Harriet Jacobs and Nat Turner, as well as the writings of Jacobs's brother, John S. Jacobs, and the early fiction of Frederick Douglass and Victor Séjour, observing that Black sentimental writing can both "activate possibilities for revolt"[31] and "align [] groups across national, racial, linguistic, and cultural divides based on their common struggles against US oppression."[32] Windell's examination of sentimentalism contextualizes depictions of Black harm through the political goals of either revolution or diplomacy, an approach that corresponds with Joycelyn Moody's formulation of African American women's use of sentimentalism to mobilize pathos in persuading authorities that anti-Black violence was "intolerable and unethical."[33] In this way, sentimentalism relies on sympathy, or, as Shirley Samuels puts it, "the act of emotional response the work evokes also produces the sentimental subject who consumes the work."[34] Testimony, deployed as a sentimental device, is ultimately an act of persuasion and intimate engagement between author and reader.

As with the logics of gothic and realist literature, the sentimental frame holds significant sway, as demonstrated by these sensitive and apt readings of Black writing; acts of witnessing and testimony in nineteenth-century Black writing speak in all of these registers, and others as well. The apparent slipperiness across or between literary movements speaks to the tendency of Black literature in general to frustrate logics of taxonomy and genre, to the point in the nineteenth century that the very line between fiction and nonfiction has historically been tricky for literary scholars to parse—both because of the intricacy of Black autobiography during this time and because of anti-Black suspicion around questions of "truth" and "authenticity," questions that themselves seem to run aground on an imaginary expanse between realism and all other literary modes. It is nevertheless significant that literary scholars have gravitated toward Black autobiographical writing by locating it within or around movements—like sentimentalism and romance—that are most closely associated with fiction writing. To be clear, I am not critiquing the impulse. On the contrary, it is deeply necessary for scholarship to acknowledge the eclectic and innovative archives that Black autobiographers engaged and reimagined. Those archives included intertexts in modes and movements ranging from political speech and rhetoric to fiction, spiritual traditions, and, as this book argues, law.

Throughout the slave narrative's critical treatment, scholars—particularly Black feminist scholars—have sought to enlarge our sense of the genre's narrative possibilities and to critique its reception among readers and critics. For example, Deborah McDowell has critiqued the positioning of Douglass as originator of the genre—a move that, as she argues, obscures Black women's experience and labor in a variety of ways. But McDowell also critiques the posturing of "origination" more broadly on a second order, as she notes the tendency to figure the slave narrative genre itself as the originator of African American literature: "Assertions that the slave narrative begins the African-American literary tradition are repeated so often that they have acquired the force of self-evident truth."[35] She proceeds to note that beyond the already well-trodden examination of the genre's "discrete, formal characteristics, a reconfigured genealogical model would examine the historical and cultural function of the slave narrative, both in the moment of its emergence and in contemporary scholarly discourse."[36]

More recent scholarship on the genre has taken up McDowell's call, often by exploring less common sites of Black narrative (Eric Gardner's formulation of "unexpected places" or Nicole Aljoe's study of testimonios embedded within other historical records, for instance[37]) or by bringing different methodologies to individual slave narratives (as with C. Riley Snorton's trans readings of Harriet Jacobs and William and Ellen Craft or Katherine McKittrick's Black feminist geographical approach to Jacobs[38]). However, there persist several strains in the scholarship on testimonial literature, in particular the freedom narrative, that we might link to the genre's status as a form of autobiographical writing.

First, there has occasionally been a tendency to dwell on the "authenticity" of freedom narratives in order to preserve their status as nonfiction—a trend that has particularly haunted texts by women writers like Harriet Jacobs and Hannah Crafts, but that also plagued James Williams. There are very good reasons to be invested in preserving the nonfiction status of the narratives, which slavery's apologists and proponents originally attempted to discredit as false.[39] But as Lindon Barrett points out, the nature of autobiography renders an autobiographical text inextricable from the author who produced it, a risk of all life writing "but with recognizably greater force in African

American autobiography."[40] Because of the anti-Black stereotypes that dismiss Black writers as incapable of producing literature, the attention to the "authenticity" of freedom narratives risks discourse that, in "discrediting" the texts as authentic autobiography, inadvertently reproduces the notion that Black writers are not *authors*—that they may be documentarians, or fraudsters, but not creators of literature. As a result, Black autobiographical writing is susceptible to treatment either as purely documentarian or as misrepresentation—categories that tend to deny artistry and/or moralize it as dishonesty.

This apparent paradox signals the capacity of Black literature in general, but especially autobiographical writing in the nineteenth century, to disrupt predominantly white literary genres. As Tavia Nyong'o has written about genre, "The hybridization of genre implied in the [phrase] miscegenation of time entails not simply the splicing together of different forms but the encounter of genre with its law and therein its indeterminacy. Exposing fictions of race and progress, hybridity unsettles collective and corporeal memory."[41] Though Nyong'o uses "law" colloquially here, the semantic link holds— genres, as normative structures, are themselves legal categories in nontrivial ways. As Nyong'o suggests, what appears to the eye as hybridity actually marks a moment of rupture, of operation that ought not be possible within a given category or rule. And Nyong'o's formulation contextualizes Lindon Barrett's connections between Black autobiography and law.

As Barrett notes, the pressures on African American autobiographers demand that they "revise or recast in the terms of their lives a story that is already (unacceptably) written—and writ large—by American law and custom."[42] Barrett's linkage of autobiography to law brings into view both testimony's utility as a frame for a law and literature approach to the freedom narrative, as well as the potential limitations that arise from fixing Black autobiographers solely as witnesses. As noted above, witnessing may appear to be a liberatory posture when considered as a response to legal prohibitions against Black testimony in court—a prohibition that often specifically applied to Black testimony against a white person.[43] In this framing, the page or the court of public opinion becomes an alternate site for litigating slavery and freedom, a way of putting "slavery on trial," to borrow from Jeannine DeLombard's formulation in her tract on print culture. To put slavery on trial produces an inversion, wherein slavery, not the enslaved person, is the accused criminal. Such an inversion does tremendous work to destabilize the mythologies that arise around legal institutions and to shift narratives concerning, for instance, the figure of the Black criminal or the impartial judge.

For this reason, testimony has proven a reliable analytic in studies of Black autobiography and other sites of Black legal witnessing.

In addition to Nicole Aljoe's work on embedded and fragmented testimonios in British West Indian archives, other scholars have likewise turned to the importance of testimony in textual contexts beyond the US freedom narrative. For example, Dwight McBride has traced the ways that Black witnessing and testimony in transatlantic slave narratives, poetry, and pamphlets staged abolitionist discourses that purported to offer access to "authentic" accounts by making the Black body the equivalent of nature, the equivalent of evidence.[44] Here I want to underscore that testimony—despite the way we think of it as offering a performative rendition of agency (a construction I have attempted to trouble here)—functions as a legal *object*. As a matter of law, testimony is evidence and thus subject to the rules of admissibility. Evidence, once introduced in a trial context, is submitted to the jury for their evaluation of its reliability and veracity. In the context of Black testimony, the posture of witnessing then moves into focus the fraught relationship here between subject and object—testimony *appears* to be spoken through an agential subject, the witness.

Actually, testimony functions as a legal object that is then subjected to the rituals of verification, bias, and judgment attending the body and character of its speaker. It is obvious why testimony's subversive potential is so tempting: it offers a site of possibility for someone who, as theoretical legal property, ought to be prohibited from spoken participation in a legal proceeding but who nevertheless achieves textual and institutional visibility anyway. The paradox McBride identifies in his title, *Impossible Witnesses*, alludes to the ways that the staging of Black testimony within white abolitionist networks "produced the occasion for bearing witness, but to an experience that had already been theorized and prophesied. In this way, the slave serves as a kind of fulfillment of the prophecy of abolitionist discourse."[45] In other words, witnessing becomes a way to create the *appearance* of access to Black speech, while preserving limits on the context and nature of the testimony.

McBride documents the ways that Black writers brought the posture of witnessing to other genres and forms beyond the freedom narrative, including poetry and pamphlets. However, McBride's work also signals a potential limitation of overreliance on witnessing as a frame for reading Black writers: it reproduces hierarchies of engagement wherein Black witnesses testify in a space that remains a white-controlled zone of authority in order to tell the truth about the ways they have been harmed. If we read Black writers, particularly writers of freedom narratives, solely as witnesses testifying to their previous experiences, we run the risk of missing all the other creative, nondocumentary, and innovative things that their literature contains. Witnessing becomes, rather than a liberatory gesture, a way of perpetuating these writers' enslavement and their injury. Despite the many tactical and political urgencies that required and demanded Black testimony, witnessing is also a way of generating what Hartman reminds us are ultimately "scenes of subjection," and it tends to preserve the frame of fugitivity as the primary way of thinking about Black emancipation in the nineteenth century.[46]

Moreover, an overreliance on witnessing and testimony would preclude consideration of Black writers as lawyers themselves, relegating them to instruments of evidence in a white legal space where they never get to be the legal architects, strategists, or judges—postures that I study as specifically literary and authorial practices, but which, as I describe later in this introduction, were also extremely commonplace forms of practical Black legal participation in the nineteenth century. A perusal of almost any nineteenth-century Black newspaper, pamphlet, freedom narrative, or work of fiction is bound to contain any number of legal references, not just because legal culture was so pervasive in general—which it was—but also because Black writers, as the targets of various oppressive legal regimes, were legal *experts*. Beyond an awareness of political debates and policy proposals, Black writers, as readers and consumers of legal culture, understood that legal discourse operates within a set of textual rules—like the rules of pleader that Russwurm and Cornish reference in their opening issue of *Freedom's Journal*. Many of the nineteenth-century examples of legal form that I trace in this book are in fact susceptible to multiple readings; they are amenable to reading within the literary genres I trace in this introduction, as well as according to the more colloquial connotations of the legal forms that structure the chapters (appeal, confession, jurisdiction, and precedent). But as my readings of these texts demonstrate, focusing on legal form as a literary device of speculative fiction and Black worldmaking both facilitates novel readings of antebellum Black literature and honors the depth of legal expertise that these authors possessed.

That legal knowledge, a matter of Black survival, circulated widely through popular and print culture, and much of my work in this book involves identifying the places where its signature lives in a text's use of legal form, though this volume does not itself study the means and modes by which that circulation occurred.[47] The deployment of legal forms is nuanced and varied, evincing lawyerly strategies that responded to the material conditions of legalized slavery and disenfranchisement, often during prolonged flight, and a rapidly evolving legal profession. And, as I elaborate in the third pass in particular, these lawyerly strategies often introduced elements of the speculative in Black autobiography and fiction by overidentifying with the pliable possibilities of law's spatiotemporal fluidity.

These literary consequences would be much harder to see, if at all, if we read Black writers' legal engagement as primarily testimonial. The testimonial frame has and continues to offer numerous, rich points of entry into works of Black literature, and scholars have read testimonial writing through every imaginable literary genre and movement. As a by-product of that generic capacity, however, literary scholarship that reads Black works of testimonial violence faces several practical challenges, challenges that speak to the very nature of Black literature—first because testimonial literature may resist taxonomy within available literary genres and movements, second because it often seems to perform many or *all* of the available literary genres and movements at once, and third because the liberatory authorial possibilities that live on the pages of these texts sit uncomfortably alongside other forms of spectacular suffering that tend to reproduce Black authors as objects rather than subjects. This book attends to the use of legal form as (1) a Black authorial practice that *produces* genre disruptions by mystifying available taxonomies and (2) a critical frame that productively grapples with all three of these challenges in analyzing antebellum Black testimonial literature alongside and as an early source of Black fiction.

Before turning to the second pass, advocacy, it is necessary to differentiate legal form from either the content of specific laws or the overwhelming tendency of legal systems, like other white supremacist institutions, to mask their technologies of oppression through what Kimberlé Crenshaw has named as the accumulation and collaboration of multiple discriminatory regimes.[48] Nor is legal form synonymous with, as Ravit Reichman puts it, "the pains legal discourse takes to address its affective thickets in neutral terms, scrubbing and sanitizing, distancing and depersonalizing."[49] By contrast, to think and write in legal form is deeply, sacredly personal. To deploy legal form is to experiment and improvise, not in service of the state, but in spite of it. Fluency in legal form requires one to recognize patterns and craft responses to them, to formulate definitions that challenge the logics of the state, to identify strategies that *evade* subjection to hostile structures, and to offer up these strategies through language and narrative. It requires both expert knowledge of an applicable set of rules, and a detachment from convention so that one can experiment and remake rules precisely to avoid being bound by them. In short, lawyers work pragmatically, identifying unwelcome rules and engineering ways around them.

As capacious, fluid, and adaptable containers for legal imagination, legal forms are also extremely portable, making them suitable for the fugitive movements that formerly enslaved authors often charted. That portability is essential because, as Justin Simard has observed, although the vagaries of slave codes and other laws differed widely in different places, legal form supplied technical rules and customs—established through community standards—that could be applied regardless of state, county, court, or jurisdiction.[50] It is for this reason that legal form is both so potent and so useful to Black writers communicating across networks of constraint, oppression, and surveillance. For writers so often severely constrained in mobility and movement, the adaptability of legal form meant that it could be approximated or duplicated *anywhere*. These latent affordances of lawyerly thinking, to use Caroline Levine's theory of form, permitted the writers in this book to experiment with various creative practices both within state-run judicial proceedings and on the pages of newspapers, in works of fiction, and in other works of literature entirely outside the "official" armature of what we think of as "the law."[51]

This framing of legal form helps us transcend witnessing as a dominant lens for locating Black authorial agency, it facilitates readings of testimonial literature's fictive possibilities, and it helps us take seriously the conditions under which enslaved and free African American writers were laboring without reproducing the subject/object binary through which these writers have so often been read. Instead, a focus on legal form promotes transcendence of resistance as the dominant paradigm for Black life, a paradigm that Black studies scholarship on nineteenth-century literature has productively challenged and unsettled. For example, Saidiya Hartman's constructions of consent and subjection arose through her grappling with the hardest edges of slavery's archives, modeling new ways of theorizing forms of subjecthood within the constraints of law, custom, and history.[52] Likewise, Emily Owens's study of antebellum New Orleans documents how fictions of consent structure Black women's survival strategies in a deeply constrained legal landscape.[53] Marisa Fuentes, in her study of Caribbean archives of slavery, similarly formulates strategies of reading fragmented archives in an effort to elucidate "the production of 'personhood'" for enslaved Caribbean women "while troubling the political project of agency."[54] Similarly, Uri McMillan envisions frameworks of Black objecthood in order to theorize it "as a way toward agency rather than its antithesis, as a strategy rather than simply a primal site of injury."[55] Hartman, Owens, Fuentes, and McMillan challenge us to reckon with the grim realities of subjection and objecthood while recognizing that these categories themselves are surprisingly capacious, complex, and versatile.

In an effort to hold these competing realities in equipoise, I close read the opening from *Freedom's Journal* two more times, developing with each pass a different gloss on Black literature and law in the nineteenth century. This first pass established witnessing as a context and point of departure for this book, whereas the remaining two passes develop the book's stakes and interventions. In the second pass, advocacy, I particularly attend to the ways that Black writers, steeped in legal culture, were suited to serve as pro se advocates (both literally and discursively), meaning to act as their own lawyers. After all, to plead one's own cause is not merely participation in litigation, but a way of navigating and remaking hostile terrain through improvisation, innovation, and craft. In the third pass, worldmaking, I describe how legal form functions as a technology of dreaming a future world into being, and I elaborate on the expansive approach this book takes to the category of "the legal." In making these three passes—witnessing, advocacy, and worldmaking—I set the stage for this book's claim that legal form is a definitional and inherently speculative element of antebellum African American literature through which Black writers innovated existing literary genres and reimagined structures of belonging and liberation.

The Second Pass: Advocacy

"We wish to plead our own cause. Too long have others spoken for us."[56] Now that I have traced the reading of this passage for its testimonial qualities, it becomes necessary to read it for its legal engagement. The language of pleader and pleadings in a legal context refers to the submissions made to a court to initiate litigation and to disclose the general positions of each party. In the criminal context, pleadings consist of indictments (or informations) and the offering of a plea (depending on the jurisdiction, the plea usually derives from a menu that resembles something like guilty, not guilty, or no contest). For civil cases, the corresponding pleadings are complaint and answer (as well as any replies and counterclaims). Pleadings are crucial because these documents assert the charges being made, including the relevant facts of the case, as well as the basis for denying or disclaiming those charges; moreover, litigants are bound by the assertions they make in these documents, which can shape the future course of the litigation. For instance, failing to allege all of the elements of a crime or a tort in the pleadings can cause a case to be dismissed altogether; the framing of facts, allegations, and defenses in the pleadings might also determine which types of punishments or damages are available at later stages of the litigation.

The process of framing is the way that lawyers give narrative force to the relevant facts in a case—they build a story about those facts, returning to that story to generate a theory of the case and/or a defense. As Cheryl Harris and Devon Carbado note, that process generates "interpretational structures" that require the framer to both interpret the situation carefully and assist the audience in interpreting the situation correspondingly.[57] Thus, while these documents may seem somewhat rote or boilerplate, they require a depth of legal knowledge and strategy to ensure that the offered claims and defenses have the stamina required to last throughout the many stages and contingencies of litigation. While the term "pleadings" technically refers to the documents that initiate a formal legal proceeding, the phrase "to plead a case" also functions metonymically to refer to case strategy more generally, in alignment with the far-reaching effects of these pretrial documents. For example, if you have watched but one episode of *Law & Order*, you have likely observed a judge ask a defendant, "How do you plead?" and further observed the defendant answering this question personally, as opposed to through a lawyer. These televisual representations oversimplify the significance and the minutiae of pleading, which mostly depend on carefully constructed documents consisting of numbered paragraphs and a demonic precision of language; but they also signal the ways that pleading refers to a general strategy or theory of a case (often, though not always, a defense).

This kind of lawyerly thinking requires more than a good sense of logic and a gift with words. In order to generate pleadings, a lawyer must be able to anticipate counterarguments and cross-claims, they must possess a deep knowledge of the relevant case law and precedent, they must be able to improvise and adapt when unhelpful facts or arguments arise, and, above all, they must be able to navigate all of these things while weaving a coherent and persuasive narrative. Pleading is both highly technical and also deeply creative labor, a combination that highlights how Russworm and Cornish's language signals legal thinking as a way to both honor and evade rules—a hallmark of lawyerly thinking and an echo of Black literature's tendency to frustrate genre taxonomies.

When Russwurm and Cornish use "plead our own cause" as a legal referent, they signal litigation generally ("cause" is shorthand for "cause of action," a legal term to describe a case warranting litigation), and more specifically they deploy a legal phrase that extends back to the Judiciary Act of 1789. That statute establishes the right to pro se litigation, or as the statute describes it, "that in all courts of the United States, the parties may plead and manage their own causes personally or by assistance of such counsel or attorneys at law as by the rules of the said courts respectively shall be permitted to manage and conduct causes therein."[58] Thus, when Russwurm and Cornish assert their wish to "plead our own cause," they reference the very specific legal concept that entitles parties to litigation the right to represent themselves and/or the right to manage their own litigation with the "assistance" of a lawyer.

Given that this mechanism extends back to the founding of the republic and the law that established the US judicial system, it would not be outlandish to think about the right to pro se representation as intrinsic to US-American concepts of legal liberty and fairness. Drew Swank has described the right to self-representation this way: "Having its roots in the British common law, the right to pro se appearances evolved as a combined proposition of 'natural law,' an early anti-lawyer sentiment, and the egalitarian 'all men are created equal' concept that 'financial status should not have a substantial impact on the outcome of litigation.'"[59] Swank further points out that the right to pro se representation, while not clearly a constitutional right (but arguably covered by the Sixth Amendment right to counsel), "has been tied to the rights of indigents to have access to the courts. Open access to the courts for all citizens has also been viewed as being important for the development of law and public policy and the avoidance of citizens' resorting to non-judicial self-help."[60] Although Swank's history of pro se litigation does not proceed from a critical race theory perspective and thus does not discuss race specifically, his article does nevertheless address the perception that pro se representation is more common in what he describes as "poor people courts," or those "that handle traffic, landlord/tenant, and child support or other domestic relations issues."[61]

The connection to indigent representation has tangible overlaps in the legal history of slavery specifically via the mechanism of the freedom suit, or the form of litigation wherein an enslaved person could bring a lawsuit if they could claim to have been wrongfully enslaved—crucially, the legal mechanism still recognized the rightfulness of slavery as a general matter and under a set of conditions that protected the property rights of enslavers. States and often specific municipalities maintained their own procedures for freedom suits. To offer just one example, in Virginia, procedures for freedom suits had been in place since the eighteenth century, when the Statutes at Large of Virginia provided, "that when any person shall conceive himself or herself illegally detained as a slave in the possession of another, it shall and may be lawful for such person to make complaint thereof." The statute further prescribed the means of a freedom petition, noting that the slave should "petition [ ] the said court to be allowed to sue therein in *forma pauperis*, for the recovery of his or her freedom."[62]

Though this statute *appears* to grant enslaved people standing to sue in a court—a privilege of personhood and citizenship that was denied in other cases, and one that sounds a great deal like pro se representation—the designation of indigence is significant. This legislative sleight of hand denies an enslaved person's legal personhood even as it provides a substitute: the slave, not a citizen and thus not a proper civil plaintiff, may sue *as though he or she is a poor person*. Proceedings in forma pauperis, which typically waive court costs and other filing fees, are primarily the domain of indigent and incarcerated plaintiffs seeking judicial relief. In making this type of pleading available to enslaved persons, the statute also limits its application—the designation of in forma pauperis occurs only for these freedom petitions and not to any other type of civil proceeding. The analogy links the enslaved person explicitly to both poverty and incarceration. While appearing to "make room" for the wrongfully enslaved at law, this judicial procedure actually signals a lack of citizenship rights and collapses the enslaved person's status as property with their condition as having no property of their own.

The proximity between pro se representation and the eighteenth-century in forma pauperis freedom suit mechanism helps explain how a legal ideal that ostensibly began as a means of extending rights and access to justice has transformed, over time, into a racialized and classed signifier of judicial inferiority and even ignorance in the present day. There is even a saying, oft quoted in law schools and among the bar: "A lawyer who represents himself has a fool for a client." This legal proverb on one hand roasts lawyers as being overly confident about their legal prowess but also reveals, in quite sinister ways, how commonplace it is to think of legal representation as a commodity and a marker of privilege. Even the lawyer, with all of his (this proverb is always gendered in this way) expertise and legal training, requires an expert interlocutor to act as his representative—the law, the proverb suggests, functions best when legal argument and advocacy are one step *removed* from personal investment, much like the surgeon who may not perform surgery on a loved one. The pretense of objectivity masks the ways that the *appearance* of objectivity is not just an aspirational value but part of the product a client pays for when hiring a legal representative. As an apparatus of various kinds of privilege and personhood rights, access to legal representation has become increasingly racialized and classed over the years.[63] Mass incarceration and the wealth gap have become firmly entrenched in legal culture and deepened this divide; policing practices have resulted in diminishing confidence in the legal system writ large at the same time that Black defendants are more in need than ever of legal representation and have limited access to the wealth that is needed to hire lawyers.

Despite the ways that pro se representation has evolved into a racialized signifier of a *gap* in legal resources, in 1827, for Russwurm and Cornish, the notion of pro se representation was much closer to the 1789 aspirational ideals of judicial access. And it certainly supposed a degree of agency and personhood that far exceeded various local prohibitions on Black participation in litigation. If that initial call to plead their own cause might merely resemble pro se rights coincidentally, an echo later in the same column makes plain that Russwurm and Cornish position themselves as advocates and specifically as lawyers presenting a case: "Is it not very desirable that such should know more of our actual condition, and of our efforts and feelings, that in forming or advocating plans for our amelioration, they may do it more understandingly? In the spirit of candor and humility we intend by a simple representation of facts to lay our case before the publick, with a view to arrest the progress of prejudice, and to shield ourselves against the consequent evils."[64] Their language here sets up "the publick" as a potential jury;[65] juries are responsible for evaluating facts, and Russwurm and Cornish specifically describe their intention to present the facts to the public, a sign of their familiarity with trial procedure.

The embrace of pro se litigation is not limited to *Freedom's Journal*, however. Just over a decade after Russwurm and Cornish's 1827 column appeared, another Black newspaper, *The Colored American*, published a report of a Poughkeepsie, New York, meeting before an upcoming Colored Convention. That report likewise borrows the language of pro se representation. A group of men led by Uria Boston issued a resolution at that meeting: "That in common with our friends, it is of the utmost importance that we have a newspaper of our own, through which we can plead our own cause, and of the rights of our brethren in bonds."[66] Like Russwurm and Cornish, Boston and his fellow signatories used the written word as a speech act to enact their status as their own legal representatives. Also like Russwurm and Cornish, they drew a distinction between themselves as free men and their "brethren in bonds," even as they set out to serve as advocates for Black people everywhere.

At least one other scholar has identified another point of contact between pro se representation and a Black writer in the antebellum period. Jason de Stefano's synthesis of Frederick Douglass's constitutional interpretations draws connections among Douglass's turn to writing fiction, the concept of *persona ficta* (the legal category of entities, like corporations, who are treated as if they are persons), and pro se advocacy in Douglass's interpretations of the Constitution. In particular, de Stefano cites Douglass's capacious sense of fiction as a site that "could provide a legitimate medium for authoritative personation as much in his literary project of self-authorship as in his antislavery advocacy."[67] De Stefano's attention to Douglass's movement between fiction and antislavery advocacy helps establish the broader claims this book makes about these forms of legal authorship being a pervasive *feature* of antebellum Black writing, though de Stefano focuses primarily on legal interpretation and personhood in his analysis. He notes, "Douglass recognized in the nexus of legal interpretation and fiction a means of aesthetic self-making that was equally an expression of political authority."[68] For de Stefano, Douglass's legal interpretation "emphasized the creative dimension of language in general and recognized in the law's personating power in particular an exercise of formal authority that is thoroughly aesthetic."[69] This analysis of Douglass accords with the claims I make in this book about how other Black writers during the antebellum period also took a deeply creative approach to their legal and literary conjunctions—which I discuss more fully in the next section of this introduction—though de Stefano's reading of Douglass very specifically focuses on how Douglass interprets the constitutionality of slavery and the philosophies of personhood, including fictive personhood, that would open up or foreclose various possibilities.

Like de Stefano, I lean into law's creative possibilities and the ways that Black writers seized on fiction in particular in their engagements with law. This relationship does not always occur in fictional literature, however; rather, as I argue, the *process* of fictionalization is accessed through legal form in order to rescript existing histories. For example, in chapter 1, I argue that the appeal form is a container for literary texts that indict and overturn oppressive regimes, whereas in chapter 4, Hannah Crafts encodes numerous nonfiction narratives within her novel *The Bondwoman's Narrative*, rehearsing an earlier version of Saidiya Hartman's "critical fabulation" by re-presenting fragments from her own archives of slavery in a way that suggests alternative histories of the US nation-state and the real-life enslavement of a woman named Jane Johnson.[70] Thus, it is not *only* that Black writers turn to fiction as a way of interpreting law; rather, it is quite often the case that their use of legal form mystifies the border between the "legal" or "historical" and the "fictional" at all.

In taking up legal advocacy, this book engages and builds on scholarship from Black studies, literary studies, law, and history. Much of this work might be termed "law and literature" studies, though scholars doing work in law and literature do not always necessarily claim that field. This is particularly true of work in Black studies, in part because, as a field, "law and literature" has been slow to embrace intersections with Black studies and ethnic studies, though law and literature scholarship by Wai Chee Dimock, Jeannine DeLombard, and Imani Perry, among others, is increasingly broadening that field.[71] Work in adjacent fields like legal history, critical race theory, and citizenship studies, however, contributes to scholarly conversations on the relationships between law and literature and elucidates the legal historical context for the writers in this book, whose participation in antebellum legal culture was persistently robust across geographies and legal fields. Elaborating that history is a crucial step in warranting the frame of pro se advocacy—the nature of Black legal participation in the early nineteenth century contextualizes a pro se posture in a hostile legal regime by honoring the depths of Black legal knowledge, the fluidity of law, and the rise of the legal profession.

In this introduction, I have already alluded to some of the testimonial constraints on Black litigants and witnesses in the antebellum period, as well as the ways that mechanisms like the freedom suit carved out exceptions to those constraints and permitted limited Black participation in litigation. In the United States, the laws of slavery or so-called slave codes varied by state and local jurisdiction, rendering the particularities of slavery deeply localized and often subject to the vagaries of local custom—a feature that, as discussed, rendered fluency in legal *form* a valuable transjurisdictional skill. Despite the differences in specific slave laws, there were nevertheless several common strains. As described by the Library of Congress, "All slave codes made slavery a permanent condition, inherited through the mother, and defined slaves as property, usually in the same terms as those applied to real estate. Slaves, being property, could not own property or be a party to a contract. Since marriage is a form of contract, no slave marriage had any legal standing. All codes also had sections regulating free blacks, who were still subject to controls on their movements and employment and were often required to leave the state after emancipation."[72] This legal regime obviously sought, on several fronts, to enclose and dehumanize Black life, and to limit Black civic participation and enfranchisement. However, the codification of these prohibitions does not necessarily reflect the actuality of Black participation in legal culture any more than the pervasive anti-literacy laws of the period accurately squelched Black reading and writing—as evidenced by the proliferation of Black-authored texts in the antebellum period, many of which were created without the use of an amanuensis. Moreover, what consistency there is in these frequent prohibitions is belied by the fluidity and often chaotic application of law during this historical moment.

While law absolutely touched everyday life extensively during the decades before the Civil War, it would be a mistake to assume that law was mobilized behind a strong, consistent, unified "state" presence. In her study of North Carolina legal history, Laura Edwards has described antebellum law as revealing deep tension between state and local authorities, tension that was resolved unevenly and often on ad hoc principles intended to produce "the peace, a legal concept that sought to maintain community order as it was defined in specific areas."[73] The gap between the "official" legal regime and the full measure of Black legal participation described below speaks to the dissonance Hendrik Hartog identifies as a tension between "the multiplicity of our social practices and normative identities . . . and the values we impute to legal order."[74] In other words, statutory prohibitions might communicate one set of values, but those values often do not correspond to the actuality of local and social customs.

Legal history projects by Kimberly Welch, Dylan Penningroth, Emily Owens, and Kelly Kennington have traced the numerous ways that Black people participated in litigation in the first half of the nineteenth century, including by bringing lawsuits as plaintiffs (even in the South, where they were ostensibly widely forbidden from doing so), and suing for their freedom. Kennington's work focuses on freedom suits[75]—where Black participants were more likely to appear in the testimonial mode that the first pass of this introduction traced. By contrast, Owens's study of Black women's survival practices in antebellum New Orleans considers, among other things, how Black women worked within the constraints of in-court testimony to use the language of "cruelty" to record sexual violence and secure judicial protection.[76] By contrast, Welch focuses on how Black litigants in Mississippi and Louisiana theorized and practiced law through "claims-making and the language used to that end: the language of property."[77] Welch examines, for instance, cases where free Black plaintiffs sued white men who had beaten them, even where the plaintiffs were (falsely) alleged to be fugitives from slavery—an allegation that arguably would have been sufficient under slave codes to cut off their right to bring suit. As Owens, Welch, and others demonstrate in their studies, Black litigants took advantage of legal mechanisms that permitted their open participation in court, as well as gaps in more restrictive legal regimes. The informal and improvisational quality of local legal practice in the antebellum period in general meant that many legal proceedings occurred in contradiction to or ignorance of even the more onerous regulatory networks. In many places, judges were neighbors or friends, court sessions occurred inconsistently, and the legal system functioned mainly to, in Laura Edwards's formulation, "keep the peace." Even in communities with stricter rules of procedure, geographical, financial, and educational resources might not guarantee a steady supply of professional local lawyers. In these cases, many tribunals and courts simply relaxed or ignored existing rules in the interest of efficiency.

This mode of more frequent but casual legal participation, despite cutting against the narratives of the slave codes, was hardly an outlier during the period. As Dylan Penningroth observes, many so-called low-level legal documents (in this case, Wisconsin newspaper items on late nineteenth-century justice of the peace proceedings) offer "clues about legal culture and legal consciousness."[78] Penningroth's rumination on legal thinking specifically references complaints, the type of pleading encompassed by Russwurm and Cornish's exhortation for Black readers to "plead [their] own cause," with Penningroth noting, "The act of going to law was, in a sense, a declaration of 'what the law is' by ordinary people, or what actions warranted a legal remedy or sanction."[79] Both Penningroth and Welch assemble archives that encompass "official" legal records (typically statutes, regulations, and judicial opinions) as well as more quotidian, informal, and ephemeral traces of Black advocacy, thus challenging the notion that Law is a proper noun and applying the category of "legal" to materials generated alongside or outside state institutions. For example, in tracing the "ubiquity of law in the daily life of the Old South," Welch demonstrates how the staging of "court week" in antebellum Natchez made law both public spectacle and social event, mingling adjudication with commerce, entertainment, and rights discourse, and serving as a legal training ground for Black litigants.[80] And in examining the thousands of Black divorce proceedings in the decades *after* the Civil War, Penningroth stresses the improvisational aspect of Black legal participation in "engagements that were much more common and, arguably, just as important" as the more well-known appellate court proceedings on civil rights.[81] In other words, in the nineteenth century, many litigants understood law not as some pervasive and insurmountable external force, but as something that they could directly shape. This relaxed relationship to law as the stuff of everyday life contextualizes its relative accessibility in the nineteenth century for litigants from all walks of life, and it nuances the reasons that legal thinking may have felt available and potent to Black writers during this period.

Penningroth's emphasis on improvisation signals another body of scholarship to which my project is deeply indebted: citizenship studies. In particular, in highlighting the quotidian nature of law, Penningroth and Welch align with

The Practice of Citizenship, where Derrick Spires explores the ways that antebellum Black print culture rehearses and innovates citizenship as practiced in everyday life and through activist efforts such as the Colored Conventions Movement.[82] There, Spires analyzes a wide range of print sources to explore how Black writers in the nineteenth century theorized citizenship "not just from the perspective of law and its framing of black people and others but also from the perspective of black Americans, who were some of the most important theorists of citizenship, both then and now."[83] Spires is in deep dialogue with other scholarship on citizenship and Black litigation, including Martha Jones's study of Black Baltimoreans' nineteenth-century claims to birthright citizenship, and Koritha Mitchell's situation of citizenship through Black women's homemaking practices.[84] Likewise, Carrie Hyde's study of citizenship's "speculative origins" both marks the ubiquity of citizenship discourse in the nineteenth century and theorizes citizenship as "an elastic site of political fantasy and debate."[85] Crucially, Hyde's work historicizes notions of citizenship and law, noting that "in the period before the Fourteenth Amendment, the law was not yet the default tradition for asking and answering questions about citizenship."[86] As Spires and Hyde have demonstrated in their studies of citizenship, the pliability of law and literature in the nineteenth century meant that legal discourses, legal experiments, and expressions of legal advocacy often occurred out of courts and legislatures and on the page.

Consequently, and in following the examples of Penningroth and Welch, my work in this book construes the category of "the legal" very broadly. That broad construction operates in some defiance of taxonomies that would vest legal authority in the violent institutions and "official" records that tend to elide, erase, or downplay the forms of "unofficial" or "extralegal" practices of improvisation, quotidian habit, and custom that nevertheless participate in and structure legal culture. In referring to "legal culture" as often as possible instead of "the law," I also make a practice of treating law as a common noun rather than a proper one; I regard law as the public sphere wherein normative rules and rights are performed and contested. Law is, as Kimberly Welch observes, a site where one can "envision a [new] social order."[87] While Welch traces the use of narrative in antebellum Black litigation,[88] this book examines the capacious use of legal form in Black autobiography and fiction. In structuring rights and belonging via normative logics, I argue that legal form does something more specific and more speculative than articulate existing political ideas and investments.

By embracing legal form as the specific type of political engagement that structures my analysis in this book, I also underscore the public nature of legal culture and the ways that it implies expertise and authority. While I am inclined to be suspicious of reliance on expertise and authority as a general matter, these valences of legal culture matter tremendously as contexts for antebellum Black literary production; the etymological proximity of "author" and "authority" nuances the historical suspicion of Black writers as literary authors and experts, meaning that the embrace of legal form has the potential to invest Black writers with both authorship and authority. Moreover, legal culture, unlike political discourse more generally, is inherently *textual*—it produces meaning through language and text (one might argue to the point of fetishization), rendering legal language capable of what Patricia Williams describes as "Word Magic."[89] The attachment to language as a site of magical meaning-making is, of course, a trait that legal culture shares with literature, an intimacy that further warrants this book's reliance on legal form in particular as opposed to political theory more broadly.

While my third pass, worldmaking, more fully addresses the worldbuilding potential of legal language, it is worth noting here that the focus on legal culture as a specifically literary form of advocacy also corresponds with the status of the legal profession during the antebellum period. While a number of law schools did exist in the antebellum United States, the practice of law remained rooted in practices of apprenticeship and study by "reading law." Calling it a "bookish profession," M. H. Hoeflich describes antebellum legal practice as requiring access to a library large enough to house "the full range of legal sources that lawyers of the period used in drawing their arguments and documents."[90] In echoing other assessments of the highly localized nature of law, Hoeflich also points out the inchoate nature of US law during this period early in the republic's legal life. Noting the "syncretism" of British and American law during this period where US independence had broken with British common law but retained its history as foundational legal philosophy, Hoeflich writes that, in addition to being responsible for knowing British legal history, "American lawyers of this period were cosmopolitan in their thinking and writing. If they could not find relevant English or American law they would gladly look to the law of ancient Rome, and of contemporary France or Germany.... The new nation in its formative period offered lawyers unparalleled freedom to look widely for their authorities."[91] According to Hoeflich, the explosion of practicing lawyers during the antebellum period also coincided with the uneven emergence of circulating law books, as the legal publishing industry struggled to gain a foothold in the print economy.[92] At the same time, even as law books were rare, newspapers and pamphleteers regularly published judicial opinions, petitions, policy proposals, and even court transcripts. Combined with the social dimensions of events like "court week," legal culture proliferated, if somewhat chaotically and unevenly, providing informal but consistent access to legal language, form, and policy. As an eclectic, cosmopolitan, and rapidly evolving discursive sphere, legal culture required improvisational navigation of legal forms not only by insurgent Black litigants but from "official" legal authorities and professional practitioners as well; these qualities rendered legal form and legal advocacy ideally suited to the equally diverse literary strategies practiced by Black authors.

The Third Pass: Worldmaking

"We wish to plead our own cause. Too long have others spoken for us."[93] I have spent considerable time in this introduction historicizing the glosses on witnessing and advocacy contained in this column from *Freedom's Journal*. In the third pass, I consider how Russwurm and Cornish, in naming themselves as their own legal advocates—and indeed as legal advocates for a broader Black community, both enslaved and free—position themselves as architects of legal possibility. In a twenty-first-century context, the notion of "legal architects" has a sinister connotation that hints at, for example, responsibility for the construction of legal systems that are, in their design, racist, sexist, ageist, ableist, homophobic, transphobic, and so on. But by "architects of legal possibility," I refer here to legal imagination in its most expansive, radical terms, to the dreaming of entire logics and structures of belonging. This relationship to legal imagination acknowledges the writerly practices and material conditions facing antebellum Black writers that I traced in the first pass (witnessing), as well as the fluid nature of antebellum legal culture that I outlined in the second pass (advocacy), and it takes seriously the capacity of legal form to imagine and enact whole worlds. This approach finds common ground with Jennifer Nash's call to observe the ways that law "can be a location of radical freedom-dreaming and visionary world-making rather than simply a deathworld and *the* paradigmatic site of antiblackness."[94] Whereas Nash grounds that call specifically in Black feminism's relationship to intersectionality, an inherently legal frame, my work in this book makes visible the ways that Black writers have long recognized the worldmaking capacity of law, well before the coinage of intersectionality or the creation of critical race theory as a scholarly field.

For Black writers in the first half of the nineteenth century, thinking like a lawyer meant projecting visions for future possible worlds and sites of belonging—these visions, though routed through legal *form*, did not necessarily derive from or retain existing structures of state *governmentality*. In thinking about the use of legal form as a kind of legal ritual, it is useful to revisit Colin Dayan's discussion of an 1871 case about civil death. Dayan writes, "To think in law means to reason in a special kind of way, and, as I seek to show, the application of legal rules could and did create a universe unto itself."[95] Notice the scope and scale of legal possibility here—applying legal rules achieves a worldmaking effect by bringing an entire universe into being. Likewise, Robert Cover has described law as both "a world in which we live"[96] and "the projection of an imagined future upon reality."[97] Both Dayan and Cover remind us of law's capacity to make entire worlds, and not just to rule this one. For this reason, the seeming contradiction of Cover's two formulations—the world we live in versus an imagined future—is of course a false opposition.

As Cover reminds us, law is both the actual material conditions of life under a legal regime—which can often be quite violent and unjust—*and* a project of ongoing worldmaking in which lawmakers enact "rules" that, by design, try to bring an imagined world into being. That temporal orientation to worldmaking proceeds in a futurist mode but recognizes the future as deeply intertwined with the present, a posture that acknowledges the ways that antebellum Black writers were both (1) laboring in the moment to achieve specific rights of personhood, civic status, and freedom *and* (2) envisioning future forms of belonging that refused to accept existing legal regimes as mandatory, natural, or inevitable. Kimberly Welch describes this both-and-ness of Black legal storytelling by pointing out the ways that courtroom narration "was ostensibly historical (it explained what had happened in the past), but it was simultaneously anticipatory and future oriented."[98] This description of legal storytelling captures some of law's polytemporal affordances. The procedural shape of adjudication or litigation, as a simultaneously retrospective and prospective process that resolves disputes and redresses harm, emerges as a surprisingly apt container for Black worldmaking projects laboring to imagine Black futures while accounting for ongoing violence and genocide.

It also contextualizes legal worldmaking as a speculative practice, which deepens one's sense of law's suitability as a literary device and also previews the ways that this book relies on legal form to read as speculative not only works of early African American fiction but also antebellum autobiography and testimonial texts. As explored in the following chapters, antebellum writers frequently practice worldmaking by fictionalizing *past* events in ways that suggest alternative *futures*. These worldmaking experiments are less counterhistories than they are counterfactuals, a distinction that stresses again the investments of this book in the fictional dimensions and possibilities of antebellum Black writing. Moreover, the use of counterfactuals to practice worldmaking from within and beyond a genocidal context thus also resonates productively with work by Justin Mann, who describes twentieth- and twenty-first-century Black speculative fiction's capacity for "world-breaking," or unmasking state frames of security and securitization.[99] The spatiotemporality of worldmaking is a through line in this book, and I extend this discussion more deeply in the coda. But as a threshold matter here, worldmaking functions in this book as an example of law at its outermost reaches of literary and imaginative possibility. It is in that register that antebellum Black writers enact worldmaking experiments.

Take Russwurm and Cornish for instance. In this first column from *Freedom's Journal*, they pose the following:

> If ignorance, poverty and degradation have hitherto been our unhappy lot; has the Eternal decree gone forth, that our race alone, are to remain in this state, while knowledge and civilization are shedding their enlivening rays over the rest of the human family? The recent travels of Denham and Clapperton in the interior of Africa, and the interesting narrative which they have published; the establishment of the republic of Hayti after years of sanguinary warfare; its subsequent progress in all the arts of civilization; and the advancement of liberal ideas in South America, where despotism has given place to free governments, and where many of our brethren now fill important civil and military stations, prove the contrary.[100]

Though they begin by posing a rhetorical question about the supposed inevitability of a permanent Black undercaste, Russwurm and Cornish immediately shift to a set of global examples of Black culture and belonging. By connecting centers of Black life in Africa, South America, and Haiti, Russwurm and Cornish practice literal worldmaking, this time not in the language of time but of space—they remap the world according to its Blackness and in particular via the possibility inherent in the establishment of a Black republic as a result of the Haitian Revolution. This Black mapping of the world turns on the overthrow or rejection of existing nation-state models, whether in Saint-Domingue or South America—a trope that recurs throughout many of the texts in this book, from David Walker's *Appeal to the Coloured Citizens of the World* to Victor Séjour's vision of revolutionary vengeance to Harriet

Jacobs's imagination of an American nation governed by a sword-wielding queen. More than simply grafting legal concepts onto their writing, antebellum Black writers persistently stake their worldmaking practices in legal form.

For example, in an 1849 editorial published in *The North Star*, and as part of his ongoing discussion of the constitutionality of slavery (a debate that was bound up in complicated ways with his affiliation and then separation from Garrisonian abolitionism), Frederick Douglass writes that, as a formerly enslaved man, he must confine his constitutional analysis to "coolness and clearness," of which he is considered capable. He writes, "We cannot talk 'lawyer like' about LAW—about its emanating from the bosom of God!—about government, and of its seat in the great heart of the Almighty!—nor can we, in connection with such an ugly matter-of-fact looking thing as the United States Constitution, bring ourselves to split hairs about the alleged legal rule of interpretation.... We have to do with facts, rather than theory. The Constitution is not an abstraction. It is a living, breathing fact."[101]

I have long puzzled over this editorial, confused by the distinction that Douglass draws between talking "lawyer like" and dealing in facts. It is confusing, first, because dealing in and parsing facts is perhaps the most lawyer-like habit I can imagine, and second, because Douglass proceeds to parse the Constitution in a deeply lawyerly way in the remainder of the editorial. But his separation here between facts and theory speaks to the privilege he understands to attach to lawyerly discourse, and his critique of it as a profession founded on fantasy, big ideas, and highly stylized metaphors about natural law and government. He juxtaposes this way of talking about law with the supposed pragmatism of a legal text like the Constitution, which he regards as more functional than theoretical—a characterization that would no doubt send generations of jurists into despair. This contrast suggests that to talk "lawyer like" for Douglass was less about litigation and more about imagination, even though he *also* performs the precise and careful interpretive analysis that we still associate with legal reasoning.

What I want to draw out here is the distinction between legal reasoning and legal imagination, and to suggest that other Black writers likewise understood and worked with that distinction. The legal reasoning skills of these writers are self-evident from their uses of legal form, and as such do not require a great deal of parsing. And of course these writers are good at legal reasoning: their lives depended on it. Rather, I am drawn especially to texts that do not necessarily appear, at least on their surfaces, to be interpreting law so much as performing and *creating* it. I focus in the book on the ways that law's imaginative possibilities surface in Black literature, often erupting as moments where the legal thinking gets very "big"—"lawyer like" in Douglass's framework—and radically reorders existing legal landscapes and futures.

Douglass's positioning of thinking "lawyer like" throws into relief once more the importance of a pro se posture for thinking about legal imagination. To represent oneself pro se is to refuse to yield the imaginative terrain of advocacy to someone else—to plead one's own cause, in Russwurm and Cornish's formulation—is to retain *imaginative* and *creative* control. This connection is one that Lindon Barrett has made in examining Lucy Delaney's post–Civil War narrative and its depiction of her freedom suit proceedings. Barrett traces the relationship between legal representation through an advocate and representation as a narrative matter, noting that Delaney's lawyer "'represents' her, not just as her advocate, but also as one more practitioner of the law who wields its power to construct and construe her life in accord with its letter."[102] Barrett's formulation brings together Dayan's and Cover's figurations of law as an instrument with incredible power to construct or make worlds, but under the sign of legal advocacy and representation as a limitation on the Black expression of that worldmaking capacity. Thus, we arrive finally at the possibility for pro se representation not only as a form of advocacy in a rights-seeking posture but as an act of creative expression, narrative experimentation, and textual worldbuilding.

Worldmaking, particularly when it relies on language, is regarded as something like magic in legal and literary contexts. Both Patricia Williams and M. NourbeSe Philip have theorized the magical and alchemical possibilities of legal language, framings that signal the potency of using legal form in works of literature. In a parable that precedes the 1991 text *The Alchemy of Race and Rights*, Williams imagines a city where priests "could learn ascendingly intricate levels of Word Magic" which was eventually trivialized as useless. Those priests "donned the garb of pilgrims, seekers once more, and passed beyond the gates of the Celestial City. In this recursive passage they acquired the knowledge of Undoing Words." Their pilgrimage eventually brings them to "a place Beyond the Power of Words" where "they let down their anchors, the plumb lines of their reality, and experienced godhood once more."[103] I have lingered on this origin story many times, and truly, I am never sure exactly what to do with it. But Williams's description of Word Magic as a sport that the priest-gods would play savors strongly of legal argument and the masturbatory word games that it cultivates as it stomps and stamps out the rights of the human beings under its sway.

And her image of the priests undertaking recursive passage to learn a skill of Undoing Words resonates as well with Philip's distrust of language—and antebellum Black writers' recursions to the historical past. In the Notanda of *Zong!* (her collection of experimental poems based on the Zong massacre), Philip observes, "In its potent ability to decree that what is is not, as in a human ceasing to be and becoming an object, a thing or chattel, the law approaches the realm of magic and religion. The conversion of human into chattel becomes an act of transubstantiation the equal of the metamorphosis of the eucharistic bread and wine into the body and blood of Christ. Like a magic wand the law erases all ties."[104] Both Williams and Philip write about the undoing of language as a way of engaging law. Philip notes that her poems, precisely through the posture of "not-telling," have a magical power of their own: "In *Zong!*, the African transformed into a thing by the law, is re-transformed, miraculously, back into human. Through oath and through moan, through mutter, chant and babble, through babble and curse, through chortle and ululation to not-tell the story."[105] In her creative process as a poet, Philip literally scrambles the legal text of the *Gregson v. Gilbert* judicial opinion[106] and then reassembles the history of the event through what she refers to as "anti-meaning"[107] to conjure a Black world and a form of the human that has been lost to law's violence.

The writers in this book, writing from the first half of the nineteenth century, are likewise engaged in projects of undoing and remaking, though their processes look quite different from Philip's experimental poems. They do not scramble words or superimpose text on top of itself, as Philip does, but they do apply pressure to governing legal documents, regimes, institutions, and literary forms. They frequently reverse the order of operations, shift the poles of the operative legal hierarchies, and imagine other, not yet existent, but arguably more just judicial entities and offices. These nineteenth-century writers' approach, of envisioning other Black worlds and ways of belonging, also seizes on the magical potential of law, turning law back around on itself, producing—similar to the three passes in this introduction—a circular or cyclical motion that makes new worlds by mingling retrospection with futurity.

My focus on legal form's capacity for literary worldmaking underscores this book's payoffs for reading the African American literary tradition through a legal frame and for identifying law as a technology of spatiotemporal literary experimentation. This frame of literary worldmaking is not without other limitations, however. While I attend as carefully as possible throughout this book to the legal and material realities facing Black writers and litigants, its primary intervention is ultimately as a work of literary criticism rather than a historiography of legal writing or a study in networks of print culture or media circulation. My hope is that historians, especially legal historians, will read and engage this book, and that my literary analysis will be useful to others who undertake cultural and legal histories of some of the people and texts examined here. Likewise, while this book's ethical and political investments are grounded in Black feminist frames—which I have endeavored to make visible in my archive, methodology, and citational praxis, and in my commitment to honoring Black women's work in legal and literary spheres—this book does not claim to be a study of gender and/or sexuality in relation to antebellum writers' relationship to legal culture. A deeper engagement with gender and sexuality in the legal sphere is an area I particularly look forward to exploring in future projects and in dialogue with scholars in Black sexuality studies and queer of color critique.

Chapter Summaries: Appeal, Confession, Jurisdiction, Precedent

Keeping in mind these possibilities and limitations, I have organized this book around four different legal forms or practices: appeal, jurisdiction, confession, and citation to precedent. Not every category resembles a form as discrete as an appeal; however, each form is a portable container for legal culture and literary experimentation, and each form contains unique affordances. For instance, as a means of challenging and redressing a previous wrong, appeal is a site of potential for inverting existing hierarchies and repairing or redressing injury. By contrast, jurisdiction has different affordances; it is a way of defying place-bound logics, of evading specific power structures, and remapping logics of organization and belonging. Confession, as a ritual of acknowledging various past "wrongs," is a site of cleansing and rewriting. Finally, precedent, as a means of carrying forward ideas and rules from other contexts, affords the possibility of encrypting and remaking legal narratives; it treats history with reverence but also as an opportunity for revision. All of these forms generate spatiotemporal pliability, calling attention to antebellum Black literature's speculative dimensions and the capacity of legal culture to work in distinctly Black registers. This spatiotemporal pliability also speaks to Karla Holloway's rumination on the question, "how is literary blackness made?" and her answer: "[It] is both structural and spatial. It is, in fact, most evident in narratives that explore what happens when rules are contested, absent, or irregular."[108] Legal form is the mechanism by which Black writers in the nineteenth century practiced innovation, evasion, and exploitation of the operative legal rules.

Chapter 1, "Appeal," considers this legal and rhetorical form as the book's entry point into nineteenth-century Black literature and print. Appeals are common enough literary forms during the early nineteenth century, where that term often refers to their general meaning as nonlegal documents. Appeals to sympathy or logic are always forms of persuasive writing, but in their legal context, they mean something slightly more specific: a legal appeal is a request made, to a higher authority, for redress of a wrong committed at some other stage of the justice system. A legal appeal therefore incorporates the element of sympathy but in the form of argument before an institution of power—a legal appeal acknowledges the power of the institution it addresses, and it seeks reconsideration of something that has already happened or been decided. In addition, this chapter considers how an older meaning of appeal establishes a legal process whereby a private citizen can bring a prosecution to redress a grievous harm or injury.

Chapter 1 considers several African American texts that use appeal to recast and reimagine the hemispheric dimensions of the antebellum legal landscape. This chapter treats as a point of departure David Walker's *Appeal to the Coloured Citizens of the World*, an 1829 manifesto that urges people of African descent to resist their oppressors and traces the history of enslavement to its ancient roots. By Walker's logic, the Black reader exists as his fellow citizen, as well as the party able to prosecute the grievous harm of slavery, *and* the higher authority capable of adjudicating existing legal rulings. In this chapter, I show how Walker uses the form of appeal to shuffle expected legal hierarchies and reorganize the system of US political power while imagining other, global forms of Black belonging. After briefly framing Walker's *Appeal* within its transatlantic legal historical context, chapter 1 turns to two works of early Black fiction: Victor Séjour's 1837 short story "The Mulatto," and the short work of serialized fiction entitled "Theresa, _____ a Haytien Tale" that was published in *Freedom's Journal* in 1828 under only the name "S." Both works of fiction are set in Saint-Domingue, with the Haitian Revolution as the explicit context for the latter and the implicit context for the former. This chapter explores the ways that these two fictional works use the logic and form of appeal to enact revolutionary vengeance and to reimagine the history of the Haitian Revolution—given that both works were published decades after the Haitian Revolution ended, this posture of review and retrospection elaborates the legal form of appeal as a technology of temporality, diasporic mapping, and speculative storytelling.

Chapter 2 turns to confession as a legal form that initiates experiments in imagining non-place-bound forms of Black sovereignty. Whereas a confessor typically *serves* legal systems by accepting criminal classifications for past misdeeds and submitting oneself to the proscribed future punishment, each confessor here *rejects* positive law, instead using the confessional performance to posit alternative forms of Black sovereignty. Here I place *The Confessions of Nat Turner* (1831) in conversation with Charles Henry Langston's 1859 speech at the Cuyahoga County Courthouse and Harriet Jacobs's *Incidents in the Life of a Slave Girl* (1861). The confessions by each writer in this chapter deploy some of the same characteristics as those used in chapters 1 ("Appeal") and 3 ("Jurisdiction"), particularly relating to claims of Black legal or moral authority. In the case of Turner, his confession to leading the Southampton Rebellion is the gesture that authorizes his imagined spiritual sovereignty. While he freely confesses to the "crimes" alleged, he disrupts the expected operation of confession as a ritual of legal cleansing by refusing to offer expressions of remorse or apology. In other words, he confesses to the *actions* alleged without acceding to a characterization of those actions as crimes. By leveraging confession in this way, Turner appears to be cooperating with or obeying law's procedures, even as his inhabitation of that legal space asserts his spiritual sovereignty as the true legal authority.

In the case of Charles Langston, what appears on the surface to be a confession likewise inverts expected hierarchies of state legal authority. In his 1859 speech at the Cuyahoga Courthouse, Langston addressed the court after his conviction under the Fugitive Slave Act of 1850 for his role in helping an enslaved man escape from a US marshal in Ohio.[109] His speech followed a widely publicized trial, and the trial court gave him the opportunity to speak before sentencing. As such, the "confession" that he offered to the judge appeared out of typical sequence, since it followed his conviction, and it inverted the expected power structure of that legal space. In rejecting the basis for the Fugitive Slave Act in the first place and willingly submitting to state punishment, Langston creates a Black jurisprudential logic that positions himself as occupying the legal and moral high ground; he performs both a claim to citizenship and an admission of outlawry. In echoes of the appeal form's capacity to invert and overturn, Langston's performance—in court but after his trial has ended—reclaims the judicial space as a site of Black sovereignty.

Finally, for Harriet Jacobs, confession verifies her claim to sexual sovereignty and structures logics of kinship that sidestep generations of white ancestors and histories of sexual abuse. In narrating her enslavement, Jacobs describes the sexual trauma she experienced, and she periodically offers "confessions" to her readers about the ways she leveraged her own sexuality in order to achieve freedom. However, the confession examined in greatest depth here is an incomplete confession she makes to her daughter, in which she attempts to disclose the details of her relationship with her daughter's (white) biological father. Instead, her daughter halts the confession before it can be completed, renouncing any meaningful connection with her white paternal relatives. By refusing to permit a completed confession, Jacobs and her daughter recast the narratives of crime in their bio-family networks, discursively divesting themselves of their white relations and transforming confession into a shared affirmation of their sexual sovereignty and embodied authority.

I turn in chapter 3 to jurisdiction, the second of two chapters that examine frameworks for Black sovereignty. At law, jurisdiction commonly depends in particular ways on place—whether specific courts or other law enforcement bodies are entitled to adjudicate matters that come before them, or whether civil plaintiffs have a right to bring claims for injury in specific places. Jurisdiction is about process and forum in one, a legal concept that governs the propriety of litigating certain types of matters in certain specific places. Chapter 3 considers jurisdictional thinking as a technology of Black authorship in ways that challenge place-bound constructions of sovereign power. The main texts in chapter 3 are *Incidents in the Life of a Slave Girl* (1861) and *Narrative of James Williams, an American Slave* (1838). In each text, the author deploys jurisdictional thinking through textual experimentation with presence and absence. For instance, in *Incidents*, while hidden for years in a nearby attic crawl space, Harriet Jacobs sends letters to the North to be postmarked from those jurisdictions before they are mailed to her enslaver in North Carolina. Williams, on the other hand, constructs and deploys various personae, some of whom exist only as traces in legal opinions where courts struggled to adjudicate his status by virtue of his multiple "identities" and aliases.

In this chapter, I consider how these writers created geographies of privacy through staged disappearances that nevertheless depended on their continued inhabitation of enslaving spaces: Jacobs through her continued, if secret, presence in a space of legalized slavery; Williams through an overidentification with the expectations of servitude that attended his embodiment while he posed as a waiter aboard a steamship. I argue that these Black geographies of dissent mark spaces of private Black life while largely abandoning the state—and arguably the slave narrative genre—as available sites of Black belonging. For Jacobs and Williams, the occupation of enslaved spaces registers their refusal of law's existing logics, and also imagines a world beyond plantation jurisdiction. By removing their *legal persons* from this jurisdictional regime, even as their *bodies* remained within it, Jacobs and Williams theorize jurisdiction beyond place and instead as a form of human relation they can create and revise.

Given that sovereignty links the central two chapters together at the literal heart of the book, I offer a few words here about its relationship to the book's broader arguments. Sovereignty has been a key term in Black culture and Black studies both historically and conceptually, as a sign of autonomy, agency, and self-determination. For example, of the many things that were significant about the Haitian Revolution, chief among them was the establishment of a Black sovereign state and the ways that this event functioned to offer both a literal and symbolic vision for Black self-governance and liberation. But of course sovereign power has often been used as an instrument of colonial and imperial violence against Black and Indigenous people. It functions as a technology of war-making, a justification for force, and a metaphor for the kind of autonomy that can live not just in a nation but in an individual body or human being. Thus, sovereignty—a concept often attached to the nation-state, to geopolitical or juridical entities, or to legal constructions of personhood—is a surprisingly pliable construct that is often at the heart of the innovations being deployed by the writers I study in this book. The paradoxical pliability of sovereignty is that it functions both as bulwark against intrusions and an assertion of self-determination. It can of course be wielded and weaponized by oppressors, but it can also be claimed and reimagined by the oppressed as a source of agency or authority that does not necessarily depend on forms of territorial (geographic) jurisdiction or "state" power. Given the constraints on Black writers during the antebellum period—in terms of their mobility, as well as their participation as civic or legal subjects of the geographic jurisdictions in which they were enslaved and to which they escaped—sovereignty thus becomes visible as a powerful intellectual and *literary* form of self-determination and worldmaking, a literary technology of Black liberation. As I argue here, writers during the antebellum period persistently experimented with worldmaking practices through their innovations of legal forms and concepts that might otherwise be understood as merely oppressive; their engagement with sovereignty is similar.

Chapter 4, "Precedent," posits a practice of citation through which African American fiction and autobiography encode and rescript legal histories. At law, the common law system of precedent depends on a citational discursive practice that evokes intricate legal histories by condensing them into narrative-rich case citations. This form of intertextual encryption claims to leave precedent undisturbed and promote coherence in legal reasoning across time, even as it conceals the complexity of legal doctrine within shorthand legal citations. As I argue in chapter 4, African American citation to precedent during this literary period tended to expose the malleable and fragile system of legal citation and rescript existing precedent to imagine alternative legal histories and new Black futures.

My main text in chapter 4 is Hannah Crafts's 1850s fictionalized autobiography, *The Bondwoman's Narrative*. I read that text alongside trial materials from the case of Jane Johnson, a formerly enslaved woman briefly referenced by Crafts who famously testified at the Philadelphia trial of several white abolitionists who assisted her self-emancipation. Encoding is a process that puts information in a readily accessible format that is legible because it follows a set of knowable and stable rules. Encryption, by contrast, *conceals* information so that it only becomes accessible if one is in possession of the appropriate decrypting knowledge or key. I argue here that the processes of fictionalization in *The Bondwoman's Narrative* encode legal narratives by referencing existing legal process or history and then encrypting alternative logics of power.

For example, in referencing Jane Johnson, Crafts citationally engages Johnson's legal history. In Crafts's hands, however, this legal history takes place in the nation's capital (as opposed to Philadelphia, where Johnson actually testified), transforming Johnson's fugitivity into a matter of federal jurisdiction—this jurisdictional question thus extends the arguments made in chapter 2. The novel also returns Johnson to the place of her actual birth, which her legal testimony connects to a significant contemporaneous historical event: the burning by the British of the US Capitol in 1814. Crafts thus uses fictionalization, I argue, to undo existing legal histories and reimagine them in such a way that makes room for redress and restorative justice, including the possibility of an alternative US history in which the Capitol did not survive. This chapter thus takes up processes of literary fictionalization through citational practices that resemble legal precedent but deploy that logic in radical ways. The chapter also briefly considers a document on precedent written by Mary Ann Shadd Cary, who, beyond her career as an abolitionist, activist, and newspaper publisher, also completed a law degree at Howard University Law School.

Finally, in a brief coda, I revisit some of the through lines in this book and offer several possibilities for how my readings of legal form in antebellum Black literature might be productively mobilized around readings of more contemporary Black fiction. I use the work in this book to broaden out in particular onto questions of nonlinear temporality and speculation, suggesting law as a constitutive context not only for antebellum Black writing but for

African American literature as a whole, thus extending Karla Holloway's argument that "nearly all African American fiction inevitably engages some dimension of the legal."[110] In particular, in the coda, I consider the implications of this project as a bridge to treating law as an unexpected context for Afrofuturism. My work in the coda suggests Afrolegalism as a possible term for Black legal thinking that collaborates with Afrofuturism to envision Black liberation. As you read the intervening chapters, hold in mind these circuitous transits across time and place, and notice the ways that these nineteenth-century writers simultaneously labor in service of immediate legal relief and at the limits of law, in anticipation of new legal worlds.

CHAPTER ONE

Appeal

The appeal form is deceptively familiar. In nineteenth-century print, it is as capacious as it is ubiquitous, particularly among antislavery activists. As a persuasive rhetorical posture—a multipronged plea targeting emotion, logic, and ethics—the appeal as a genre sustains countless essays, articles, and pamphlets engaged in various forms of advocacy. In the abolitionist context, the rhetoric of appeal typically coheres around advocacy on a particular case or policy, and it often doubles as a fundraising appeal—another familiar gloss on the term and one that points to the function of sentimentalism in appeal's deployment.[1] For example, an 1839 item from *The Colored American* entitled "Appeal to the Friends of Liberty" addresses the newspaper's readers on the matter of thirty-eight enslaved Africans from the *Amistad* revolt who were "incarcerated in jail to await their trial for crimes alleged by their oppressors to have been committed by them."[2] In titling their appeal, the authors—a trio of white abolitionists that included Lewis Tappan and who were known as the Amistad Committee—implicitly and automatically characterize their request as aligned with liberty and, at the level of address, invite the newspaper's readers as accomplices in the pursuit of liberation for a group of "unfortunate men" who "are ignorant of our language, of the usages of civilized society, and the obligations of Christianity." The article notes that these men are "destitute of clothing" with "scarcely a rag to cover them," rehearsing the prisoners' abjection as the thing that both authenticates their status as victims and verifies the request for financial support.[3] Between their literal nakedness and their ignorance of the language and customs necessary to navigate their incarceration and trial, the enslaved men are narrated as both needing and deserving assistance from the authors and the newspaper's subscribers.

The rhetorical framing of an emotional appeal is as familiar in the twenty-first century as it was in 1839. These appeals for charitable assistance affirm the donors' ideology and affiliation with a common cause (in this case, emancipation), reify Blackness as abject, and position philanthropy as the solution to systemic oppression. But then the article proceeds to note that "several friends of human rights have met to consult upon the case of these unfortunate men, and have appointed the undersigned a Committee to employ interpreters and able counsel, and take all the necessary means to secure the rights of the accused."[4] This reference to legal counsel, which promises specialized legal representation as the tangible outcome that a financial contribution will help realize, links the rhetorical appeal as a *literary genre* to the *legal form* and significance of appeal as a specialized forum in which to challenge a previously completed legal action.

Note the ways that this article mystifies the distinction between "friends of human rights" who "consult upon the case of these unfortunate men" but who appear to be distinct parties from the "able counsel" appointed to secure the men's rights. That porosity between the categories of "legal counsel" and "political consultant"—counseling versus consulting, advising versus opining—points to the relaxed professional status of lawyering in the 1830s, when many lawyers entered the profession after a period of individual study and apprenticeship as opposed to the highly regulated law school and bar examination protocols familiar today. It also demonstrates the nuanced difference between the valences of political and legal; in this distinction, the "friend of human rights" evinces a political form of affiliation, while "able counsel" is a professional, fiduciary relation.[5]

That distinction also presses the altered stakes for subjects of legal oppression; while political affiliation can protest that oppression and argue for policy changes, navigating the intricate system of legal procedure requires the labor of a professional legal advocate who is fluent in that world and its textual rules. By the time an appeal is on the horizon, several conditions have already been met: a legal action has recently concluded, with an unfavorable result, an outcome that under modern rules of appellate procedure initiates a legal clock or deadline by which litigants must either announce their intention to appeal that previous outcome or forfeit their right of appeal altogether. I have taken some license here to pursue this train of thought a bit beyond the contours of appeal that are superficially visible in this 1839 newspaper article, in which the prisoners have yet to proceed through the trial phase of litigation, much less an appeal phase. But I do so in order to foreground the temporal pressures and exigencies that arise around appeal in general—one imagines how those stakes increase if the action being appealed is, for instance, a conviction resulting in a sentence of death by execution. These pressures haunt an article like this one in *The Colored American*, which deploys the language of appeal in an ostensibly emotional register even as it anticipates an actual future legal appeal, if only as a contingency, a worst-case scenario. In fact, in the case of the *Amistad* captives, the case was actually appealed all the way to the Supreme Court; a number of the captives died in custody amid the lower court litigation before the surviving captives were ultimately granted freedom by the Supreme Court two years later, in 1841.[6]

These pressures surrounding appeal also signal the ways that the burden of acquiring professional legal assistance during this process demands an outlay of labor and expense amid an ongoing legal emergency. From a litigant's perspective, pro se legal representation might be tempting both as a practical solution to dwindling resources during a time of crisis and because the person subjected to legal process is often the single greatest expert on the underlying factual scenario and relevant legal procedural history. Moreover, as described in the introduction and traced through work by Dylan Penningroth, Kimberly Welch, Emily Owens, and others, nineteenth-century African Americans frequently participated in litigation and consumed legal culture via print, meaning that they often possessed professional legal expertise as well as factual knowledge.[7]

As an example of legal culture's ubiquity in print circulation, abolitionist newspapers in the 1830s and 1840s are replete with items styled as "appeals" that alert the reading public to specific legal issues ranging from disenfranchisement to the right to jury trials. The prevalence of these appeals, and their frequent linkage to jury trial rights, underlines two simultaneous truths: (1) the extent to which criminal procedure rights and rules occupied, as an urgent matter of survival, the legal vernacular for Black people in the nineteenth century; and (2) the extent to which abolitionist networks mobilized this urgency as a strategy of public relations and policy influence. It becomes obvious after reading a dozen or so similar items how uniformly they operate and how effectively the appeal functioned as an instrument of ethical and emotional persuasion; it creates urgency and drama, unambiguously establishing the high ethical and moral stakes, even as it promises the reader the opportunity to feel powerful and benevolent.[8] While these two valences of appeal operated simultaneously, I attempt in this chapter to disentangle the legal qualities and possibilities of appeal from its more general political and rhetorical dimensions, and to show how early Black fiction writers in particular took up the legal appeal as a literary form that offered enticing[9] possibilities for engagements with counterfactuals and speculative history, possibilities that afforded creative constructions of Black history and creative mappings of local and global Black communities.

This chapter examines the longer history of appeal as a legal mechanism before turning to several antebellum examples of Black writing that use the legal form of appeal, including (1) David Walker's *Appeal to the Coloured Citizens of the World*, (2) Victor Séjour's short story "The Mulatto," and (3) the serialized short story, "Theresa, _____ a Haytien Tale," (written by "S."). Each text explores the possibility of revolution: Walker's political pamphlet references and reframes the American Revolution, while both short stories use the Haitian Revolution as either the primary setting or an implicit context for the rearrangement of familial and political structures and the reimagination of past events. It stands to reason that these writers would avail themselves of legal appeal as a literary container for their work—legal appeal, at its core, operates to review past events before determining whether and/or how to overturn them and start anew. It necessarily grapples with the material realities and consequences of what has already happened, but it also retains the ability to redress past wrongs through its capacity to reimagine and enact new legal worlds. It is unsurprising, then, that the appeal form would arise consistently in the specific context of revolution.

As alluded to above, the most familiar modern legal definition of appeal is as a form of judicial review; following the outcome of a legal proceeding in one court, a dissatisfied litigant can, under certain circumstances, petition a higher court to review and reconsider the original result. Typically, an appeal of this nature relies on claims that the original trial proceeding was inherently flawed or unjust. In a nineteenth-century treatise on appellate proceedings, Thomas Watkins Powell notes that this legal mechanism protects individuals by providing recourse to poorly adjudicated outcomes, but he claims that "the great value of appellate proceedings is not only in the preservation of the rights of the individual, but also in establishing upon just and correct principles, the constantly recurring new questions in the administration of the law, in which the public is interested, that they should be so settled, as to be consistent with sound principles of justice and in harmony with the existing body of the law."[10] This process of judicial review, then, serves two functions: (1) to protect an individual's right to a fair proceeding, thus ensuring that there is a process for reconsidering badly decided judgments; and (2) to protect the legal system as a whole as a public resource. This second function of appeal speaks to public confidence in legal process and legal principles both because that confidence props up the perpetuation of the legal system and faithful adherence to it, and also because the potential for misuse and abuse of the system would threaten the so-called public good. As Powell further observes, "It is of the utmost importance, in giving satisfaction and confidence in the administration of the law, that litigants should know and feel that their case has been decided upon consistent and uniform principles; so that the like cases and the like facts produce the like results."[11]

These logics of appeal rehearse some well-worn principles of the judicial system in general as entangling and making interdependent the rights of the individual and the interests of the state or the public. But Powell also calls our attention to the interest in judicial efficiency, the need for law to assimilate aberration and to produce the appearance of a harmonious coherent whole. This appearance of a harmonious whole sustains the appearance of the system's integrity, but it also helps produce results in different cases that will be consistent with one another. That normalization, the creation of norms applied to "like cases and ... like facts," tends to support a process of naturalization, wherein legal norms are treated as inherent, naturally occurring, and arising from a somewhere else that both is the state and is bigger than the state. Therefore, while Powell's formulation of the appeal suggests that it produces judicial efficiency as a means of ensuring sound results in individual cases, it is important to remember that this function also serves the system itself, by normalizing what Derrick Spires has referred to in the context of citizenship as "the assumptions that make current social and political arrangements seem natural, timeless, and desirable."[12] Appeal functions then as a check on aberrant or inefficient results, and in doing so it entangles the interests of the litigants with those of the state, bringing their interests into alignment under the signs of concepts like "integrity," "efficiency," and "consistency."

As Powell's treatise further illustrates, this concept of appeal as judicial review is also deeply rooted in theories of injury—it imagines that the judicial process itself may fail to make whole the victim of some other crime, and it concedes that the judicial system may actually inflict its own harm in rendering a poorly or improperly decided case. The process of seeking a judicial appeal, then, is fundamentally about redress. It is an opportunity to repair or compensate for a wrong or harm that has occurred in the course of litigation or legal enforcement. This reparative capacity of appeal as a legal form underscores its imaginative and liberatory possibility for Black writers in the nineteenth century, who were living under a system of legalized genocide and dispossession. As a mechanism that concedes the possibility for judicial action to produce harm and to offer correctives to that harm, legal appeal holds the imaginative promise of relief and protection under law in a profoundly oppressive legal regime; the practice of overidentification with law's protective capacities has persistently been a legal strategy among Black litigants, and particularly Black women. Emily Owens has traced the ways that nineteenth-century Black women in New Orleans improvised legal performances in pursuit of protection from sexual abuse, while Thavolia Glymph has documented Black women's claims to rights as refugees during the Civil War.[13] The latter example shows how Black women identified refugee status as a legal mechanism of redress and identified or overidentified with that mechanism as part of a rights-seeking strategy. Both historians illuminate these practices as examples of Black legal culture that, in construing law as a possible shield from other forms of legalized violence, seek refuge within what Harriet Jacobs describes as the protective "shadow of law."[14]

The framing of legal appeal as a route to legal protection emerges in even sharper relief when we consider some of the specific legal history around rights of appeal in the United States. Beyond functioning merely to correct errors in the judicial process, "appeal" in the colonial period "referred to a procedure under which a higher tribunal could completely and broadly rehear and redecide not only the law, but also the entire facts of a case."[15] While this remarkably inefficient system of judicial review largely gave way by the nineteenth century to the error-centric writs model that we recognize in modern judicial review, as Mary Sarah Bilder notes, "the word 'appeal' and arguably some of its broader jurisprudential connotations never completely vanished from the American legal system."[16] This haunt of colonial appeal matters especially to my consideration of Black writers' use of legal appeal as a literary form—the capacity to review and renarrate the full factual world of a case in addition to the relevant legal rule is worldmaking at an almost fantastical scale. Understanding legal appeal as a hierarchical review with the ability to annihilate whole legal worlds helps frame the literary relationship between appeal and revolution.

To further complicate matters, there is a separate overlapping genealogy of American legal appeal that arrives through English common law and which William Blackstone references in his *Commentaries on the Laws of England*. The *Commentaries*, originally published between 1765 and 1770, were perhaps the most widely read legal texts in the nineteenth-century United States, despite their specific affiliation with English legal history. The US Supreme Court *continues* to cite Blackstone well into the twenty-first century; in the nineteenth century, reading the *Commentaries* was a critical component of legal training at a time when the legal profession largely used an apprenticeship model to train practitioners. Abraham Lincoln famously read Blackstone by candlelight, and the *Commentaries* were widely accessible and familiar to the antebellum reading public in general, whether or not they were training as lawyers. *Freedom's Journal*, for instance, the first African American newspaper—with which David Walker was affiliated—contains several references to Blackstone from the late 1820s,[17] demonstrating Blackstone's influence among Black as well as white audiences.

The *Commentaries* were widely read for several reasons. First, as a practical matter, the United States "inherited" English common law as precedent. That body of law had governed colonial legal proceedings up until 1776, at which point, post–Declaration of Independence, the US American common law system formed its own branch of law that grew out of, but departed from, British precedent. So all of the legal history that Blackstone martialed in the *Commentaries* supplied both the theoretical and philosophical underpinnings of US American law, as well as many actual areas of overlap on theories of trespass, inheritance, and so forth. Second, legal reading among laypeople, as I discuss at several points throughout this book, was a much more commonplace nineteenth-century reading practice than it is today. Between the detailed legal news that appeared in periodicals and pamphlets and the inchoate development and regulation of law as a profession, the need to consume legal information as news, human interest, and even entertainment was much higher during this time period. And finally, given the relative newness of the United States as an independent republic in the 1820s—barely fifty years beyond the American Revolution—Blackstone was also a remarkably "current" reference source at the time.

The type of legal appeal outlined in Blackstone is essentially a private criminal prosecution rather than a rehearing of an earlier case. Typically, crimes are prosecuted by the government; the victims of the crime often appear as witnesses in such prosecutions, but the victims themselves are not responsible for staging the trial or crafting the prosecution's theory of the case.[18] The available forms of punishment in a criminal prosecution typically include imprisonment and imposition of fines; these punishments redress the public good but do not provide tangible financial compensation to individual victims. Victims in contemporary law maintain a separate mode of recovery to collect damages for their injuries—typically, we refer to these private, or civil, causes of action as torts. In general, a "bad act" is considered a crime when a governmental body has declared that act punishable as against the public interest. A tort, on the other hand, is a civil action where a person who has been injured by someone may, under certain circumstances, recover compensation for their injuries, whether or not the conduct in question is also a public crime. This distinction matters here only insofar as tort law was not widely developed or practiced in US law until the mid- to late nineteenth century, despite concepts elsewhere in Blackstone that allude to private wrongs.

On the contrary, this form of appeal identified in Blackstone's *Commentaries* appears in the volume dedicated to "Public Wrongs." This form of legal appeal, according to Blackstone, "when spoken of as a criminal prosecution, denotes an accusation by a private subject against another, for some heinous crime; demanding punishment on account of the particular injury suffered rather than for the offence against the public."[19] While Blackstone concedes that it is used far less commonly even in the late eighteenth century, he notes that the private appeals still in use at that time were appeal of felony (larceny, rape, and arson) and mayhem,[20] alluding by extension to the conception of these specific crimes as having the potential to interfere with or degrade the public good. In the case of murder, designated family members of a murder victim could bring prosecution in their stead. Significantly, citizens bringing these private appeals did not need to wait for a government to issue any indictment. This form of legal appeal identified the crime that gave rise to it, identifying the injury suffered as the basis for prosecution (rather than relying on a prosecutor to identify harm done to the public good by the conduct in question—note the ways that, like pro se advocacy, this mechanism attempts to dispense with a legal "middle man"). This form of appeal, though less common, has retained its visibility in sources other than Blackstone as well. For instance, both *Black's Law Dictionary* and the *Oxford English Dictionary* include entries for this form of legal appeal. In *Black's Law Dictionary*, it is defined in criminal practice as "a formal accusation made by one private person against another of having committed some heinous crime."[21]

All of these definitions of legal appeal—whether a reconsideration of a lower court's error, relitigation of a proceeding's entire factual landscape, or a private indictment of a heinous crime—contemplate the role of the legal system in redressing harm and injury, offering a mechanism for an ostensibly disempowered legal subject to name legal violence and seek legal repair. These qualities of legal appeal suggest why the form is inherently relevant to African American thought and culture in the antebellum period. We know that African Americans—enslaved as well as free—in the antebellum period well understood the nuances of their legal statuses, and that they regularly developed strategies of legal participation that worked within and beyond the ostensible limitations on civic and legal life that "official" legal records often enumerated via anti-literacy laws and prohibitions on legal testimony. We also know that the stakes of law were huge and high for enslaved and free African Americans in the first half of the nineteenth century. Facing a legal regime that routinely sought to either exclude or enclose, Black legal culture as a practice of survival and freedom had to at once respect the law's violent reality and seek ways to exploit the protections it had to offer. Legal appeal, with its theoretical potential to wipe the juridical slate clean, to renarrate both history and future, extended one such possibility.

This chapter takes seriously this potential of legal appeal by reading texts like *Walker's Appeal to the Coloured Citizens of the World*, "The Mulatto," and "Theresa, _____ a Haytien Tale" not just for their deployment of rhetorical persuasion but also as sites of strategic imagination that seek redress by imagining alternative histories and revolutionary futures. I read Walker's use of the legal appeal form in conjunction with his well-documented deconstruction of Thomas Jefferson, suggesting Walker's use of appeal as a primer for experimentation with legal forms that literally overturn rhetorical, legal, and fictional hierarchies. After briefly considering Walker's *Appeal*, this chapter considers how Victor Séjour's 1837 short story "The Mulatto" and S.'s 1828 short story "Theresa, _____ a Haytien Tale," considered two of the earliest works of African American fiction, deploy the appeal form as a technology of revolutionary overthrow and of counterfactual experimentation, marking these texts' speculative qualities.

DAVID WALKER—a Black abolitionist, subscription agent for *Freedom's Journal*, and Boston shop owner—mounts a series of legal arguments through his *Appeal to the Coloured Citizens of the World* (1829), an antislavery pamphlet published in three separate editions between 1829 and 1830 and distributed throughout the United States.[22] It is difficult to overstate the *Appeal*'s influence or its range. Between 1829 and 1831 alone, physical copies of the *Appeal* traveled up and down the Eastern Seaboard, while publications ranging from *The Liberator* to Georgia's *Statesman & Patriot* (and of course *Freedom's Journal*) reprinted excerpts from the *Appeal* and published commentary on it.[23] The circulation model of the *Appeal* deliberately aimed to extend as far south as possible: Walker himself shipped a number of pamphlets to individual recipients in Southern cities—sometimes with their knowledge, and sometimes without—with instructions for distribution.[24] Thus, the *Appeal* infiltrated the South, producing intense anxiety where it appeared, including numerous state legislative responses that criminalized possession of the *Appeal* as a revolutionary or seditious item. White lawmakers regarded the *Appeal* as a grenade, and they determined to prevent it from "exploding" and setting off Black rebellion.

It is not a mystery why the proliferation of the *Appeal* produced this reaction. The *Appeal* calls for "coloured citizens of the world" to reject slavery and to resist slave culture in all of its forms. Generally regarded as a classic example of revolutionary rhetoric, scholars have read the *Appeal* as an example of early Black radicalism,[25] a foundational text in the Black jeremiad tradition,[26] and an example of a tradition Derrick Spires calls a "sublime appeal."[27] Walker's rhetoric influenced fellow Black antebellum public intellectuals and orators such as Maria Stewart and Henry Highland Garnet; the *Appeal* has echoed throughout Black radical and Black nationalist thought for the past 200 years. The pamphlet's defining feature as a condemnation of slavery has sustained its afterlife as a critical context for antebellum Black rebellion and as a necessary postscript to the founding documents that it responds to (the Declaration of Independence and the Constitution), as well as Thomas Jefferson's *Notes on the State of Virginia*.[28] To the wealth of scholarship on Walker's *Appeal* as protest literature, jeremiad, and rhetorical masterpiece, my aim here is to bring the legal form(s) of the appeal more squarely and directly within our understanding of how the text works and how its use of this form summons the possibility of speculative history as practiced in the early Black fiction that emerged in rough contemporaneity with Walker's text. As becomes evident when we sit with Walker's *Appeal*, it functions within *all three* historical meanings of legal appeal—it produces a petition for redress of a past grievance, it seeks to overturn and remake the factual and legal realms that structure Black life in the United States (and around the world), and it formally lodges the accusation of a heinous crime. In each of these registers, the *Appeal* does what all legal appeals do in that it unsettles hierarchy.

In particular, Walker's engagement of the legal appeal form as an instrument of literal overturning amplifies the logical and moral aberrations inherent in Thomas Jefferson's legal discourse in the Declaration of Independence and *Notes on the State of Virginia*. As Tavia Nyong'o has argued, "Jefferson's discourse on racial governmentality, unlike that of 'hate speech,' was not intended for a black audience at all." Nyong'o further notes (and uses Walker as an example) that "black subjects eavesdropped on an anxious discourse of white superiority, black inferiority, and the dangers of racial contamination. Overhearing this discourse, they replayed and refracted it, precisely in the hopes of shaming whites about it as well as using it as evidence to rouse other blacks out of their acquiescence to the present state of affairs."[29] As Nyong'o shows, Walker's "refraction" of Jeffersonian legal theory functioned as a type of public shaming—an indictment of a crime—as well as a rebuke. In this sense, in responding to Jefferson in a way that demands review and revision of *Jefferson's* legal imagination—and to extend Nyong'o's formulation of refraction—Walker's use of petitionary appeal demands review and reconsideration by a higher authority. Who or what constitutes that higher legal authority? Walker's *Appeal* displaces white legal institutions (a court of judicial review), instead vesting moral and legal authority in the titular "coloured citizens of the world." Walker's text positions people of African descent *as* the higher authority capable of hearing and ruling on that question. The "coloured citizens of the world," as the addressees of the *Appeal*, are the equivalent of an appellate court, or perhaps the Supreme Court; in the same way that one appeals *to* a judicial body, this *Appeal* is made to "the coloured citizens of the world, but in particular, and very expressly, to those of the United States of America."[30] In making these addressees the highest legal authority and the most esteemed judges, this posture of Walker's legal pleading upsets and overturns expected individual and institutional hierarchies, whether or not it "succeeds" in overturning any of the documents or systems it challenges.

In other words, the framing of the *Appeal*, which challenges several specific features of US law and Jeffersonian legal doctrine, *also* discursively overturns the entire legal system by reversing the relational positions of those with the most and the least legal power. This mode of overthrow and reinvention of operative norms is an example of legal worldmaking.

Walker's nimble use of language in the titling of his *Appeal* is emblematic of the duality that characterizes the text as a whole. At once specific and general, inciting and condemning, the *Appeal* moves back and forth in its engagement with, and resistance to, prevailing law. This oscillation or ambivalence is part of the performance of legal appeal, a mechanism that recognizes legal review as a valid juridical procedure even as it skeptically regards law as fallible, reserving the power to invalidate and overturn previous legal proceedings. He argues that the "almost universal ignorance among us" is the result of laws and customs that prevent the education of African-descended people in the United States.[31] In this context, Walker's distribution scheme—he mailed the *Appeal* to locations throughout the South with directions that those too poor to pay for a copy ought to receive it for free, and those unable to read should have it read aloud to them[32]—is legible as part of the *Appeal*'s project of educating and organizing his fellow "coloured citizens" around the call for a revolution that doubles the American Revolution and Jeffersonian legacy, reimagining Black revolution as an appellate technology of reversal and redress.

In his consideration of Walker's contributions to discourses of citizenship, Derrick Spires identifies the power of the legal appeal as a worldmaking device through which, from a position "outside of official state institutions," "restrictive notions of belonging can be contested and ... alternate models can be theorized and practiced."[33] In thinking about how Black writers experimented with alternative models of belonging, Spires alludes to the ways that the legal form of appeal supports and sustains Black creative possibility;

indeed, it is not a long journey from practicing alternate models of belonging to experimenting with alternative histories and ultimately experimenting with speculative literary imagination. In his work on the "Appeal of Forty Thousand Citizens" and the 1848 Appeal to the Colored Citizens of Pennsylvania, Spires further makes a compelling case for the form of the legal appeal as central to convention organizing and forms of public belonging, whether state-sanctioned or not. His work here exposes how conventions' appeals shift the focus away from supplication and onto advocacy.[34] Thinking about this connection between appeal and advocacy productively returns us to the concept of pro se litigation. A pro se framework is especially helpful here in that it picks up the strain of entrepreneurial and improvisational engagement with hostile legal structures but also foregrounds legal form (and specifically the form of legal appeal) as an innovation of authorship and a technology of spatiotemporal possibility.

Walker's *Appeal*, while pleading for a more just future and asking African Americans to become allies in that project, adopts a rhetorical posture that, because it wears the clothing of legal appeal and thus addresses past wrongs, appears initially to be more *retrospective* than futurist. Each of the four articles that follow Walker's preamble traces what he terms "our wretchedness" to a different root cause—slavery, ignorance, religious hypocrisy, and the colonizing plan. But Walker's *Appeal* is forensic in the way that legal appeals must be; it identifies African American "wretchedness" and, in a methodical four-part approach, it develops arguments about the causes and sources of that pain. It acknowledges the pain without reducing African American identity to an abjected or helpless posture—rather, by addressing his fellow "coloured citizens" as the audience for his *Appeal*, Walker makes Black Americans not only advocates of their own resistance, but the *judges* of their oppressors and the architects of the world to come.

As much as Walker's *Appeal* thus practices futurity through retrospection—a temporal feature of legal appeal—it also uses the form of legal appeal in order to remake and remap a Black world. The title's term of address to the "coloured citizens of the world" suggests on one hand that Walker situated his text within proto-Pan-Africanist or diasporic discourse; he refers not to the United States, but to "the world." Despite focusing his pamphlet particularly on African-descended people in the United States, in overturning the existing US legal regime, Walker clears space to rebuild that legal world around a global form of belonging for all African-descended people. His normative "rules" for that new legal world contemplate civic and social membership on the basis of shared Blackness, as opposed to national identity. However we read "coloured citizens of the world," it seems most significant to register that label's incompatibility with geopolitical nationalism and its elevation of non-white subjectivity as a marker of moral and legal superiority.

It is evident from the framing of the *Appeal*, and from its formal conventions and content, that the adversarial division of the text as a legal appeal has people of African descent on one side of the "v." and white Americans on the other. Toward the end of the pamphlet, Walker writes, "Americans! notwithstanding you have and do continue to treat us more cruel than any heathen nation ever did a people it had subjected to the same condition that you have us."[35] This example of Walker's use of pronouns underscores the way that the legal appeal form inflects his work. As above, if we read this moment in the text as part of a conventional legal appeal, in which a petition requests a rehearing, this moment reads as a fairly conventional legal argument. On the other hand, reading it not only as a straightforward appeal but also as an indictment of a heinous crime, Walker's use of vocative direct address here performs a speech act that, rather than *beginning* a process of review, *completes* the work of accusing. In the equivalent of a courtroom gesture that points at a witness, a gesture echoed throughout the *Appeal* in the persistent use of the manicule (☞), Walker issues the accusation, while carefully using "you" and "us" pronouns to make clear that African-descended people are categorically excluded from the signifier "American." It is for this reason that I have been careful here to refer to Walker's primary audience as people of African descent rather than African American—as his text exposes, the category of "African American" has no place in Walker's geopolitical understanding of Blackness and its relationship to the US nation-state. This distinction is in some ways a function of the fact that "African American" as a term only achieved widespread cultural use much later, but the distinction in Walker's text is so visible and persistent that it would be a form of rhetorical violence to merely substitute a contemporary signifier like "African American" when Walker himself takes such pains to refuse to marry those adjectives to one another.

Whether thinking about Walker's *Appeal* as a petition for redress or an accusation of a heinous crime, legal appeal is suitable to Walker's purposes precisely because that legal form contains the potential to undo or reverse the "scriptive" qualities of a legal text like the Constitution or the Declaration of Independence, or to redefine conduct as illegal. Indeed, Nyong'o argues that the *Appeal* "is a scriptive thing for undoing white racial innocence," a claim that deploys a broader connotation of innocence as a narrative but nevertheless also returns us to the realm of criminality and sutures innocence explicitly to whiteness.[36] This scriptive potential to undo hews very closely to the colonial form of appeal that permits a higher judicial authority to review and rewrite both the legal and factual case being appealed. As the analysis of the framing already suggests, at a very general level, it is possible to read Walker's *Appeal* as not just attempting to overturn a single previous decision or document but to overthrow the entire United States. Even passing references in the *Appeal* suggest a preoccupation with the precarity of the United States as a viable national project. For instance, Walker opens Article IV of his *Appeal* with a relatively lengthy response to Henry Clay and the far less famous attorney, Elias Caldwell, whose opinions on colonization Walker had encountered in the *National Intelligencer*.[37] In work on Walker and Douglass, Babacar M'Baye observes that Caldwell was, in addition to a proponent of colonization, a former clerk at the US Supreme Court, two items that are relevant to Walker's interest in him as an object of appeal.[38] First, Walker's opposition to colonization is the subject of Article IV, in which he takes Caldwell to task. But, second, Caldwell's affiliation with the US Supreme Court—literally the highest appellate court in the United States—makes him an especially alluring target of appeal.

In fact, in addition to having clerked at the Supreme Court, Caldwell was perhaps most famous as the *savior* of US jurisprudence when he rescued the Supreme Court library from its then home at the Capitol before the British set that building on fire in 1814 during the War of 1812.[39] This specific historical event (the burning of the Capitol) resurfaces again in chapter 4 in connection with *The Bondwoman's Narrative* and the case of Jane Johnson—its afterlife among antebellum Black writers is suggestive of a nagging fantasy about how close the United States had come in 1814 to having actually burned down. In any case, Caldwell's connection to appellate practice and his reputation as having salvaged Supreme Court jurisprudence imbue Walker's address to him with a layer of dramatic and legal irony. Despite addressing this symbolic figure of Supreme Court jurisprudence, Walker does so not as a supplicant seeking Caldwell's judicial authority or a request for Caldwell to perform judicial review; Walker instead approaches Caldwell in a pro se posture, acting as his own advocate, *and* as the prevailing judicial authority in solidarity with the legal and moral authority he has already established with other non-white people around the world.

In engaging one of Caldwell's speeches, Walker begins by inhabiting the posture of the reviewing authority, writing, "I shall now pass in review the speech of Mr. Elias B. Caldwell, Esq. of the District of Columbia."[40] Walker maintains a formal distance from Caldwell as he disassembles Caldwell's embrace of colonization; this disassembly reproduces the "undoing" or "unmaking" that judicial review enacts in overturning a previous proceeding on appeal. Despite positioning himself as the reviewing authority, Walker also maintains the posture of advocate throughout this section of the text, staging the review of Caldwell as though he stands before a judicial audience during appellate arguments. In this way, in the section that follows, Walker effectively duplicates himself, occupying multiple locations or roles at once and using the theater of legal appeal as an occasion to experiment with its spatiotemporal affordances.[41]

Caldwell had claimed that it was pointless to educate African-descended people because they would never be able to put their education to any use, which would transform the intended "blessing" of education "into a curse." "Let me ask this benevolent man," Walker writes of Caldwell, "what he means by a blessing intended for us? Did he mean sinking us and our children into ignorance and wretchedness, to support him and his family? What he meant will appear evident and obvious to the most ignorant in the world."[42] Walker places a manicule immediately after this sentence, as if to literally point the finger at Caldwell. Walker pauses here in the sort of rhetorical flourish that arises during appellate argument where confrontation is *performed* in front of the judicial authority being petitioned/addressed but never carried out in direct dialogue with one's adversary. In other words, appellants do not speak directly to those they are opposing; all arguments on appeal are presented to and through the judging body. The adversarial component of a judicial appeal is abstracted out by a degree so that, rather than actually arguing with one another, the parties to an appeal each *separately* present their arguments to a reviewing body and attempt to persuade or convince the appellate court of their position's superiority. Rather than simply addressing Caldwell directly, by asking "what did *you* mean?" Walker uses the third person to refer to Caldwell ("Let me ask this benevolent man what *he* means"), suggesting that, in the preceding moment, Walker addresses someone or something *other* than Caldwell. This apparent address to a reviewing authority marks the way that Walker, in this staged appellate argument, has slipped out of his role as judicial arbiter and into his role as advocate.

This rhetorical toggling, like the move back and forth between "us" and "you," once again underscores the pamphlet's function in multiple senses of legal appeal—as plea for judicial review and as the indictment of a heinous crime. When Walker shifts into the rhetoric of "you," he moves out of pleading for rehearing and into the form of legal appeal as indictment, or accusation, of a heinous crime. By performing the directly accusational version of legal appeal, Walker turns the language of culpability directly onto his white oppressors, charging them with responsibility not only for the harm done directly to enslaved people but also for the social conditions that have arisen among all African-descended people as a result of slavery. He writes, "Have you not . . . entered among us, and learnt us the art of throat-cutting, by setting us to fight, one against another, to take each other as prisoners of war, and sell to you for small bits of calicoes, old swords, knives, &c. to make slaves for you and your children?"[43] Walker thus traces a chain of responsibility for the very character deficiencies that have been alleged against people of African descent. He assigns not only blame but *guilt*, unearthing a logic of culpability that explains Black violence under a new theory of criminal liability: white Americans, through example and manipulation, are responsible for the Black violence that they then use to justify continued oppression. Walker assigns ownership to white Americans in the one way they do not wish to assert it—at a time when proslavery arguments insisted on slavery as the *natural* consequence of perceived racial inferiority, Walker gives white Americans ownership of the mechanism by which slavery is *manufactured*. Here again, his use of legal appeal is an exercise in overthrow and subsequent (re)worldmaking.

Walker's legal arguments therefore are not mere mimesis, but something closer to the mimicry that Homi Bhabha describes as "a form of colonial discourse that is uttered *inter dicta*: a discourse at the crossroads of what is known and permissible and that which though known must be kept concealed; a discourse uttered between the lines and as such both against the rules and within them."[44] Walker's *Appeal* does not simply rehearse legal form, it also deploys legal form to undermine the legal system *itself*—even as Walker's audiences witness one form of appeal at a time, multiple other appeals and meta-appeals constantly reverberate throughout the text.

Almost none of the *Appeal* rehearses the sort of biographical or autobiographical accounts of enslavement that would become so common to the slave narrative genre a few years later. Walker's exhaustive legal and historical presentation offers not one shred of personal information about his own life, his family, or his identity other than his name on the pamphlet's cover. Instead, the open accusations and assertions of the *Appeal*, despite their boldness and publicness, protect and preserve private Black life in a way that feels unexpectedly resonant with what Kevin Quashie describes as the sovereignty of quiet. As Quashie notes, "Public expressiveness is the workhorse of nationalism, and is vital to any marginalized population."[45] Quashie uses John Carlos and Tommie Smith's Black Power salute at the 1968 Mexico City

Olympics as an example of quiet—it is a highly visible and public gesture that leaves much unsaid even in its external expression. My reading of Walker's *Appeal* locates a version of quiet in his presentation of his arguments. Walker's *Appeal* certainly engages in public expressiveness, even as it challenges white nationalism and offers its own theory of Black nationalism or Pan-Africanism. There is, on one hand, the unmistakably public expression of his claims. And yet, the imaginative potential of legal appeal as a literary form leaves its traces of overthrow and worldmaking in the text—in the imagined and perhaps implausibly unsettled hierarchies; in the hint of spaces of belonging that depend not on the nation-state or the juridical but some as-yet-undefined communal practices; even in the fact that the *Appeal* ends not with a prayer for relief, as is customary in a legal pleading, but with actual prayers and verse from the *Common Prayer Book* and *Wesleys Collection*.

This closing gesture turns darkly poetic with a warning that "the Americans," a term that underscores the white racialization of US identity, will never be "vigilant enough for the Lord, neither can they hide themselves, where he will not find and bring them out."[46] This turn to the prophetic speaks to the *Appeal*'s persistent vision of overturned hierarchy. The performance of prophecy also aligns with Matt Sandler's formulation of "Black Romantic revolution,"[47] and it suggests literary points of connection with "The Mulatto" and "Theresa, _____ a Haytien Tale," both of which employ features of gothic romance. As the *Appeal* closes, its claim for redress turns to a distinctly spiritual realm, rehearsing a vision of a post-slavery world wherein the existing logics of power have already been subjected to legal appeal, or judicial review. As a result, those logics have been unmade, redressed, and reassembled to make way for a new model. This clearing and worldmaking, in its construction of future worlds out of a disassembled past, hints at the ways that Black fiction in particular might take up the speculative affordances of legal appeal. As Justin Mann notes, the speculative is particularly suited to "probe at imperial structures ... while preserving [Black] life force."[48] Legal appeal as a form also facilitates this dual practice of critique and survival through its dual operations of review and redress/rebuilding.

Before entering the world of fiction, however, Walker's final turn to the apocalyptic shares terrain with another trend in Black print culture of the 1830s that helpfully glosses the speculative and revolutionary possibilities in legal appeal and fiction. Scholars have cataloged a tendency among antebellum Black writers to deploy the language of apocalypse, particularly among those writers whose rhetoric is most deeply invested in scriptural and Christian traditions. In *Apocalyptic Sentimentalism* (2015), for example, Kevin

Pelletier considers how David Walker, Maria Stewart, and Nat Turner all draw on prophetic discourse to imagine that slavery may end when a furious god rebalances a world that has fallen so deeply out of order that it must be exploded and remade.[49] Brittany Sulzener has likewise traced the apocalyptic in Maria Stewart as offering a form of futurity that cuts against the tendency of white writers to "proleptically envision [] the ruins of a great American nation as a source of nostalgia for future generations." Sulzener argues instead that Stewart uses the apocalyptic "as a rhetoric of empowerment," as a means of narrating "a nation so inherently corrupt that it must be destroyed or transformed in a catastrophic, apocalyptic event that would leave no traces of the former nation behind."[50] These reclamations of the apocalyptic by and for Black writers suggest a relationship between ruination and futurity refracted through the language of prophecy. But one trend in Black print culture from the 1830s specifically confirms this nexus of prophecy, futurity, and ruination through a single biblical verse that speaks these things through the language of legal appeal.

A survey of African American newspapers from the 1830s and 1840s yields a number of references to Ezekiel 21:27, a biblical passage that includes Ezekiel's prophecy about the fall of Jerusalem. References to this verse are not always visibly cited as such but are recognizable through variations on the phrase "overturn and overturn." For example, an 1837 article in *The Colored American* includes the following prophetic claim: "God will turn and overturn, and put down one and another, until right and righteousness shall occupy the throne, or anarchy and misrule devastate the government."[51] The full language from Ezekiel is translated in places as "A ruin! A ruin, I will make it a ruin!" or "Overthrown, overthrown, I will make it overthrown, until he comes whose right it is," or "I will overturn, overturn, overturn it: this also shall be no more, until he comes whose right it is."[52] These various translations link up the concepts of ruination (which recalls Mann's formulation of "world-breaking"[53]) and reversal or overturning; overturn is, of course, the same language that describes what happens when one judicial authority, on appeal, reverses the decision of a lower authority. As the verse tends to get referenced in abolitionist newspapers, it frequently appears in the language of overturn specifically. And yet, as with David Walker's turn to the apocalyptic and the prophetic, it appears to be more focused on the "after" than on the destruction of eliminating the current order.

For example, in an 1844 article from *The Liberator*, an author writes that society was "radically false in its structure," and "it ought to be REORGANIZED." This author envisions this reorganization as "a oneness of spirit in righteousness which shall 'overturn and overturn,' all that is oppressive and unjust, until the form of society shall be simple, beautiful, the outward symbol of an inward redemption."[54] Here again, despite the outwardly expressive call for radical societal reorganization, this 1844 article uses this same spatial binary—outward vs. inward—to suggest to the reader that the "success" of a revolutionary project, a liberatory project, depends on a "oneness of spirit" that itself becomes the divine authority capable of overturning that which oppresses.

The attachment to ruination, then, is not an attachment to nihilism or even annihilation but a form of imaginative possibility. Framing the apocalyptic as a practice of Black futurity and prophecy both underwrites the status of African-descended peoples as "chosen" by a Christian god and indicts the US nation-state for its crimes against those people. That the attachment to this verse from Ezekiel so frequently appears in phrasing that uses a legal cognate—overturn—speaks to a tradition of apocalyptic futurity in language that we must also construe as legal. While this single example may be read as coincidental, note that a number of other items from the same time period repeatedly label slavery as "a heinous crime"[55]—the same legal language verbatim that authorizes the ancient practice of appeal described in Blackstone's *Commentaries*, and through which I have read David Walker's *Appeal*. This constellation of terms that operate in both divine and legal frameworks remains preoccupied with reversing the poles of existing power structures as a means of redressing crimes against humanity.

This broader turn to apocalyptic futurity demonstrates how appeal, despite its retrospective process, remains a future-oriented practice. It also links Walker's *Appeal* with other literary forms and genres that take up the legal form of appeal. One of the main consequences of Walker's *Appeal* is that it exposes the legal fictions that enable and sustain the US national project—fictions of equity that mask enslavement and genocide; fictions of legal classifications of African-descended people as subhuman; fictions of law's stability that Powell describes by noting, "Each principle and maxim of the law must agree and harmonize with each other, or the law becomes a mass of disconnected fragments instead of a harmonious and scientific whole."[56] Walker's dismantling of these legal fictions exposes law as harmonious and scientific only when read as deliberately engineered genocide and oppression—a stark contrast to the "oneness of spirit" envisioned in the pages of *The Liberator*. Given how nimbly the *Appeal* navigates different elements of fiction—how it dissects and displays fictions of law, and how it experiments with its own worldmaking possibility—it stands to reason that writers would also experiment with legal appeal as a literary form in early Black fiction.

In the remainder of this chapter, as a case study in how the legal form of appeal functions in early Black fiction, and to note the ways that this form reimagines place-bound sovereign logics, I examine Victor Séjour's experimentation with appeal and apocalyptic futurity in his 1837 story "The Mulatto" and then turn to S.'s use of counterfactuals to reimagine revolutionary pasts and futures in the 1828 story "Theresa, _____ a Haytien Tale." These texts each perform legal appeal's tripartite process of reviewing, overturning, and rebuilding, demonstrating judicial review's utility as a site of speculative imagination in fiction. As works of fiction, these texts already share narrative affiliation with legal form (and specifically appeal) as a technology of world-making. It is significant that each of these texts, generally considered the first two works of African American short fiction, deploy historical fiction, setting their events in the historical past and even more specifically in pre-Revolutionary Saint-Domingue. This shared emplacement signals the importance of the Haitian Revolution in Black culture and Haiti's symbolic legacy as a Black sovereign state even decades after Haitian independence, and it speaks to the amenability of legal appeal—as a kind of sanctioned revolution—to fictive experimentation and innovation. These stories take up appeal from different angles, but in both cases appeal operates as a futurist practice that is enacted through retrospective review and redress. The situation of that process in Saint-Domingue calls attention to appeal's temporal pliability, and it remaps the world according to a hemispheric or diasporic consciousness.

Victor Séjour's 1837 short story "The Mulatto," originally published in French in the *Revue des Colonies*, depicts an act of vengeance that redresses an enslaved woman's execution. Set in Saint-Domingue, pre–Haitian Revolution, with a post-Revolution external frame narrative, the story primarily narrates the life of Georges, an enslaved mixed-race man who is the living product of his mother's rape by her (and Georges's) enslaver.[57] The knowledge of his father's identity, contained in a pouch that his mother has sworn him not to open until his twenty-fifth birthday, is the lever across which the tragedy of Georges's life unfolds. Without access to that history, Georges spends his early life forming a perverse sense of loyalty to the enslaver who is his biological father—and, unbeknownst to him, also potentially the father of his own mixed-race wife, who is executed for striking the enslaver as he attempts to rape her. This nexus of deranged familial connections, in addition to being visible as an early example of what has come to be known as the "tragic mulatto" genre, indexes the multiply disordered social networks wrought by plantation slavery in the Americas and specifically Saint-Domingue. Georges's family history is legible to the reader, as though it has been presented to the reader for a version of judicial review or appeal. But that history remains inscrutable to him up until the end of the story; as vengeance for his murdered wife, Georges strikes a decapitating blow, and Alfred's last words acknowledge his paternity. Finding confirmation in the pouch from his mother and tormented by the revelation of his father's identity, Georges takes his own life.

This act of patricidal vengeance—the decapitation of Alfred—is visible to the audience as an intervention that supplies a gothic linkage between the sexual violence of slavery and the mythological echoes of an Oedipal tale. By the time the paternal revelation eventually reaches Georges, he has already planned and carried out the attack as revenge for the murder of his wife (and potential sister), Zelia. Crucially for my analysis of legal form, this act of vengeance is the extension of a legal proceeding in the story: the legally sanctioned execution of Zelia for striking Alfred in self-defense. When Georges kills Alfred, he redresses not only the loss of his wife but specifically the legal proceeding that sentenced her to death by hanging for her "violation" of the slave code. Though the story does not depict trial proceedings, per se, it is nevertheless evident that legal process has been mobilized to punish Zelia's alleged offense. As they await her sentencing and punishment by a separate executioner, Alfred repeatedly rehearses what Robert Cover describes in *Justice Accused* as the "judicial can't"—a strategy used by judges to passively allow law to achieve violent means, even when they personally disagree with its substance, by professing that the individual judge is "bound to apply the law, immoral as it may be."[58] In response to Georges's pleas for Zelia's life, Alfred claims, "There's nothing I can do," and "It is no longer up to me to pardon her."[59] Ironically, it is Alfred's failure to exercise his available legal discretion that both marks him as a judicial authority and transforms him, in Georges's theory of the case, into the true criminal of these proceedings.

At this point, following Zelia's death, Georges is in the posture of legal appeal. There has been a legal proceeding (Zelia's execution) that he desires to appeal; unfortunately, as an enslaved person he lacks legal standing to challenge Zelia's sentence, and he lacks the time or other resources to mount any other kind of appeal because she is executed almost immediately. Georges's dramatic situation thus highlights the importance of legal appeal as a rights-seeking and rights-protecting mechanism, and it presses on appeal's temporal sensitivity—in order to perform judicial review, an appellate authority must first pause a legal clock before irreparably punitive harm occurs (as it does here, with Zelia's execution).

In another gloss on engagement with legal appeal, Georges persistently reframes the impending execution not as a legal punishment but as a heinous *crime*: "'What! you can leave her to be killed, to have her throat cut, to be murdered,' said the mulatto, 'when you know her to be innocent ... when, like a coward, you wanted to seduce her?'"[60] Here, like Walker, who makes the white nation culpable for slavery, Georges mystifies the language of culpability, narrating Zelia not only as guiltless (in the sense that she committed no crime and in fact acted morally by resisting Alfred) but innocent (in the sense that she is the victim of murder at Alfred's hand). Though Georges preemptively appeals (legally) to Alfred as a pardoner, Alfred's position atop that judicial hierarchy is in the same breath inverted; over the course of a single conversation, Alfred transforms from the highest available legal authority into a murderer. Georges initially performs legal appeal as an indictment of a heinous crime. But in what follows, this version of legal appeal collides in interesting ways with the other form of appeal, the pursuit of redress by contesting and requesting the review and overturn of a previous judicial proceeding.

Aware that legal process holds no redemption for Zelia or himself, Georges abandons the judicial mechanisms of the plantation and the slave codes—which may or may not be in concert with one another—while claiming appellate authority for himself from a space outside of law and its reach. Without waiting for Zelia's execution, Georges gathers up his young son and flees to a maroon camp deep in the forest surrounding the plantation. This extralegal space "of slaves who fled the tyranny of their masters" materializes almost as an oasis after Georges spends six hours walking through the forest.[61] By "extralegal," I mean that a maroon community definitionally operates outside the legal strictures and logics that attach to the plantation, the colony, the state, or even the nation-state—a status and practice that Neil Roberts, in *Freedom as Marronage*, has theorized in order to reframe marronage and fugitivity not merely as escape but as strategies of ongoing liberation.[62]

Georges's retreat to a maroon settlement in the story is a geographic relocation that in turn alters the relevant legal framework.[63] In the space of marronage, Alfred is neither a judicial nor a moral authority; the slave codes have no practical application among the maroons. Instead, the maroon community, its own sovereign space, is a version of an overturned or dismantled plantation logic. It is a space of possibility where Georges can access a new form of belonging, detached—or, more accurately, liberated—from the juridical structures he has left behind. In this place, the literary and spatial manifestation of legal appeal, Georges becomes the highest authority over his life, his wife's murder, and the appropriate form of redress. It is fitting that he forms his plan for revenge from this "recess,"[64] a space that echoes the sanctuary of the pimento grove in "Theresa, ____ a Haytien Tale," Nat Turner's pre-rebellion retreat to the forest, Henry Blake's repeated "seclusions" among

Black revolutionaries throughout the diaspora in Martin Delany's 1859 novel *Blake*, and Harriet Jacobs's "loophole of retreat."[65] In "The Mulatto," this retreat to the maroon community and its revolutionary possibility is marked by the greeting Georges extends to the maroon leader upon arrival: "'Africa and freedom'" and then, "'I'm one of you.'"[66] This greeting, which links Blackness, freedom, and belonging, speaks to Neil Roberts's formulation of marronage's sovereign possibilities. By proclaiming himself as a member of this group, Georges performs a speech act that eradicates his juridical status as nonperson and instantiates him as a member of a sovereign Black space. In relocating here, Georges effects a legal appeal and overturning of his enslavement, if not (yet) Zelia's murder.

This invocation of Africa, uttered from the heart of the forest in Saint-Domingue, authorizes his confident claim, "I am one of you," as he calmly brushes away the gun that is pointed at him. In this moment, this text—written by a free man of color from New Orleans, published in French in Paris, documenting an African sense of belonging from a maroon community in pre-Revolution Haiti—signals the forms of global, diasporic Black belonging suggested by David Walker in his *Appeal*, published just a few years before "The Mulatto" appeared in the *Revue des Colonies*. This space of African belonging is not only a place of sanctuary and liberation for Georges, it is where he becomes the authority capable of redressing his wife's murder. Read this way, his revenge against Alfred is not only vengeance or bloodlust; it is an extension of the legal proceedings for which Georges's original legal appeal (his petition to Alfred) failed; replacing Alfred with Georges as the highest judicial authority also serves as a corrective to an unjust legal regime. As Georges and Alfred reverse their hierarchical positions, the structure of their relationship, like the basis for Zelia's execution, is overturned.

This unconventional extension of the legal proceedings that condemned Zelia to death might be referred to as vigilantism, or extralegal revenge, but scholars have been more inclined to read this plot event as insurrection, a reading that aligns Georges's narrative trajectory with the revolutionary dimensions of legal appeal. For example, despite thinking about this text alongside Walker's *Appeal* and eighteenth- and nineteenth-century petitions by enslaved people, Christopher Michael Brown theorizes "The Mulatto" as participating in a tradition of "seditious prose" in which Black literature grapples with "the irresolvability of [enslaved African Americans'] doubled roles as patriots and traitors."[67] I do not dismiss the fact that, from one angle, Georges's murder of Alfred is undeniably a form of insurrection, but I read insurrection as revolution as opposed to treachery; why should we reproduce the legal logics of the system that enslaved Georges in the first place by reading his resistance only through the lens that system prescribes? In fact, one of the payoffs of legal appeal as a literary form is its capacity to alter the terms of existing legal regimes, as Georges does in this story.

But it also makes sense to consider Georges's actions as a literary reworking of legal appeal because he responds directly to Zelia's prosecution and execution by imagining an appellate judicial authority that exceeds—if only through pure force—any authority that the plantation legal system could produce. Additionally, the story marks that process by stationing Georges among the maroons and identifying a distinctly Black space in which the response to Alfred can be imagined, nurtured, planned, and brought to fruition. Georges implements the logic of judicial appeal as an extension of Zelia's execution, and though he does not name it that way, he does maintain focus on the task at hand by recalling that "he had come to the house of his master, not to learn the name of his father, but to settle accounts with him for his wife's blood."[68] It is worth noting the slippage here, as Georges has this thought *before* learning that his master *is* his father. The use of the word "him" in this sentence refers both to "his master" and "his father," and there is a suggestion here that, on some level, Georges already knows that these two men are one and the same. But additionally, the metaphor of "settling accounts" makes clear that Georges understands this vengeance as a form of redress—that Zelia's execution has created an injury that positions Alfred as a debtor. This positioning of Alfred not as a creditor but a debtor inverts the expected relationality between enslaver and enslaved. As Saidiya Hartman has noted, "The literal and figurative accrual of debt recapitulated black servitude within the terms of an emancipatory narrative," constructing even an emancipated person as maintaining a status of indebtedness to their former enslaver.[69] In reversing that status relationship, the story returns us to the ability or end goal of appeal to overturn and upend as a form of redress, a goal envisioned as well by the final verses quoted in Walker's *Appeal*.

"The Mulatto" marks these valences of appeal and overturning in other ways, as well, including Alfred's apparent recognition that Georges's appearance relitigates their earlier conversation in which Georges sought Zelia's pardon from Alfred. In a moment of symmetry that perhaps suggests some of the other reformulations and dissonances produced by overlapping colonial and jurisdictional regimes that generate conflicting rules and procedures, Alfred now pleads with Georges and explicitly positions Georges as the pardoner: "'Oh! mercy . . . please take pity on me,' said Alfred, throwing himself at the feet of the mulatto."[70] Here, both legally and visually, Georges has assumed an elevated position while Alfred has been cast down below at Georges's feet. Unlike Alfred, however, Georges occupies the position of both judge *and* executioner, and Alfred's final sentence now names him as such ("Strike, executioner . . . strike"[71]).

Perhaps, however, the most salient references to Black appeal and apocalyptic futurity rest with the story's setting, which straddles pre- and post-Revolution Haiti. The external frame narrative signals this temporal status in the opening sentence: "The first rays of dawn were just beginning to light the black mountaintops when I left the Cape for Saint-Marc, a small town in St. Domingue, now known as Haiti."[72] The spatiotemporal situation of this introduction signals at once the capacity of appeal as (1) an overturning of a criminal regime and (2) the intermingling of pastness and futurity thus encompassed by appeal. This framework, in which the reader witnesses dawn rise above the black mountaintops, augurs a new beginning, even as it references the Haitian Revolution as a precursor to this text ("a small town in St. Domingue, now known as Haiti"). Although the events narrated in the story take place prior to the Haitian Revolution, the telling of it in the external framework seems to have been authorized somehow precisely through this overturned system, this radical reorganization that has been produced by the Haitian Revolution, a revolution that prosecuted the heinous crimes of slavery, colonialism, and empire.

As a mode of legal relation and review, appeal can structure intimate forms of connection, and it can serve as a check on abuse. For one thing, appeal (whether operating as indictment or petition for review and redress) unambiguously identifies a wrongdoer, making it difficult or impossible for enslavers to avoid personal culpability if not legal responsibility for their crimes. This quality of appeal illuminates the ways that it functions, as I have suggested, as legally sanctioned revolution. Appeal disrupts and overturns systems by seeking recourse both for the wrongdoer and the victim. Moreover, as a legal form and structure of advocacy, appeal is inherently discursive—it catalyzes redress and worldmaking through language and speech, which makes it a particularly hospitable form for Black fiction writers, whose work on the page is inherently interested and invested in language's ability to produce material, as well as rhetorical, consequences. The fictional potential of legal appeal here is twofold. First, given the life-threatening risks of revolution for enslaved people, fiction is a site that can safely catalyze and sustain experiments in revolutionary appeal. Second, for a work of historical fiction like "The Mulatto," fiction, like appeal, permits the retrospective revisitation of events from the historical past. Fictional worlds, like legal appeals, facilitate counterhistories, counterfactuals, and opportunities to "do" history differently in order to generate alternative futures; fictionalization, like appeal, thus permits imaginative speculative experimentation.

This speculative experimentation is visible as well in the ways that "Theresa, ____ a Haytien Tale" uses a (presumably) fictional account of the Haitian Revolution to creatively remake events from the historical past and produce counterfactual thought experiments. Serialized in *Freedom's Journal* in 1828 and written by an author identified only as S., this text predates "The Mulatto" by nine years.[73] The story follows a free Black woman named Madame Paulina and her three daughters as they become refugees during the French military occupation of Saint-Domingue, or St. Domingo. When one of these daughters, Theresa, overhears French soldiers' tactical plans, her sense of solidarity and revolutionary duty moves her to risk her life to deliver this intelligence to Toussaint L'Ouverture, who is encamped nearby. After successfully delivering this information, "her thoughts reverted to the deplorable state of her country; with a prophetic eye she saw the destruction of the French, and their final expulsion from her native island. She entreated the Creator, that he would bless the means, which through her agency, he had been pleased to put in the possession of her too long oppressed countrymen, and that all might be made useful to the cause of freedom."[74] This passage situates the titular character as an instrument of Black liberation, and a spiritual or moral authority within the text. Nevertheless, she immediately follows this moment with a critical self-examination of her actions as injurious to her mother and sister and possibly as violations of her duties to gendered norms of respectability and propriety. Performing a self-review of her actions, Theresa weighs "the important services[ ] she had rendered her aggrieved country and to the Haytien people... [and] felt that her conduct was exculpated, and self-reproach was lost in the consciousness of her laudable efforts to save St. Domingo."[75]

While the rehearsal of legal appeal is perhaps more tenuous here than in "The Mulatto," I want to underscore several registers in which we can locate legal appeal as a literary device in "Theresa." First, in following the tripartite structure of reviewing, overturning, and rebuilding, the elements of legal appeal are all present. The most visible of these in the text is review. As noted above, the narration actually positions Theresa—like Walker in his *Appeal* and Georges in "The Mulatto"—as *both* the reviewing judicial authority and the petitioner or pro se advocate. Having established her moral and spiritual bona fides, the text allows Theresa to both plead and adjudicate her own cause; she reviews her actions to determine whether a crime has been committed, and ultimately she exonerates herself.

The text's more significant practice of overturning, however, occurs in the way the story modifies or overturns the narrative of the Haitian Revolution. On first reading this story, I assumed it was performing feminist counterhistory by highlighting the revolutionary labor and spirit of Black women and girls in the Haitian Revolution and suggesting that Theresa, not L'Ouverture, was the true hero of Haitian independence. That reading remains a plausible one. However, I have eventually come to an alternative reading of the text as performing counterfactual as opposed to counterhistory. There is no reason to assume that this text purports to merely supplement the official historical record (the function of counterhistory); while it is possible to read the story as a supplemental or corrective fictionalized account that adds to the history of the Haitian Revolution without altering its outcome, it is actually quite ambiguous in its relationship to known historical events. Since it does not fix the temporal setting with absolute specificity, it is impossible to know whether, for instance, the story reimagines L'Ouverture's fate. L'Ouverture, who died in 1803 before witnessing Haitian independence, was captured by the French and imprisoned for the last year of his life. "Theresa" could be set well prior to L'Ouverture's capture, imagining a fictional encounter in the earlier part of his military career. The other, somewhat more intriguing, possibility is that Theresa's fictional intelligence mission altered the course of L'Ouverture's life and career; in this narrative world, the story could function as a counterfactual that permits an alternative history wherein L'Ouverture survived to see Haitian independence. In either reading, the text, bound up as it is in the spirit of revolution, performs an overturning—a sanctioned revolution—of the history of the Haitian Revolution. Like legal appeal and judicial review, it operates correctively, whether by supplementing Haitian history with a more complete account of women's revolutionary labor or by redressing the violence of L'Ouverture's capture and eventual death.

These narrative possibilities are largely inextricable from the text's performance of appeal's third element, rebuilding. Rebuilding a normative world happens within the text, as Theresa reunites with her family under the promise of Haitian independence—St. Domingo has transformed from a site of dispossession to a site of possibility. As Mary Grace Albanese notes, in language that precisely corresponds with my formulation about legal appeal's temporal affordances and futurist possibilities, the story "runs backward and forward along multiple axes, reliving pasts and imagining futures. Much like the Haitian revolutionary calendar, the tale's temporal dislocations confound rectilinear time, resurrect the revolution's foundational energies, and index both the past and future to the ever-reverberating rupture of 1 January 1804."[76]

Albanese's assessment of the story presses on time as well as place, observing that the narrative reimagining of the Haitian freedom struggle "requires that the reader imaginatively identify with the past in order to recognize not simply Haiti's independent existence but its *futurity*."[77] These qualities of retrospective futurity correspond to legal appeal's temporal situation of judicial review (retrospective) as a means for redress and rebuilding (futurist). And Albanese notes that, even in 1828, twenty-four years after Haitian independence, "Haiti was legally still a futuristic construct"[78] for US readers because the United States did not formally recognize the independent nation until 1862. Thus, "Theresa, ___ a Haytien Tale," deploys the affordances of both fiction and legal appeal to construct a postrevolutionary imaginary and site of Black refuge—a space that Albanese describes as "a consciously mystical topography."[79] Albanese's reference to mysticism and its effects on space and time in the text elaborates the power of legal form as an engine of worldbuilding that often signifies, in the Black abolitionist imagination, as mystical or magical.

As M. NourbeSe Philip writes, "In its potent ability to decree that what is is not, as in a human ceasing to be and becoming an object, a thing or chattel, the law approaches the realm of magic and religion. The conversion of human into chattel becomes an act of transubstantiation the equal of the metamorphosis of the eucharistic bread and wine into the body and blood of Christ." For Philip, this sacred and magical potential of law makes it not just an empty vessel of power, but something that can be reappropriated, cultivated, practiced, and put to different—more just—use. In *Zong!*, Philip characterizes her poetry collection as harnessing that language magic so that "the African, transformed into a thing by the law, is re-transformed, miraculously, back into human."[80] Overturn, overturn, overturn. It is this same quality that Patricia Williams calls "Word Magic"[81] and imagines as the sacred practice of a society of priests. It is the same with legal appeal as a literary form. There is retrospection in appeal, but there is also futurity, and there is ancient craft.

While my focus in this chapter has been on the appeal form specifically, the constellation of consent, autonomy, and authoritative hierarchy across these texts moves us toward theories of sovereignty, which itself expresses a paradoxical relation of power, obligation, and freedom. Chapters 2 and 3 in turn take up the legal forms of confession and jurisdiction, respectively, by thinking through their capacity to provoke various forms of Black sovereignty. In the subsequent chapters, I move from the appeal's tendency to overturn existing hierarchies to the capacity of confession and jurisdiction to create alternative strategies of Black survival and sanctuary in hostile terrain.

CHAPTER TWO

Confession

This chapter turns to the ways that Black writers leverage confession as a site of Black possibility, despite the confession's ostensible performance of culpability and capitulation to institutions of punishment and criminality. The ritual of confession, as the testimonial speech act that authorizes the transition from investigation to prosecution or from trial to punishment, vests the confessor with tremendous power. As an opportunity for public, Black-voiced participation in legal culture, antebellum confessions were strategies for certain kinds of legal visibility, though the practice carried obvious, significant risks of incarceration or worse. With roots in religious as well as legal traditions, confessions have historically occupied a liminal space. They have certain straightforward legal consequences for criminal defendants, often marking a procedural and strategic point of no return: once uttered and/or introduced into evidence, it is extremely difficult to alter, revoke, or exclude that official statement. At the same time, a strategically negotiated confession sometimes carries an almost magical capacity to neutralize punitive consequences by functioning as a symbolic cleansing ritual that purges the confessor of punishable liability. As with appeal's capacity for temporal malleability and worldmaking, confession operates both retrospectively and prospectively: definitionally, a confession addresses past actions (it is not legally possible to confess to a crime that has not yet occurred), even as it moves prospectively to initiate resolution or the transition to a punishment or restitution phase of adjudication.

Before turning to the nineteenth-century texts that occupy the center of this chapter, we must first consider where confession fits into the relevant literary and legal historical frameworks and how it surfaces in legal proceedings—most commonly in criminal trials. As a threshold matter, confession's association with criminality and anti-Blackness renders it deeply relevant to the legal history of the nineteenth-century United States and to the ways that, post-Emancipation, the structures of anti-Black oppression were often transferred automatically to the criminal sphere as a means of perpetuating the social and hierarchical conditions of legalized slavery. Moreover, as it is intended to be a recitation of facts and expression of remorse (as opposed to a legal argument), confession is also a form of testimony that must be spoken directly by a defendant and not through the defendant's attorney. For this reason, confession—which I focus on in this chapter as a literary mode—is, like other forms of autobiographical writing, susceptible to liberatory optimism as well as essentialist fantasies of unmediated access to a confessing person's interior. And confession's overlapping relevance to spiritual, as well as legal, traditions further complicates the amount of latitude given to confession as discursive expression and to the highly moralized uses of confession as part of a project of spiritual conversion. As Joycelyn Moody observes, "The early prison confession, a subgenre that is perhaps intrinsically sentimental, also took the form of a Christian conversion narrative."[1] The religious overtones of confession thus produced a kind of spiritual commerce in criminality, with hints and promises of "forgiveness" offered in exchange for confession and repentance.

However, most criminal confessions are (and were) extracted out of court by interrogators and law enforcement officials as opposed to during a trial, where procedural rules and rights against self-incrimination exist as protections for defendants. As a result, antebellum confessions were frequently subject to ad hoc and informal protocols as opposed to consistently applied or coherent rules, particularly where they were being solicited either by justices of the peace or as part of the terroristic regime of plantation abuse. In the case of justices of the peace, the impulse driving confession-gathering was an interest in promoting legal efficiency and keeping "the peace," or "community order," a loaded term that often defined order in racialized terms.[2] In the case of plantation abuse, by contrast, coerced confessions functioned as part of the daily abuse of enslaved people and as a way of compelling submission to the logics of hierarchical plantation rule. In any case, the informal nature and inconsistency of these rules made it even more dangerous for criminal defendants to trust interlocutors who promised them leniency or even exoneration in exchange for confession.[3]

For these reasons, confessions in all of their possible contexts ought to be and often were regarded with an amount of suspicion. And though the suspicion of confession may feel like a more modern artifact of police violence and corruption, for several centuries there has been concern about both coerced confessions and abuse of power by legal officials in obtaining confessions. As early as the 1790s, some state courts began requiring that confessions be corroborated, and by the 1840s, "at least three states—Arkansas, Missouri, and New York—had committal statutes that required magistrates to warn the accused of his right not to answer questions and his right to consult with counsel."[4] To be clear, rather than suggesting that this type of regulation established unbreachable protections for defendants, the existence of these statutes rather confirms that the potential for abuse in obtaining criminal confessions was, at a minimum, an open secret.

A survey of newspaper coverage during the mid-nineteenth century confirms that concerns over coerced and false confessions ran high during the period. Black and white abolitionist newspapers documented ongoing legal cases in their pages, frequently lingering on questions about dubious confessions, their evidentiary value, and their stakes. For example, an 1859 item in *The National Era* reports on the Indiana lynching of Joel Gresh, who had been a suspect in a string of robberies. The lynchers "hung [him] up to the limb of tree by the neck, with a view of forcing him to confess. When let down he still asserted his innocence. Up he was run again, and nearly strangled. He then confessed his only chance to live. The confession afterwards proved to be an entire fabrication, and Gresh was innocent of the crimes charged upon him." This brief article demonstrates the porosity of the legal process for Black defendants, for whom a "state" criminal investigation could be, at least partially, carried out by the extralegal violence of so-called lynch law. As the article points out, "Extorted confessions are uncertain evidence," a claim that speaks specifically to the *admissibility* of confession and the inherent unreliability of confessions elicited through threat, violence, or torture.[5] Though the article does not explain how or why Gresh was ultimately exonerated, it demonstrates that the legal process itself had been appropriated by lynchers, making it impossible for Gresh to receive a fair trial.

The *Provincial Freeman* reports in 1856 on a similar case of forced confession, this time in a murder trial from India. That article documents a case of three men who had confessed to committing a murder and who were exculpated only when the supposedly murdered victim appeared at the trial, very much alive. The article concludes, "It would seem most probable that the confessions in question had been extorted by the violence of the subordinate native police," again marking the danger of admitting out-of-court confessions to authorities with the means of coercing or extorting specific testimony.[6] This reference to coerced confessions in India, rather than signaling an unusual international practice, functions to rehearse how commonplace confession coercion was, a claim pressed by Black abolitionists and writers. In an 1860 article on Black insurrection, for instance, *Douglass' Monthly* prints, "Confessions are being extorted from the negroes by the free application of the lash, and the slaves on several plantations have taken fright at the excitement prevailing about them, and have fled to the woods."[7] This characterization of extortion is pervasive in the Black press during the midcentury, including an 1851 article from *The North Star* that documents the use of a so-called shower bath to torture a prisoner at Sing Sing—essentially the article describes the deployment of water-boarding "for the purpose of extorting confession."[8]

But despite these many concerns over forced and false confessions and the very good reasons to be suspicious of compelled confessions, Black defendants and legal participants have also historically found ways to appropriate the public space of confession to creative ends. For example, in conversation with Joycelyn Moody's observation about prison confession as Christian conversion narrative, Laura Edwards notes that, in nineteenth-century Carolina legal culture, confession (plus repentance) often functioned as a prerequisite for "forgiveness," and served as a way to evade harsher punitive consequences.[9] In the context of debt recovery suits, Kimberly Welch notes that Black plaintiffs brought suit against white debtors in part to compel in-court "confession" from these delinquent borrowers and establish a repayment plan.[10] And, as Emily Owens demonstrates in the context of Black women's survival in antebellum New Orleans, any occasion in which a Black woman offered official testimony was an occasion that could be leveraged a site of public claims-making, an opportunity for information transmission whether to the legal record, an individual judge, an enslaver, or the public.[11]

I offer these competing examples of confession's nineteenth-century legal contexts for several reasons: first, to demonstrate the ubiquity of confessions discourse as a contested site of testimonial "truth" and, second, to illustrate that Black writers understood that the very things that made confession unreliable as an evidentiary device vested confession as a genre, like appeal, with the potential for worldbuilding. Gallows literature is largely beyond the scope of this chapter, but its existence as a body of literature is relevant to the context of legal confession and helpfully links the materiality of criminal litigation with Black literary production. As a common exception to nineteenth-century prohibitions on Black in-court testimony, gallows confessions both depended on and unsettled perceptions of Black subjects as achieving legal visibility primarily through criminalization. In her 2012 book *In the Shadow of the Gallows: Race, Crime, and American Civic Identity*, Jeannine DeLombard, citing William Andrews, specifically identifies the significance of gallows literature and criminal confession to the African American literary tradition, describing the criminal confession as the "'obvious literary ancestor' to the slave narrative."[12] The link in the generic genealogy makes sense: these first-person narratives established a narrow route to forms of public Black authorship, while relegating that authorship to the testimonial/documentary, and ultimately sustaining the anti-Black associations of Blackness with criminality.

While the genre of the freedom narrative sought to cast off the affiliation with the criminal, these other authorial attachments remained, albeit in increasingly experimental and innovative forms as the genre evolved. *The Confessions of Nat Turner* might properly be termed gallows literature—though I prefer to include it in the lineage of confession outlined in this chapter—because of its attachment to offering a presumably white reading audience a Black subject who has been (1) sensationalized by lurid criminal context and simultaneously (2) rendered "harmless" by his inevitable execution. The sensational dimension of gallows theater gruesomely "ritualistically reminded the assembled spectators of the simultaneously punitive and redemptive power of God in the life of the individual and the community even as the day's carefully orchestrated exercises vividly displayed the terrifying power of local authorities."[13] And yet, despite the narrowness of this path to public Black authorship, and the spectacular display of Black death, gallows literature nevertheless, in DeLombard's words, "imagine[d] an unprecedentedly autonomous [Black self]."[14] DeLombard has offered a robust study of this genre of Black literature, marking the significance of confession within the African American literary tradition, a trope that gets taken up in nineteenth-century freedom narratives more commonly under the general rubrics of disclosure, witnessing, and testimony. While freedom narratives may have sought to reframe confession away from its historical associations with criminality, it is worth lingering on confession as a specific form to consider why antebellum Black writers remained invested in its affordances and possibilities.

In this chapter, while I honor the material pressures that confession placed on litigants, and despite the fact that two of my main texts involve legal proceedings, I specifically examine the legal form of confession as a site of *literary possibility*, as opposed to generating a historiography of antebellum criminal confessions and litigation proceedings. This posture may be an unfamiliar engagement with an unconventional archive, but by focusing primarily on confessional form as a site of literary potential, I am able to more fully explore the ways that confession operates not only in the gallows or as a mere metaphor, but as a public textual and legal strategy that, like the appeal form, mobilizes retrospective review as a futurist mode of worldmaking. Each writer examined in this chapter seizes these transcendent affordances of the confession form to infiltrate and unsettle the relevant hierarchy (law, patriarchy, respectability) demanding confession in the first place. This approach to confession as a literary form also allows me to go beyond criminal confessions to, for example, analyze Harriet Jacobs's intimate intrafamilial disclosures as assertions of sexual and familial sovereignty.

This chapter thinks of confession as a strategic *textual* and *literary* inhabitation of legal form (even when that inhabitation occurs in an official legal proceeding), inhabitation that transmits creative forms of possibility for Black life and freedom. The antebellum authors in this chapter, each of whom labors at the nexus of legal, spiritual, and social precarity, offer admissions of wrongdoing in ways that superficially and technically conform to the practical legal requirements of confession. But they also refuse to perform confession's expected expressions of remorse, regret, or submission. Thus, while performing compliance with confession's legal requirements, these writers also deploy confession in a separate literary register, in which confessing becomes an instrument of Black argument, worldmaking, and ethical sovereignty.

This chapter turns to three specific instances of literary confession—Nat Turner's published *Confessions* in connection with the 1831 Southampton Rebellion, Charles Langston's 1859 Cuyahoga County Courthouse speech following his conviction under the Fugitive Slave Act for assisting in the rescue of a formerly enslaved man, and Harriet Jacobs's 1861 autobiography, *Incidents in the Life of a Slave Girl*—to examine how Black literary performances of confession (1) attend to the legal and cultural demands of the form and (2) rewrite the terms of these events as creative and argumentative expressions of sovereignty. As I read each of these texts, I pay careful attention to the legal historical contours of confession that shape these literary expressions; I situate these texts as literary strategies that use confession's legal affordances to alchemize sovereignty from within spaces of apparent normative violence, which is to say, spaces that ostensibly seek to compel subjection and subordination.

These nineteenth-century literary confessions complicate frameworks of dissemblance and quiet in surprising ways, suggesting that confession holds abundant potential for formulations of Black survival, legal strategy, personhood, and sovereignty. As a frame both here and in chapter 3, sovereignty is a term that presses us toward the productive friction of overlapping boundaries among persons, groups, and, in some cases, states. That frictional ambiguity vests a sovereign variously as a person, a state, and/or a theory of rights that precludes interference from elsewhere. The relationship of sovereignty to nation, rights, and property signals its capacity to function productively both as a legal term and as a theoretical one. As Samantha Pinto observes, "Sovereignty holds a dual distinction of being a key site of and for the enforcement of rights. It is also a key node of debate about the bureaucratic, cultural, and ideological perils of claiming 'autonomy' as the key virtue of a rights-bearing entity. As a synonym for autonomy and independence, but also power and authority, sovereignty is at the heart of the struggle over discussions of human rights and black freedoms."[15] This sovereign constraint on, and possibility for, Black freedom helps explain why it has been taken up in so many different contexts, including *The Sovereignty of Quiet* (Kevin Quashie) and *The Sovereignty of the Imagination* (George Lamming). As this is the first of two chapters that examine forms of sovereignty, it is necessary to trace this term's significance as a structure of Enlightenment philosophy that has been both an object of critique and a site of reappropriation, particularly in Black and Black feminist studies.

Sovereignty is, in crucial ways, a legal form itself. For Imani Perry, sovereignty, along with property and personhood, is a "juridical form" that "consistently structured patriarchy."[16] Tracing the concept of the sovereign through John Locke, Perry identifies the "juridical nature of patriarchy . . . in both the coercive power of legal words—to distribute, to punish, to kill, to reward— and the clarity of the constructedness of all juridical decision making."[17] Perry demonstrates how Locke's formulation of the sovereign both claims a preceding property scheme under natural law *and* constructs that natural law (which established gender, race, and class hierarchies) in terms that cannot exist or be enforced without sovereign authority. In other words, though the concept of sovereign authority is ostensibly a positive law construction, the natural law construction of property relation relies on a circular definition that requires sovereign authority to affirm its own existence. And as Samantha Pinto observes about sovereignty in Enlightenment thought, "The sovereign both represents the people, but is also answerable to them and to the law that the people enact as their description of political will. As such, sovereignty has much to do with the social contract and the overreaching promise of contracts."[18] Contract has at times—particularly in the nineteenth century—been posited as a framework for the extension of rights (i.e., the suggestion that the capacity to contract is the badge of a "free" subject); constructing the sovereign as a benevolent contractual party facilitates the illusory suggestion that "the people" have consented to a sovereign authority to whom they are actually incontrovertibly and vulnerably bound.

In tracing the hegemonic violence of Lockean theories of sovereign authority, both Pinto and Perry also note the ways that this strain of sovereign theorization shapes feminist traditions. As Perry observes, "Hortense Spillers's theory of the vestibular, Gloria Anzaldúa's borderland theory, and Gayatri Spivak's subaltern are theoretical tools that emerge directly out of the human lacunae of Locke's ideas."[19] Moreover, Pinto points out that "when scholars such as Saidiya V. Hartman (1997) identify the coercion to consent to one's own brutalization and injury, they are identifying black subjects, particularly black women subjects, at the very heart of sovereignty rather than its antithesis."[20] Emily Owens's work in *Consent in the Presence of Force* further elucidates the fiction of consent as an available bulwark against violence for nineteenth-century Black women; Owens presses the weaponization of consent as a falsely promised path to sovereignty that instead imagines Black women "as culpable for their own violation."[21]

Thus, sovereignty, in its pressure on the border between collective and personal, is a theory of contestation and paradoxical power, of mutually constituted spheres of belonging that are nevertheless at odds with each other. As Pinto writes in relation to shifting constructions of Victorian British sovereignty, "These formations of black women as, in, and through concepts of sovereignty reveal resistance tactics that rely on the language of sovereignty and autonomy (state and self) to imagine black freedoms. These might be stretched to think of black women not as excluded from sovereignty but as the builders of alternative models and networks of sustained and sustainable vulnerability."[22] I enter this capacious construction of sovereignty here, to think in this chapter and in chapter 3, about how these nineteenth-century writers use the forms of confession and jurisdiction to theorize and enact their own articulations of civic, sexual, and spiritual sovereignty. *Incidents in the Life of a Slave Girl* is a through line across these two chapters and a textual link that theorizes sovereignty using both confession and jurisdiction. Jacobs's presence as a hinge between chapters 2 and 3 also calls attention to the ways that Black women's labor brings us to, in Pinto's words, "the very heart of sovereignty rather than its antithesis."[23]

Whether uttered out of court and admitted into evidence during a trial or uttered in court, a confession has significant stakes for a defendant's sovereignty and safety, a circumstance that a confessor navigates through their various audiences. The initial audience for an out-of-court confession is often an investigator or other official, and when that out-of-court confession is introduced into evidence, the jury becomes a second audience for the confession. Where confession is not offered directly during trial but is made in court during an allocution (following a guilty plea), the audience in this case is the judge or court. These distinctions among audiences matter because, while confession is often idealized as a moral and spiritual purification ritual, the truth is that most confessing parties are keenly aware of their audiences and the relative power that each audience wields. Most people making confession, whether in a religious or legal context, will pitch their confession at their audience's assumed soft spots. This subjective quality of confession reminds us of confession's inherently authorial and literary dimensions (which warrant the analysis of confession as a literary device), as well as its persuasive dimensions (which warrant its inclusion here as a strategy of pro se advocacy).

In moving through several different types of confessions, this chapter begins with out-of-court confessions as a general legal historical matter and then through Nat Turner, specifically, whose use of confession affirms his personal spiritual sovereignty even as it disrupts the legal proceedings against him. From there, I turn to in-court statements and Charles Henry Langston's formulation of himself, in his post-conviction statement, as a citizen-outlaw,[24] thus formulating a theory of citizenship and personal sovereignty that requires him to break the law. Finally, I turn to Harriet Jacobs and her use of confession in literary autobiography to affirm her sexual and familial sovereignty and to transmute a genealogy of sexual violence into maternal intimacy and sexual freedom. Jacobs, who so nimbly finds the overhangs and canopies within "the shadow of law" (a site of rights-bearing and protection), uses the confession form to verify her sexual sovereignty and to rewrite the unwritten "rules" of confession that serve the authorities to whom disclosure and penance are "owed" in the first place.

IMPORTANTLY, A CONFESSION acknowledges a set of conceded facts; it is a *narrative* about the deed or deeds committed by the defendant, but it is distinct from a plea, which is the defendant's formal, procedural answer to the charges alleged in an indictment or charging document. It is entirely possible, for instance, for a defendant to plead not guilty to a crime in a case where the prosecutor introduces evidence that the defendant previously "confessed" to the criminal conduct in question. In fact, as discussed in this chapter, that was precisely the procedural posture of Nat Turner when on trial for his participation in the 1831 Southampton Rebellion. In out-of-court confessions, the main legal controversy hinges on the admissibility of that evidence at trial. Although confessions or admissions against interest are typically exceptions to prohibitions on hearsay evidence, in order to protect defendants' Fifth and Sixth Amendment rights, modern courts move carefully when admitting out-of-court confessions into evidence. Over time, the specific legal standards have changed somewhat, perhaps most notably in the modern era with the *Miranda v. Arizona* decision, which established specific warning statements that must be given to those in police custody regarding their right to remain silent and thus avoid making a confession to police.[25] Obviously, given that African Americans had no codified citizenship rights in the first half of the nineteenth century, in cases involving African American defendants, and particularly enslaved defendants, courts had a great deal of latitude about which rights they elected to extend to defendants at all. But in the legal historical landscape of the nineteenth century, many people (particularly in the African American press) remained skeptical of out-of-court confessions as judicial evidence.

This suspicion stemmed, perhaps obviously, from the fact that criminal defendants and those in police custody are highly vulnerable to manipulation and exploitation, whether in the form of coercion to admit culpability or through the promise of rewards or lenience in exchange for a confession. As George Thomas and Richard Leo have traced in their 2012 book, *Confessions of Guilt: From Torture to Miranda and Beyond*, the skepticism among judges surrounding out-of-court confession was actually higher in England than in the United States during the early nineteenth century—though they suggest this difference may have been due in part to the fact that, in the 1790s, the United States, unlike England, had "no large urban underclass" and thus the exigencies of protecting those "vulnerable suspects" were different.[26] Though Thomas and Leo do acknowledge the widespread dehumanization of enslaved and Indigenous people, their implication about the lack of a "large urban underclass" rather conveniently sidesteps the burgeoning plantation underclass in the US and the fact that, for Black and Indigenous criminal defendants in particular, their extreme vulnerability to state power rendered them and their out-of-court treatment even *more* susceptible to state abuse. Despite an apparent gap in the legal historiography that might differentiate confession protections and outcomes based on the racial identity of the defendants, Thomas and Leo do conclude that, as a general matter, "What emerges from the early American cases is that voluntary, credible confessions were admissible" although often subject to burdens on the state to demonstrate that the confessions were properly obtained.[27] This general trend imposed evidentiary burdens at trial, as in an 1803 Delaware case where "the recorded examination could not be received in evidence at trial unless the magistrate appeared to 'prove the circumstances, whether by menacing, hope, etc.'"[28] It also manifested in several individual states establishing proto-*Miranda* style obligations that "required magistrates to warn the accused of his right not to answer questions and his right to consult with counsel."[29] These procedural safeguards, ostensibly designed as much to confer admissibility as to protect the rights of the accused, evince an awareness about the vulnerability of confession as a site of manipulation and coercion.

In response to this vulnerability, the Black press gathered and reported on instances of coerced confessions during the antebellum period.[30] Jurists and legal activists alike were alert to the possibility that out-of-court confessions might prove unreliable, and criminal defendants were naturally especially aware of that possibility. A false confession, or one offered under duress, could essentially sign a defendant's death warrant. But it also had the potential to disrupt the teleology of confession as a protocol that moves from an admission about a set of facts to an admission or declaration of legal guilt or culpability for a crime. When these qualities of confession are scrambled, decoupled, and re-presented, they have the potential, as in the case of Nat Turner, not only to disrupt legal systems but to safeguard forms of Black spiritual sovereignty—a mode of private spiritual autonomy that Turner asserts as a response and an alternative to the imposition of moralized whiteness as a spiritual framework.

Note that, by reading this use of confession in part as "re-presentation," I call in Saidiya Hartman's formulation of "critical fabulation," a process she identifies as a method of scholarly engagement that "strain[s] against the limits of the archive to write a cultural history of the captive, and, at the same time, enact[s] the impossibility of representing the lives of the captives precisely through the process of narration." Hartman calls attention to what is fictional about archival sources in order to "displace the received or authorized account."[31] Hartman underscores the importance of practicing restraint in this methodology to honor "the imperative to respect black noise—the shrieks, the moans, the nonsense, and the opacity, which are always in excess of legibility and of the law and which hint at and embody aspirations that are wildly utopian, derelict to capitalism, and antithetical to its attendant discourse of Man."[32]

While Hartman offers critical fabulation as a mode of twenty-first-century engagement with slavery's archives, critical fabulation's proximity to fictionalization is a useful point of reference for Turner specifically because of the highly mediated nature of his *Confessions*, which, as I describe below, was assembled and circulated by Thomas Ruffin Gray, an unscrupulous white lawyer who had represented some of Turner's coconspirators but did not represent Turner. This document has long troubled scholars who are ultimately unable to know for certain how much of the text is Turner's voice and to what extent that voice has been modified by its shady editor; in other words, it is easy for readers of the *Confessions* to be sidetracked immediately by questions about how "true" the text is. A number of scholars and writers engaging with Turner have gone well beyond the narrative restraint Hartman counsels, perhaps most notably and egregiously with William Styron's 1967 novel, *The Confessions of Nat Turner*.[33] But rather than thinking of critical fabulation as the sole domain of a twenty-first-century scholar, what if we consider the possibility that Turner, through a process of juxtaposition and evidentiary re-presentation, scrambles the archive in which he himself appears, constructing certain gaps that contain entire spiritual worlds?

By noticing the ways that Turner himself practices Hartman's combination of narrative imagination and restraint, some of what comes into focus is the intersection with Quashie's formulation of quiet as "the inexpressible expressiveness of this interior, an expressiveness that can appear publicly, have and affect social and political meaning, challenge or counter social discourse, yet none of this is its aim or essence."[34] While Turner's public expressions of confession operate on one external level, his re-presentation of a lengthy confession builds its own archive that we might think of in Hartman's terms as evincing an internal worldview that is "wildly utopian and derelict to capitalism."[35] Moreover, Turner's textual performance of confession in this pamphlet moves certain things into public view as others disappear, but his inhabitation of the legal posture of confession persistently unsettles and overturns—in echoes of that verse from Ezekiel again—the legal and literary structures that purport to hold him captive.

As legal historian and Turner scholar Christopher Tomlins writes of the Southampton Rebellion, "Some facts are not in dispute."[36] Tomlins traces these undisputed facts more or less as follows. On August 22, 1831, a group of Black men, most of whom were enslaved, attacked the households of more than a dozen enslavers in southern Virginia. These men eventually scattered until the only remaining fugitive was Nat Turner, an enslaved man who had been the ostensible leader of this event. On October 30, Turner was captured and brought to nearby Jerusalem, Virginia, for a hastily assembled trial before local magistrates (James Parker and James Trezvant). In the several days between his capture and his November 5 trial, Turner met—by what exact means this meeting was arranged is unclear—with Thomas Ruffin Gray. Gray's sole purpose in interviewing Turner was to collect his narrative of the rebellion for publication in a pamphlet, *The Confessions of Nat Turner, the Leader of the Late Insurrection in Southampton, VA.*[37]

This pamphlet, the only surviving record of Nat Turner's narrative, is mediated in a number of ways that render it a fairly cursed object for both literary scholars and historians. First, it presents itself as a formal legal record, though it was not one (the pamphlet identifies Gray as the recipient of the confession while Turner was in prison, a slippage that could lead many readers to assume that Gray was either a magistrate in the proceeding or an attorney acting on behalf of Turner). Second, it includes supplementary materials that purport to offer a transcript of the trial proceedings, as well as biographical information on the white victims of the rebellion and the Black perpetrators. Finally, and perhaps most vexingly for many scholars, the interruptive presence of Gray's narrative voice operates both as a frame and as an interlocutor throughout the *Confessions*, causing many readers to throw doubt on the "authenticity" of Turner's narrative.

In reaching his conclusion that the document offers both a confession of Turner's faith—perhaps in an inversion of a typical conversion narrative—and a criminal confession (the former of which he believes to be more or less authored by Turner, the latter by Gray),[38] Tomlins offers several useful interventions for critical analysis of the pamphlet as a mediated text. As one example, Tomlins offers this theory of the pamphlet as a more plausible version of previous interpretations that ask us to encounter the pamphlet as a trial report (Caleb Smith), slave narrative (Eric Sundquist), or gallows literature (DeLombard), in part because Tomlins's reading closely engages the paratextual aspects of the pamphlet that support his construction.[39] Tomlins's reading of the forms of narrative control and nonlinear storytelling is persuasive, and his close reading of the paratextual aspects of the pamphlet are deeply compelling. Ultimately, however, Tomlins is a historian and thus invested mainly in questions about Nat Turner the historical figure that run alongside, though not necessarily parallel or equivalent to, my own scholarly question about the narrative Nat Turner, the literary Nat Turner, the authorial Nat Turner, the textual Nat Turner. These Turners may or may not have been the direct equivalent of Nat Turner the historical actor, but unlike Tomlins, I am more inclined to work with this flawed, deeply mediated document, and to give Turner full authorial "credit" for it in the places that purport to come from him, even as I acknowledge a healthy suspicion about Gray's editorial interference.

I follow this treatment of Turner's *Confessions* as his own for several reasons. First, that is how the pamphlet announces itself, and the pamphlet signals in several places overt narrative intrusions by Gray, such as on page 18 where what Tomlins describes as "Gray's 'I' resumes full control"[40]; or on page 12 where the pamphlet briefly switches to transcript format, marking a "Q" for what appears to have been a question or prompt from Gray and an "A" for what appears to be Turner's answer or response; or on page 9, where Gray inserts "*Question—*" and "*Ans.*" to indicate where his follow-up questions interrupt Turner's narration.[41] The fact that the pamphlet marks these narrative intrusions so plainly in several places suggests that main body of the narrative (again, excluding the prefatory and appended materials) derives primarily from Turner himself. Second, though the publication of Turner's *Confessions* precedes the rise of the freedom narrative genre, the conventions of that genre are visible here: an authenticating preamble by a white amanuensis who verifies the "truth" of the main narrative—in this case, that preamble also anticipates any objection to a coerced confession by including a court clerk's pronouncement that the confession had been "fully and voluntarily made"[42]—followed by appendixes that further verify or document the substance of the narrative's main claims. The main structural difference between this text and later freedom narratives following the same convention is that this amanuensis was unambiguously acting on behalf of the so-called public (or rather, himself) and not on behalf of Turner. We should not necessarily assume that Gray would follow practices used by subsequent amanuenses, but given these stylistic similarities, it seems that Gray has made at least some efforts to mark the text with the moments where his voice intrudes.

Additionally, the opening letter addressed from Gray to "the public" asserts that Turner's "account of the conspiracy is submitted to the public, without comment. It reads an awful, and it is hoped, a useful lesson, as to the operations of a mind like his, endeavoring to grapple with things beyond its reach."[43] Here Gray shows his cards even as this gesture urges the reader to trust the substance of Turner's narrative as unaltered; how different is this, really, from Thomas Pringle's preface to *The History of Mary Prince*, also published in 1831? That preface reads in part: "The narrative was taken down from Mary's own lips by a lady who happened to be at the time residing in my family as a visitor. It was written out fully, with all the narrator's repetitions and prolixities, and afterwards pruned into its present shape; retaining, as far as was practicable, Mary's exact expressions and peculiar phraseology."[44] The prefatory language to the Prince narrative actually acknowledges through euphemism that editorial liberties have been taken to "prune" the narrative into a legible text—a metaphor of wildness that, ironically, Lydia Maria Child also turns to in her introduction to *Incidents in the Life of a Slave Girl*.[45]

While I think it eminently appropriate to acknowledge Thomas Ruffin Gray's ghoulish sense of opportunism, I do not think it productive to give white abolitionists unearned credit for being so far off that mark; there is plenty of evidence to suggest that their involvement in the publication of freedom narratives frequently derived from either a version of white saviorism and/or, as Teresa Goddu has demonstrated, a fairly predatory opportunism directed primarily toward fundraising for white abolitionist societies.[46] If we are able to accept Black authorship in freedom narratives where an author has potentially been manipulated by a white abolitionist claiming to work in service of an antislavery project, we ought to accept Black authorship from a text like Turner's *Confessions*. After all, Turner's response to the genocidal system of legalized slavery is a perfectly rational survival impulse, and he treats it throughout his *Confessions* as a predictable, common-sense response to his lived experience and his spiritual visions; there is no reason to assume that these sentiments derive from him and not Gray. If anything, the straightforward descriptions of the murders that Tomlins suspects Gray of having written display far less bloodlust and violence than Gray seemed interested in publishing. Is it not just as possible that Turner understood Gray's objective, as he understood the magistrates' objectives at trial, and simply elected to construct a confession according to his ends and not theirs?

This somewhat laborious explanation of why I treat Turner as the primary author of the *Confessions* is essential as a precedent to my argument about how he leverages the confession form to enact a spiritual disruption of state process. In other words, Turner mobilizes the form of confession in such a way that he disavows any obligation to the state even as he asserts his own spiritual sovereignty; he does so by decoupling natural law from legal punishment regimes and decoupling confessions of fact from admissions of guilt or remorse. In the first part of Turner's narration, he says to Gray: "You have asked me to give a history of the motives which induced me to undertake the late insurrection, as you call it—To do so I must go back to the days of my infancy, and even before I was born."[47] Immediately, Turner frames his narrative not as a "confession," but as a "history," despite the titling of the piece. His "history of the motives" takes advantage of confession's retrospective posture to sketch out a past record, despite the fact that animating the basis for rebellion is in fact quite a different project, legally speaking, from performing a confession; his narration is far closer in this case to a legal justification (like self-defense or defense of one's property), a subtle distinction that suggests Turner's occupation of the text as a pro se advocate and not merely a confessing criminal.

Likewise, while Turner's confession admits relevant underlying facts and conduct, it stops short of expressing guilt; in the pamphlet's summary of the trial, at his arraignment, Turner "pleaded *Not guilty*; saying to his counsel, that he did not feel so," despite also saying that he had "made a full confession to Mr. Gray, and [had] nothing more to say."[48] This bifurcation of confession and admission exposes the importance of defense. At law, a justification defense concedes certain factual events (for instance, the physical attacks on enslavers that Turner acknowledges) but proposes mitigation of punishment on the grounds that those events were warranted or justified by the extenuating circumstances and should be regarded as reasonable or proper as opposed to criminal. To reach back to and beyond his earliest memories, Turner the confessing party makes room for Turner the pro se advocate, who crafts a justification defense by establishing not merely a description of the rebellion, but an elaborate *context* for it. Rather than solely admitting the underlying facts, Turner creates a narrative of it—this practice of legal storytelling is available to Turner by virtue of confession's affordances, including the opportunity it provides a confessing defendant to introduce other information into the legal record.

Here, Turner frames the *Confessions* with a history not only of his own motives, but one that began before his birth, one that eventually extends out into the cosmos and his skyward visions of "the forms of men in different attitudes—and there were lights in the sky to which the children of darkness gave other names than what they really were—for they were the lights of the Saviour's hands, stretched forth from east to west, even as they were extended on the cross on Calvary for the redemption of sinners." This spiritual context, using language that references Christianity, also indexes a more syncretic, African-descended spirituality, as when he encounters "on the leaves in the woods hieroglyphic characters, and numbers, with the forms of men in different attitudes, portrayed in blood, and representing the figures I had seen before in the heavens."[49] Turner establishes this otherworldly backdrop for a series of messages he receives urging him to "commence the great work" and "fight against the Serpent," to "slay [his] enemies with their own weapons."[50] This prophetic cosmology follows descriptions of his seemingly supernatural abilities as an autodidact and an agent of physical transformations on white listeners who manifest bleeding lesions on hearing Turner's visions, and it precedes the narration of the 1831 rebellion. I read this not, as Tomlins does, as a separate "confession of faith,"[51] but as an affirmative defense of the rebellion that naturalizes Turner's actions through these arguably supernatural provocations. Turner subordinates his own will to a divine or sacred interlocutor, situating the rebellion as a rational, appropriate response not only to his enslavement but also to the instructions received from his spiritual guides. In legal terms, this rationalization is a justification.

Identifying these spiritual guides and cosmological influences illuminates how Turner mobilizes the confession form to assert his own spiritual sovereignty—his *personal* access to the divine, unobstructed by state interference—rather than to appease his captors or to express remorse. Makungu M. Akinyela has framed Turner's spirituality as "Africanized Christianity" that might be read as "an example of the worldview of enslaved

Africans generally in the nineteenth century."[52] While I do not purport to extend Turner's cosmology to enslaved Africans as a class, nor do I cosign the assertion that this part of the pamphlet "could be of no legal or investigative value," Akinyela explains that Turner's cosmological exegesis "is a testimony learned in the Turner family in the hidden spaces far from the ears of White oppression."[53] This framing of Turner's spirituality as arising in hidden familial spaces marks Turner's visions as a birthright; this framing is also affirmed by Turner's own repeated descriptions of how he "studiously avoided mixing in society, and wrapped myself in mystery, devoting my time to fasting and prayer."[54] This form of Christianity is, at a minimum, marked by an unusually ascetic devotion, as well as traces of African ritual (for example, while Turner disavows "conjuring and such like tricks,"[55] his use of leaves and herbs and his visions of hieroglyphs on crops suggest a connection to rootwork practices based in African spiritual traditions[56]). Even in his descriptions of apparently Christian references, which Tomlins documents extensively (and persuasively), Turner's images are, as Akinyela notes, "interpreted in an African cosmology where deity is expressed through nature rather than from outside it."[57]

Holding in mind this cosmology, which at a minimum maintains deep dialogue with Christian and African traditions, consider how Turner's context for the rebellion depends on a spirituality in which he requires no intermediary to the divine—much like Martin Delany's Henry Blake, Turner's spirituality, connected though it may be to forms of white Christianity, completely bypasses white participation or intercession. In his *Confessions*, Turner constructs a narrative world in which he bears no obligation to either his white oppressors or their God; rather, his spirituality has divested itself of whiteness and, by extension, of positive law. It is for this reason that Turner can with one hand offer a "full confession to Mr. Gray"[58] and, with the other, disavow any feelings of guilt or any pressure to enter a guilty plea. Thus, Turner's "confession" actually rearranges the legal proceeding; the appearance of disclosure shuttles along with it a vision for a Black elsewhere—what J. T. Roane calls "a wider world *otherwise*."[59]

This multivalent inhabitation of the confessional "space" enables Turner to persistently scramble the expected legal order, even as it leaves traces in his public performance of the concealed, the withheld, the wildly alive forms of Blackness. Once Turner finally proceeds to his account of the rebellion, he spends pages documenting his *failure* to commit murder ("I could not give a death blow"; "I struck her several blows over the head, but not being able to kill her,"[60] etc.), which Eric Sundquist has described as his "notorious inability to carry out some of the deeds himself,"[61] before finally confessing to a single act of murder on page 14: "I killed her by a blow on the head, with a fence rail."[62] Rather than a detailed description of his own culpability, Turner's *Confessions* tend to describe, first, the spiritual context for his leadership of the rebellion and, second, the general scene once the rebellion was underway. Because these component parts do not easily fit together, and even rely on different narrative styles and tones, I see the appeal of Tomlins's bifurcation into spiritual and legal confession.

At the same time, their incommensurability is what endows the *Confessions*—the plural signifier of the title already hinting at the doublings and proliferations inherent in the text—with worldmaking potential. Indeed, the pamphlet as a whole is entitled *Confessions*, while the main narrative by Turner within the pamphlet retains the singular format of "Confession." Though this titling convention is almost certainly an inadvertent allusion to the varying levels on which Turner "confesses" and the multiple audiences to whom these confessions are legible,[63] it nevertheless gestures once more to the ways Turner's presence within the pamphlet produces excesses and surpluses that cannot quite be imagined by either the legal form or the literary document. The pamphlet itself, in its appendixes, indexes the way that Turner decouples guilt (his not-guilty plea in court) from disclosure (his assertion that he has made a "full confession"). This decoupling demonstrates how Turner's apparent willingness to participate in a confessional process actually frustrates the judicial procedure, which is designed to extract expressions of remorse from subjected defendants. Moreover, the confession Turner acknowledges making is not addressed to a judicial actor in his proceedings at all, but to Thomas Gray, an extralegal publishing opportunist, through whom Turner ultimately addresses a much wider audience. Therefore, even what appears to be his "surrender" to the state is actually an act of surrender to himself and his spiritual vocation.

Recall that Kevin Quashie describes a "quiet subject" as one "who surrenders, a subject whose consciousness is not only shaped by struggle but also by revelry, possibility, the wildness of the inner life. Quiet is not a performance or a withholding; instead, it is an expressiveness that is not necessarily legible, at least not in a world that privileges public expressiveness. Neither is quiet about resistance. It is surrender, a giving into, a falling into self."[64] Given his notoriety and charisma and his apparent willingness to speak to Gray, it might be tempting to read Turner as an excessively public figure. Such readings may even feel liberatory, given the overt and violent forms of silencing to which Turner and other enslaved people were subjected, particularly in the legal context. But notice all that his seemingly public confession covertly brings along with it—a distinctly Black cosmology, a peacefulness and resignation to what he regards as his divine purpose, and the wild unknown interior contours of a man scholars have continued to try to "solve" because he so "wrapped [himself] in mystery"[65] and because his widely disseminated *Confessions* actually reveal remarkably little about his planning or execution of rebellion.

These mysteries about Turner arise precisely because he understood how to leverage overidentification with legal procedure. His earnest and matter-of-fact pronouncements of his actions and his justification for those actions superficially signal a level of participation in the legal process. But Turner was well aware that, given the political climate, no justification of his actions would realistically spare his life. And despite the ways that he claims access to certain forms of prophecy, he is careful to class his ability as divination rather than foresight. When Gray asks if Turner coordinated a rebellion then underway in North Carolina, Turner responds, "I see sir, you doubt my word; but can you not think the same ideas, and strange appearances about this time in the heavens might prompt others, as well as myself, to this undertaking."[66] Thus, Turner once more offers up his actions not as divine warfare but as a *rational response to his environment*. Here again, we see that Turner has no use for the logics of his oppressors—he gives his "full confession" to Thomas Gray, perhaps in part because all of these men are indistinguishable, as equally irrelevant to him.

This willingness to disclose is thus, from the court's point of view, somewhat misdirected—in other words, Turner has made his confession, but arguably to the "wrong" audience. How does a court square what appears to be a willingness to participate in a ritual of confession with a refusal to confess to the "proper" authorities? Or, as Peter Brooks puts it: "Herein lies the problem: what is the relation of the act of confessing to the reliability of what is confessed?"[67] If the act of confessing is meant as a cleansing ritual, an expression of remorse, and a submission to the legal order, can it really be said that what Turner provides constitutes a confession at all? Brooks writes, "Confession of wrongdoing is considered fundamental to morality because it constitutes a verbal act of self-recognition as wrongdoer and hence provides the basis of rehabilitation."[68] In his confession, Turner expresses deep fluency and interest in self-recognition but absolutely no interest in state "rehabilitation" whatsoever. As a result, Turner's ostensibly earnest participation in the tribunal proceedings utterly deflates their intended purpose. In this sense, Turner's confession poses real problems for the magistrates overseeing his case. He has confessed, but he has declined to do so in a way that would grant the tribunal any moral authority, and he has absolutely refused to admit guilt for the things to which he has confessed. In one sense, this is immaterial, because Turner's fate was sealed from the moment of his capture, as he well understood. But in another sense, at this moment, Turner has become the most powerful actor in this exchange, and the court appears remarkably impotent in comparison, despite the fact that it holds the power to order his execution.

Tomlins describes this shift in power as "countersovereignty," where Turner's rebellion "called the regime's own sovereign legality into question. The justices' job was to restore that sovereign legality by doling out death to whatever extent necessary to do so."[69] In fact, in carrying out the sentencing, Jeremiah Cobb claimed that Turner's only plausible defense was misguided fanaticism. Cobb's consideration of this hypothetical defense follows:

> If this be true, from my soul I pity you; and while you have my sympathies, I am, nevertheless called upon to pass the sentence of the court. The time between this and your execution will necessarily be very short; and your only hope must be in another world. The judgment of the court is, that you be taken hence to the jail from whence you came, thence to the place of execution, and on Friday next, between the hours of 10 A.M. and 2 P.M. be hung by the neck until you are dead! dead! dead and may the Lord have mercy upon your soul.[70]

First, it is important to note that this account of the sentencing from Turner's *Confessions* almost certainly did not reflect a verbatim transcript of the tribunal proceedings. It is through the *Confessions* that Cobb's tripling enters the cultural imagination; the official court record of the sentencing excludes the verbatim transcript, noting instead simply that the court ordered Turner's execution.[71] Nevertheless, this ritual enters the public domain through the *Confessions*, where it reflects the tribunal's urgency in ordering Turner's death as a means of restoring its own sovereign authority. In the *Confessions*, Cobb reinforces this premise; rather than announcing, "You are sentenced to death," he frames the official act with the court as the subject and Turner as the object: "The judgment of the court is, that you . . . be hung by the neck." This dual shift—from personal to "court" and from Turner as subject to Turner as object—reveals the mechanism by which legal language enacts violence. While discussing his personal feelings, Cobb allows Turner to exist as a subject ("you have my sympathies"). It is only after shifting from the personal to the rhetoric of "the court" that Cobb transforms Turner into the denatured object ("hung by the neck until dead! dead! dead!") that law is determined to produce and then execute.

The violence of law comes into sharper relief in Cobb's tripling of Turner's eventual death. This striking moment of the opinion departs from typical judicial protocol, and it also creates a fissure in the rhetorical work Cobb has just done in shifting the burden of Turner's death onto the institution of law: "The judgment of the court is, that you ... be hung by the neck until you are dead! dead! dead and may the Lord have mercy upon your soul." Rather than expressing the cool, formal posture of the "court," Cobb is unable, in the *Confessions* at least, to resist killing Turner a total of three times in the single judgment. This rhetorical "overkill" of Turner's body not only enacts a legal ritual but also produces an excess that sets the stage for that ritual's repetition through the circulation of the *Confessions*. Cobb's tripartite announcement of Turner's imminent death reveals a ritualized aspect of the sentencing that transforms it from secular court action into vanishing ritual—a ritual occasioned precisely by the intensely spiritual language of Turner's confession, his claims of religious visions, revelations, and astrological messages. By insisting three times on Turner's death, Cobb seems to engage in a superstitious purge of any supernatural qualities Turner may possess.

As much as Cobb relies on characterizations of Turner as delusional and fanatical, this tripartite condemnation evinces a tacit *acceptance* of Turner as possessing supernatural force. He deliberately tries to denature Turner and empty out any possibility of his divinity. The use of "hung" as opposed to "hanged" underscores the depersonalizing gesture of the sentencing: people are hanged, while objects are hung. This unfleshing exemplifies what Colin Dayan describes as "the occult revelations of law's rituals."[72] The very thing that enables law's sacred status is its ability to produce unnatural effects from within a secular space. But as law dispossesses Turner of his body, one of the material residues of that dispossession is *The Confessions of Nat Turner*.

Moreover, Turner's ostensible participation in the legal process, in addition to unsettling the operative legal hierarchy, affirms his spiritual sovereignty by effectively dismissing the tribunal as a temporary state obstacle between himself and his spiritual guides. This instantiation of Turner's spiritual sovereignty would not have been possible in the same way had he expressed remorse or had he refused to participate in the legal process altogether. Rather, in mustering the literary and spiritual power of confession as a legal form, he exerts a different kind of power over his confessional space. Turner's inhabitation of the confessional space ultimately forces Thomas Gray and the tribunal to hold space for him and his spirituality. In a contemporary context, when we "hold space" for others, it is a way of sitting with and before them, nonjudgmentally; it is a practice of generosity and support, of letting others be heard and known. Obviously Gray and the trial magistrates did not intentionally extend generosity or nonjudgment to Turner, nor did they have the capacity to know or understand him; but his performance as a confessor functioned legally as a procedural "magic word" that opened a site of possibility. Notice the ways that Turner's words continue to "wrap [himself] in mystery,"[73] in the language of an elsewhere that continues to haunt the *Confessions*—a set of disclosures that mystify as they clarify, asserting formidable spiritual sovereignty.

While Turner uses out-of-court confession to imagine forms of sovereignty that are not state-bound or place-bound, Charles Henry Langston uses the legal space of the post-conviction sentencing statement—yet another mode of retrospective futurist speech—to imagine forms of civic sovereignty that position him as a citizen-outlaw. The category of citizen-outlaw consists of a subject obligated to violate or break the laws of the nation-state in order to preserve his personal and communal duties toward justice. Like Turner, Langston faced criminal prosecution; Langston, a free Black man (and the grandfather of Harlem Renaissance poet Langston Hughes), had participated with thirty-six fellow citizens, both white and Black, in the 1858 event known as the Oberlin-Wellington Rescue, technically a violation of the 1850 Fugitive Slave Act.

This particular rescue, which was widely covered in the Black press at the time, liberated John Price, a self-emancipated man who was under threat of kidnapping and re-enslavement pursuant to the Fugitive Slave Act. It is important to register Oberlin's status as an abolitionist stronghold in Ohio, which itself was a crucial transit state for self-emancipated people coming in particular from Kentucky. Thus, as word spread that John Price had been seized, a local abolitionist effort wasted no time springing into action. While Price was arrested in Oberlin, he was transported immediately to a hotel in Wellington, less than ten miles away, where his kidnappers intended to put him on a train headed for the South. As this news traveled throughout the region, a crowd of protesters gathered at the hotel in order to prevent Price from being forced onto a train, at which point it would be all but impossible to free him. Though the details of his exact rescue are somewhat unclear, the crowd in Wellington eventually enabled Price to escape from the hotel and ultimately flee to Canada.[74] While thirty-seven rescuers were indicted, only two trials proceeded: Langston's and that of a white coconspirator, Simeon Bushnell. Both men were convicted; Bushnell received a sentence of sixty days' imprisonment and a $600 fine, whereas Langston was sentenced to twenty days' imprisonment and a $100 fine.[75]

In order to understand the legal context for these prosecutions, it is necessary to revisit the provisions of the Fugitive Slave Act. That legislation, part of the broader Compromise of 1850, is best known for its requirement that all states recognize enslavers' property rights in those they enslaved by requiring all people in the United States to assist in the recapture of fugitives from slavery. The statute essentially federalized slavery; before 1850, crossing the boundary from a so-called slave state into a free state was at least a theoretical safeguard against re-enslavement. Although enslavers frequently traveled to free states in pursuit of self-emancipated individuals, these states rarely, if ever, conscripted state officials, deputies, and other legal officers into assisting those efforts. But the Fugitive Slave Act required not only all state officials, but all people *everywhere*, to assist in the re-enslavement of self-emancipated people. It accomplished this goal via several provisions that operated as proverbial carrot and stick. First, section 5 of the Act mandated that "all good citizens are hereby commanded to aid and assist in the prompt and efficient execution of this law, whenever their services may be required."[76] The breadth of this provision imposes an affirmative obligation, a duty to assist, framed around a conception or category of "good citizens." The inclusion of "good" in this context implies the existence of its inverse category, but it also implies that compliance with the legislation is the contingent condition that actually confers "good citizenship." The carrot.

Apart from imposing this duty under the banner of nationalism, the Fugitive Slave Act also imposes, in section 7, criminal penalties for "any person who shall knowingly and willingly obstruct, hinder, or prevent [an enslaver or their agent] from arresting such a fugitive from service or labor . . . or shall rescue, or attempt to rescue, such fugitive from the custody of [their former enslaver] . . . or shall aid, abet, or assist such person so owing service or labor . . . to escape from [an enslaver or their agent]."[77] This slippage, in which assisting someone in their flight from slavery is characterized as "rescue," betrays any argument that there was a notion, even among enslavers, that slavery was benign or humane. Even so, an attempt to "rescue" someone from enslavement became a crime under this statute. Section 7's incredibly broad imposition of criminal liability ensures that anyone who is not enticed by inclusion in "good citizenship" still complies with the statute out of fear of imprisonment (up to six months) or significant penalties (up to $1,000). The stick.

In addition to this general regime that federalizes enslavers' property rights and requires participation by all private citizens, there are several other statutory provisions in the Fugitive Slave Act that are relevant to Langston's specific case and his in-court statement. Namely, sections 6, 8, and 9 of the statute establish various procedural measures that govern the recapture of self-emancipated people. Under the statute, the process for detaining or arresting a fugitive from slavery requires bringing the fugitive and the case to a court or magistrate authorized under the law to hear the case and determine whether the fugitive from slavery is indeed the person sought and whether they do in fact "owe service or labor" to the enslaver in question. This requirement from section 6 also specifies that the person arresting or seizing the self-emancipated person must produce "satisfactory proof," which might consist merely of an affidavit and/or testimony. Crucially, people detained under the statute retained no right to testify on their own behalf, nor any right to present evidence demonstrating that they had been wrongly captured. Section 9 tightens this regime by providing that, once an affidavit had been submitted stating a reason to believe that a fugitive from slavery "will be rescued by force," then "it shall be the duty of the officer making the arrest to retain such fugitive in his custody."[78]

Section 8 establishes a system under which marshals and their deputies would receive financial compensation per alleged fugitive brought before a court or commission. Marshals could receive $10 for each case where the magistrate found that sufficient proof had existed; but even in cases where insufficient proof existed, marshals and deputies would still be paid $5 per person. In essence, section 8 of the Fugitive Slave Act created a system of financial incentive for kidnappers who could round up any Black person and claim that they fit the physical description of a self-emancipated person. Indeed, in his post-sentencing statement, Charles Langston references a letter found on a "counterfeiter" and conspirator in an ongoing scheme to kidnap free Black people in the North. In that letter, the counterfeiter writes, "Go among the n*****s; find out their marks and scars, make good descriptions and send to me, and I'll find masters for 'em."[79] It was against this backdrop that Langston and thirty-six of his fellow community members staged the Oberlin-Wellington Rescue.

As with Turner's confession, while I attend to the legal context for Langston's post-conviction statement, I treat Langston's "confession" as my primary text here, as opposed to undertaking a historiography of this case. Unlike Turner, Langston's confession occurred in court following his conviction. The trial itself was largely a political exercise, but in comparison with the tribunal that passed judgment on Turner, this court appears to have staged a much less improvisational proceeding. Of course, the difference in subject position between Langston and Turner contextualizes some of that difference, as does this jurisdictional and historical distance (1830s Virginia versus late 1850s Ohio), which also presses on the hyperlocal and widely divergent legal protocols that operated in different places and against different people. Langston, as a free Black man, may have been in legal peril for violating the Fugitive Slave Act, but this act of outlawry signifies very differently from Turner's status as an enslaved insurrection leader. Steven Lubet has observed that the case against Langston was relatively weak and arguably succeeded only through the collusion of several prosecution witnesses to bring their testimony into alignment.[80] Both Langston's trial and Turner's trial were examples of legal theater; in Langston's case, and partially owing to the fact that his life was not at stake as Turner's was, Langston retained much greater input into and control over the legal spectacle.

Langston's speech, directly addressed to Judge Willson, occurred in the liminal moment between conviction and sentencing. Lubet notes that, because Ohio then followed the so-called "interested party rule" (which prohibited criminal defendants from testifying on their own behalf), Langston had not been able to testify at all during the trial.[81] His post-conviction statement is, counterintuitively, somewhat analogous to an allocution statement, where defendants address a court in offering a guilty plea. Unlike in an allocution, Langston had pled not guilty. However, in his post-conviction statement, Langston conceded his participation in the rescue and swore that he would continue to violate the Fugitive Slave Act in the future. Thus, despite his failure to plead guilty, Langston's speech admits many of the underlying facts that would support his guilty verdict. Like Turner, his "confession" decouples guilt from justice.

The purpose of allocution is, in addition to ensuring that defendants pleading guilty understand their rights and plead guilty voluntarily, a space in which defendants typically contextualize their actions, express remorse, and plead for leniency or mitigation on these accounts. The American Bar Association describes an allocution statement as "an opportunity for defendants to accept responsibility, humanize themselves, and to mitigate their sentences to ensure that their punishment is appropriate for both the crime and the person who committed it."[82] How telling that humanization is required for criminal defendants pleading guilty—this purpose of allocution acknowledges the tendency to regard criminals as having forfeited personhood status, a nexus of reduced legal personality that carried additional weight in the context of a mid-nineteenth-century proceeding against a Black man, whose race further diminished his personhood. Although Langston was found guilty as opposed to pleading guilty, his post-conviction proceeding still afforded him the opportunity to make something like an allocution statement, when Judge

Willson asked, "Have you or your counsel any thing to say why the sentence of the law should not now be pronounced upon you?"[83] In the speech that followed, Langston mobilized the confessional form to both overidentify as a state subject and extract himself from state inclusion, positioning himself as both an agent of higher law and a citizen-outlaw of Ohio.

Langston begins his statement in the expected way, by purporting to seek mitigation of the sentence. But what follows is as far from an expression of remorse as one might imagine. He almost immediately invalidates the legal system as a source of justice and removes himself from its sway, stating, "I know that the courts of this country, that the laws of this country, that the governmental machinery of this country, are so constituted as to oppress and outrage colored men, men of my complexion. I cannot, then, of course, expect, judging from the past history of the country, any mercy from the laws, from the [C]onstitution, or from the courts of the country."[84] This naming of the so-called justice system offers a working definition of systemic or structural oppression—the "machinery" Langston alludes to characterizes the legal system as a human-made, industrialized, mechanized structure whose very purpose and design is the continued oppression of Black people. "Machinery" of course signifies both on one hand being within a narrative of progress and invention and, on the other hand, as the stuff that is always breaking down, requiring repair, and falling into obsolescence.

Langston contrasts this description of positive law by describing John Price's kidnapping: "on which those men, by lying devices, decoyed into a place where they could get their hands on him—I will not say a slave, for I do not know that—but a *man*, a *brother*, who had a right to his liberty under the laws of God, under the laws of Nature, and under the Declaration of American Independence."[85] The inclusion of "devices" here, though referring to the tactics of the kidnappers, recalls the "machinery" of positive law—indeed their "devices" are "machinations," or tricks used to lure Price away from his freedom and into enslavement—and stands in opposition to the free-form, almost abstract categories of natural law that, somewhat surprisingly, appear to include the Declaration of Independence. This moment of attachment to one founding document (the Declaration) and rejection of another (the Constitution) evinces the possibility that law still retained for Black thinkers at the midcentury.

For Langston, the Declaration of Independence, which untethered the colonies from England under an ideology of equality, is properly classified alongside "the laws of God" and "the laws of Nature." Self-emancipation, an act Langston describes as evidence of formerly enslaved people's "everlasting honor ... by the exercise of their own God-given powers,"[86] is in some sense a restaging of the Declaration of Independence on an individual level and thus a sacred act. For Langston, the possibility of a nation-state is not inherently an inhospitable space for Black freedom; it is through the process of white nation-building, and enactment of the Constitution and other legislation, that these divine legal doctrines of emancipation and liberation devolve into anti-Black machinery.

Langston retains this attachment of the American Revolution to Black revolution throughout his speech, noting that his "Revolutionary father" taught him "that the fundamental doctrine of this government was that *all* men have a right to life and liberty."[87] Of course, Langston's father, Ralph Quarles, was a Revolutionary father in the senses that would resonate with a white court—he had been an enslaver in Virginia and indeed was the enslaver of Langston's mother. In this reference to his father, Langston is not, however, claiming whiteness; rather, he translates his paternal biological inheritance from one form of revolution into another, holding that promise of law as an equalizing right to life and liberty at its word and applying it to the kidnapping of John Price. Langston's argument for his own interference in the Price rescue turns, critically, to a close reading of the ostensible legal procedures outlined in the Fugitive Slave Act. Langston cites those procedural requirements—the same requirements that hail all "good citizens" to assist in the enforcement of the Fugitive Slave Act—as the very things that required his action.

Specifically, Langston points out that Price's kidnappers had failed to establish the validity of their warrant. "I supposed it to be my duty as a citizen of Ohio—excuse me for saying that, sir—as an *outlaw of the United States*, to do what I could to secure at least this form of Justice to my brother whose liberty was in peril."[88] This formulation of citizen-outlaw, a citizen of a state and an outlaw of the nation as a whole, establishes the paradoxical stakes on which Langston confesses his participation in the "crime" of rescuing Price. Langston's citizen-outlaw construction recalls what Stefano Harney and Fred Moten have said about affiliation with the university, another sprawling site of systemic racism: "The only possible relationship to the university today is a criminal one."[89] To be a "good citizen" of natural law, for Langston, requires him to disavow the forms of "good citizenship" both promised in and demanded by the Fugitive Slave Act. His confession in court unfolds on multiple levels, addressing multiple audiences, each time claiming one kind of civic membership and rejecting another, asserting forms of civic belonging that cannot theoretically coexist.

On one hand, and in the dimension of this confession that most squarely addresses the court, Langston points out that the kidnappers had failed to comply with the Fugitive Slave Act's procedural requirements. This productive overidentification with the statute allows him to imply that he actually *was* assisting in the proper execution of the law. At the same time, he unambiguously denounces the entire law itself, decrying it as "unjust" and "made to crush the colored man, and one that outrages every feeling of Humanity, as well as every rule of Right."[90] This form of arguing in the alternative, rather than signifying as inconsistent at law, is an incredibly common form of legal argument and bears deep connections to the counterfactual, which is a form that Langston deploys throughout his confessional speech. Like Turner, who refused to attach his confession of specific acts to criminal *guilt*, Langston disentangles his own participation in Price's rescue from the concept of criminal liability on the theory that the Fugitive Slave Act itself is invalid. Crucially, he does not make an argument about its constitutionality ("I have nothing to do with its constitutionality; and about it I care a great deal less. I have often heard it said by learned and good men that it was unconstitutional.... I had always believed, until the contrary appeared... that the provisions of this odious statute would never be enforced within the bounds of this State"[91]). Constitutionality is not a form of legal rationale that tempts Langston, and he suggests that Ohio's local sensibilities should overrule the Fugitive Slave Act as a federal statute in any case. By framing his intervention this way, Langston implicitly asks the court to proceed as though—or at least imagine that—the Fugitive Slave Act simply did not exist.

Stephen Best has noted the freight that counterfactuals carry in both law and literature as a means of worldmaking, writing that "a counterfactual supposition allows one, in literary analysis, to imagine what a text from the past would mean if it were being reauthored in the present; it is the very conditional that permits a text to be transported to other worlds."[92] In the legal context, Best observes that "counterfactuals allow one to make inferences regarding causation, to infer not merely what happened... but, in addition, 'what *would* have been the case if some actual event, which in fact happened, had not happened.'"[93] It is not a coincidence, then, that there are so many examples throughout the chapters of this book where Black writers imagine the consequences of certain historical events either not happening or happening differently; the counterfactual as a rhetorical form is an imaginative exercise that both enables the assignation of liability and imagines entire worlds that might have arisen otherwise. For the writers in this book, in addition to the specific legal historical and literary outcomes they consider—

whether the British burning of the Capitol in 1814 (chapters 1 and 4), or the possibility of a queen who presides over America (chapter 3), or, as here, an Ohio where the Fugitive Slave Act either did not take effect or was simply ignored—these counterfactual possibilities imagine Black elsewheres, spaces of Black liberation and community and even nation that could have, but did not yet, materialize.

Langston's conception of himself as a citizen-outlaw enables him to dart back and forth between the legal reality in which he finds himself and the possible legal world that does not yet exist. It further *compels* him to maintain this relationship of lawbreaking as a structure of Black worldmaking. The figure of the "outlaw" connotes quite differently than a "criminal" or even "fugitive." Like a fugitive, there is a sense of ongoingness about an outlaw that feels closer to a permanent category than a temporary or singular one. An outlaw is flagrant, flouting violations of law in the open rather than in the shadows. Thus, by classifying himself as a citizen-outlaw, and in keeping with the tendency of rhetorical counterfactualism to rewind and replay historical progression in alternative outcomes, Langston scrambles the expected temporal posture of confession. Confession is an inherently backward-looking form that narrates past events, and *only* past events and actions that give rise to criminal liability. It is both theoretically and legally impossible to "confess" to future crimes, but Langston as self-proclaimed citizen-outlaw transforms his confession of past actions into the obligation and promise of future crimes.

Although the category of citizen-outlaw theorizes that possibility within its own terms, Langston makes this transformation explicit: "I stand here to say that I will do all I can, for any man thus seized and help, though the inevitable penalty . . . and . . . fine . . . hangs over me! We have a common humanity. You would do so; your manhood would require it; and no matter what the laws might be, you would honor yourself for doing it; your friends would honor you for doing it; your children to all generations would honor you for doing it; and every good and honest man would say, you had done *right!*"[94] Here, in addition to transforming his confession of participation in the Price rescue to the promise of future "crimes," Langston also extends the subjunctive counterfactual that builds other worlds within the text of his confession. His previous counterfactual had asked the court to imagine an Ohio where the Fugitive Slave Act either did not exist or where Ohio simply ignored it. Here, following a series of "if" conditions ("if your brother; if your friends, if your wife, if your child, had been seized by men who claimed them as fugitives, and the law of the land forbade you to ask any investigation, and precluded the possibility of any legal protection or redress"[95]), Langston asks the judge to imagine *himself* as the only force standing between his loved ones and slavery. As common as this move is, it is a strategy typically reserved for jury arguments. Instead, here, having already claimed that his Blackness precludes him from accessing a fair jury trial, Langston steps into the role of advocate and demotes the judge into the function of juror as part of this subjunctive exercise. Not only has he constructed other possible worlds, he has uprooted and reconfigured his own legal environment. The citizen-outlaw has naturalized lawbreaking as a badge of "good citizenship," rewriting the hail of the Fugitive Slave Act and the space of the courtroom.

While Nat Turner and Charles Langston leverage the confession form in actual trial proceedings, this chapter briefly turns to Harriet Jacobs's 1861 autobiography, *Incidents in the Life of a Slave Girl*, to examine how Jacobs, whose confessions occur as interpersonal interactions entirely outside judicial proceedings, mobilizes confession around forms of relation and privacy. For Jacobs, the posture of confession happens in several different registers: the moments where she "confesses" certain behavior to her enslavers, a form of confession I do not take up here; the performance of confession for white readers as part of how Jacobs, according to Samantha Pinto, "games the dictates of the politics of respectability;"[96] and, finally, the forms of confession that Jacobs stages for her family members, most notably her grandmother and her daughter. These latter two registers demonstrate how Jacobs's use of confessional form falls somewhere in between Darlene Clark Hine's formulation of dissemblance and Kevin Quashie's theorization of quiet. As ever, Jacobs has a gift for finding law's overhangs and canopies—the "shadow of law"[97] that she occupies through a combination of confessions and concealments, the rights-bearing space of protection that was not built or meant for her as a Black woman but which she experiments with and seeks as a form of sanctuary. This relationship to law marks one important difference from Turner and Langston, both of whom were occupying legal space publicly as criminal defendants.

Jacobs is linked to Turner in several important ways, however. First, like Turner, Jacobs's authorship of her narrative was the source of protracted scholarly suspicion well into the late twentieth century. It was not until 1981, in Jean Fagan Yellin's article, "Written by Herself: Harriet Jacobs's Slave Narrative," that Jacobs's authorship of the text—and thus its classification as nonfiction—was definitively established.[98] These intense anxieties around authorship, echoing the case of Turner, reflect anti-Black as well as anti-feminist assumptions about the production of literature (especially fiction) and the production of textual authority. In comparing reception of Jacobs's work to the poetry of Phillis Wheatley, Frances Smith Foster notes, "For African American women writers, the resistance to the authority of blacks or of slaves was compounded by gender prejudices."[99] Foster points to the genre of the slave narrative—a classification in which *Incidents* perpetually appears with the metaphorical equivalent of an asterisk because of how much it resembles the novel form, evidenced by the fact that it continues to appear on syllabi for courses on the novel—as itself being invested in the concept of "revelation" or disclosure and as such a site of both epiphany and suspicion among readers. Here we see how the suspicion of Turner's confessional authorship runs alongside and in collaboration with suspicion of Jacobs's authorship within a genre that readers meet with an expectation of disclosure and revelation—a (white) appetite for the revelation of slavery's "truths" through autobiography and narrativized trauma.

Indeed, as P. Gabrielle Foreman has observed, the classification of *Incidents* as "true" is the very rubric through which the text was both "dismissed" and later "resuscitated."[100] Whereas the suspicion around Turner's authorship concerned his presumed criminal liability for an insurrection, the suspicion and policing of Jacobs as an agent of "truth" is additionally rooted, as Foreman further notes, in gendered abolitionist expectations around Black women to uncritically reproduce their own violence while navigating the norms of femininity and discretion that white women readers claimed for themselves. These literary expectations extend the gendered expectations and violence that attended enslaved women in general, to whom, as Angela Davis notes, "the alleged benefits of the ideology of femininity did not accrue."[101] Thus, while the reception of Jacobs's text shares important terrain with Turner, it is additionally inflected by the pressures on her to navigate these bonds of feminine performance through what Foreman describes in productively legal terms as "an implicit contract with her readership . . . [who would] perceive (but to be 'delicate' enough not to admit that they comprehend) the sexually determined Black 'back regions' of her textual performance."[102]

Jacobs also maintains a second, more overt link to Turner's confession, however. Her text explicitly reflects retrospectively on Turner's rebellion and its aftermath in chapter XII of *Incidents*, "Fear of Insurrection." Jacobs's description of patrols explains how the surveillance structures authorized by Turner's rebellion created "a grand opportunity for the low whites,"[103] who used property inspections as occasions to enact the forms of control and humiliation typically reserved to enslavers. Jacobs thus links sovereignty, insurrection, and property surveillance on a broader geopolitical scale that operates as a doubling of the sexual surveillance to which she is endlessly subjected on the Flint plantation. These pressures between public authority and private autonomy, through the link to Turner, remind us again of the utility of sovereignty as a theoretical frame that formulates alternatives to a persistent public (white) equation of Blackness with forms of moral transgression. Jacobs repeatedly uses literary engagement, and specifically the form of confession, to address the assumptions of moral transgression and to experiment with legal ways of being that will shield her from her oppressors while also affording her the freedom and privacy to sustain and nurture herself and her family.

Darlene Clark Hine famously formulated the concept of dissemblance in her 1989 essay, "Rape and the Inner Lives of Black Women in the Middle West: Preliminary Thoughts on the Culture of Dissemblance."[104] That essay, which specifically studied Black women migrants to the Midwest in the late nineteenth and early twentieth centuries, nevertheless linked the practice of dissemblance—"the behavior and attitudes of Black women that created the appearance of openness and disclosure but actually shielded the truth of their inner lives and selves from their oppressors"[105]—to the lives and literature of antebellum Black women, including Harriet Jacobs. Certainly, Jacobs's descriptions of the sexual abuse of her enslaver appear to comport with Hine's theory of dissemblance in that her selected disclosures to her readers both signaled her vulnerability and sought to "retain or claim some control and ownership of [her] own sexual [identity]."[106] However, I am reluctant to classify Jacobs's descriptions of Flint's abuse as *confession*, per se, which is a narrower subset of "disclosure" than that which Hine imagines; and which, crucially, is a recitation of one's *own* criminal activity, as opposed to the criminal acts of someone else (which would be better labeled an accusation or testimony). Instead, this chapter considers moments where Jacobs appears to confess to her own shortcomings, moments where she creates "the appearance of disclosure, or openness . . . while actually remaining an enigma."[107]

However, as becomes more and more apparent, Jacobs reserves a more personal form of confession for her family members, whose affection for her typically obviates the need for confession. This preemptive absolution rearranges the expected order of confession—Jacobs as the confessing party persistently receives absolution *before* she can complete a confession; her family members thus shield her from subjection in ways that she repeatedly notes law is unable to. Early in the text, Jacobs writes about the disappointment of her "love-dream," a young romance with a free Black man; the term "love-dream" shows how the text makes visible but not necessarily explicit the tender joys and pleasures in the corners of Black life that manifested around, alongside, and underneath Jacobs's enslavement.[108] This reference to the sweetness of young love conceals the specifics of that relationship behind the violence of its opposition by Dr. Flint. This disappointed "love-dream" functions within *Incidents* to contextualize and dramatize Jacobs's revelation that her enslavement was a problem of sexual captivity as much as anything else. Aware that Flint would never permit her to exercise sexual agency and marry a love match, Jacobs instead identifies only one remaining path to sanctuary from Flint's sexual pursuit: a strategic pregnancy by another local white man. In framing this event for her white readers, Jacobs deftly navigates the mores of the so-called Cult of True Womanhood, which demanded various performances of domesticity and, crucially, sexual purity. For Jacobs, as for Black women throughout history, sexual agency and sexual freedom were tantamount to criminality; it is for this reason that confession is the specific rhetorical mode Jacobs turns to at this point in the text.

Here Jacobs performs an agonized confession that not only adopts the relevant legal terminology but also fully delivers on confession's extraction of subjection and remorse. Jacobs speaks of herself as a defendant pleading a case, writing "I will not try to screen myself behind the plea of compulsion from a master; for it was not so. Neither can I plead ignorance or thoughtlessness." In other words, Jacobs appears to waive her defenses, and unlike Turner and Langston, who confessed guilty actions while denying actual guilt, Jacobs seems poised to offer both, until, after carefully documenting Flint's years of sexual abuse, she writes, "The influences of slavery had had the same effect on me that they had on other young girls; they had made me prematurely knowing, concerning the evil ways of the world. I knew what I did, and I did it with deliberate calculation."[109] Here, despite having seemed to waive certain defenses, she has nevertheless shifted culpability away from herself, even as she claims that she acted with "deliberate calculation."

Where she turns next in her address to white women underscores this confessional sleight of hand while reinforcing her ideology of law as a site of protective potential. She writes, "But, O, ye happy women, whose purity has been sheltered from childhood, who have been free to choose the objects of your affection, whose homes are protected by law, do not judge the poor desolate slave girl too severely!"[110] By applying the transitive logic of her previous statements, the actions she undertook with "deliberate calculation" were nevertheless not free—Jacobs here differentiates herself from white women whose sexual freedom and thus families ("homes") benefit from law's protective capacity. Law in this moment is a form of insurance against the exercise of sexual freedom, a protective latch that preserves white women's purity and also affords them the freedom to configure their own homes as they see fit. Law is a lock that white women can place on their bedroom doors. Jacobs signals the way that her home and family status retained no such protection, cutting off her ability to configure marriage and family according to her own preferences. Indeed, in this context, the "crime" of sexual conduct, however deliberate it may have been, cannot be said to be truly consensual,[111] meaning that the criminal intent, or mens rea, could not exist.

Crucially, like Turner and Langston, who acknowledge the intention of performing certain actions while refusing to characterize those actions as criminal, Jacobs leverages this moment of confession into a moment of Black worldmaking. As in the case of Langston, she accomplishes this via counterfactual: "If slavery had been abolished, I, also, could have married the man of my choice; I could have had a home shielded by the laws; and I should have been spared the painful task of confessing what I am now about to relate; but all my prospects had been blighted by slavery."[112] In this moment of address to her readers, whom she has positioned as judge or jury, and to whom she is on some level expected to submit, Jacobs calls herself into affinity with them by briefly conjuring another world—a world where the laws protected her, where she could be "free" to enact and perform all of the rituals of womanhood that these white women readers might expect, but crucially a world where this confession is undone, erased, and unnecessary. Because Jacobs is not in court, she has no obligation to wait and receive a verdict; rather, she retains control over her text and, a few pages later, she offers an alternative: pardon.

In seeking pity and pardon, Jacobs once again deploys what Foreman identifies as a characteristic method within the text of concealment through revelation.[113] Jacobs writes, "You never knew what it is to be a slave; to be entirely unprotected by law or custom.... I know I did wrong. No one can feel it more sensibly than I do. The painful and humiliating memory will haunt me to my dying day. Still, in looking back, calmly, on the events of my life, I feel that the slave woman ought not to be judged by the same standard as others."[114] She bookends her confession with waivers of excuse or justification, performing the kinds of subjection and remorse that locate her within a white readership's "safe zone"—she has, in essence, earned compassion not by virtue of her humanity but by virtue of her willingness to offer certain injuries up for her audience's examination. Though she performs a request for absolution, she does not wait to receive it, and indeed she has already imagined an alternative history where the confession does not exist at all. Were we to stop here, it might not seem necessary to test the borders of dissemblance to understand how Jacobs uses confession. We might read her navigation of white women's expectations around respectability as evidence of her strategic use of disclosure to merely (and falsely) remain an "enigma" (Hine) or, in the parlance of Turner, to "wrap herself in mystery."[115]

However, Linda also attempts to make several other confessions, to her grandmother and later to her daughter, in which the contrast of public versus private confession is clear. Jacobs unambiguously positions both of these women in her family as authorities whose forgiveness is her paramount objective. Each of these confessions nuances Jacobs's deployment of confession and concealment (Foreman's framework of "reveals as it also conceals"), signaling forms of "quiet" imagined by Kevin Quashie as the "inexpressible expressiveness of the interior"[116] and further theorized by Shoniqua Roach "as a reading practice, a mode of reading for black intimacies forged in the space of the public."[117] In other words, Jacobs's familial confessions are moments where we see her practice a form of failed confession as a mode that authorizes radical revisions to her imagined family tree. In marking out private zones of relation, confession operates here as a signifier of intimacy, familial safety, and an assertion of Black sexual and familial sovereignty.

The confession to Linda's grandmother follows swiftly on the heels of the ostensible confession to Jacobs's readership, marking the contrast between the two confessional performances.[118] However, much like Turner who at first repeatedly *fails* to confess specific acts of violence, Linda discovers, "My lips moved to make confession, but the words stuck in my throat."[119] Not only is she unable to summon the language or justification that the readership has consumed over several preceding pages, she also experiences overwhelm out of fear of her grandmother's judgment and disappointment and also out of shame. Crucially, the source of her shame here comes not from having failed to live up to standards of white womanhood but from failing to live up to her *grandmother's* moral authority, which is suggested but not delineated in detail here. Moreover, Jacobs preserves the privacy of that encounter, shielding the specifics of the confession beneath descriptions of her desperation. The emotional significance of the moment is visible in the text, as both Linda and her grandmother weep, and Linda begs her grandmother for forgiveness. Note the contrast with the confession to her readers, where Jacobs performs a plea for pardon while "looking back calmly" on her life's events.[120] Though a confession is alluded to in the scene with her grandmother, it is not explicitly articulated.

Here, though not surrendering solely into herself, Linda literally falls into her grandmother, a familial extension of herself and her private life. Her grandmother "listened in silence" and "did not say, 'I forgive you;' but she looked at me lovingly, with her eyes full of tears. She laid her old hand gently on my head, and murmured, 'Poor child! Poor child!'"[121] Thus, her grandmother offers absolution by implication if not by speech act. It is a moment of grief and lamentation about the outer world, but not one that is necessarily rooted in resistance to that world; rather, it is a turning inward and away from public examination. These partial confessions—where the text discloses the existence of confession but not its substance—mark what P. Gabrielle Foreman has identified as the "good use of the implicit expectations of victimization that Jacobs simultaneously shuns" by "toying with the acceptable titillation and resolution of confession and absolution without ever really shedding any raiment."[122] Unlike the use of counterfactual, deployed against white readers as a worldmaking strategy, this creation of private space within the public world of *Incidents* is an example of worldmaking that becomes possible through the intimate, deeply personal rituals of confession that punctuate the text in contrast with its other public rituals of confession that explicitly address its reading audience.

Foreman has likewise identified the nexus between religious and legal (criminal) valence of confession in *Incidents*, which she reads as "convert[ing] a religious invocation of pardon into both sexual and political agency,"[123] and more specifically through what Foreman describes as the persistent choice between "silence or sale,"[124] which is the looming threat that governs Linda's enslavement. It stands to reason that silence would operate in opposition to sale, an action that threatens to irreparably dismantle Black family structures. However, Jacobs also mobilizes confession as a form that contains the potential to deliberately rewrite familial structures around Black relation as opposed to the consequences of Black women's sexual vulnerability. Perhaps nowhere is this use of confession more prominent than in a much later chapter entitled "The Confession," a chapter immediately followed by the chapter entitled "The Fugitive Slave Law." This juxtaposition reminds the reader once more that "confession" has a legal, specifically a criminal, context, and not merely a colloquial connotation.

This chapter, chapter 39, takes place in Boston, where Jacobs and her daughter spent several years after Jacobs successfully arrived in the North and secured custody of her daughter. On the eve of her daughter's departure for boarding school, Linda determines "to tell her something about her father,"[125] the white politician who had purchased the daughter. But the chapter's title is misleading, as the confession itself is rendered unnecessary. After Linda begins to describe the hardships of her youth, Linda's daughter interrupts and asks her mother to stop. Linda answers, "But, my child, I want you to know about your father," to which her daughter replies, "I know all about it, mother. . . . I am nothing to my father, and he is nothing to me. All my love is for you. I was with him five months in Washington, and he never cared for me."[126] Thus, the "confession" of the chapter's title never takes place, or if it does, Jacobs completely conceals it from her readers' view, leaving instead this reimagining of familial relation that becomes possible across the terrain of what began as confession.

Because the chapter title refers to yet another confession that does not materialize, or at least that does not complete a ritual of disclosure, like Langston's formulation of a citizen-outlaw, Jacobs's use of confession here tends to rearrange the expected temporalities and event sequences. It additionally reconfigures the hierarchy of confession, substituting Jacobs's daughter Ellen—rather than a judicial judge or juror, or other reader—at the top of the text's imagined legal hierarchy. Ellen capitalizes on this innovation by reappropriating the presumed confession as a site in which to rewrite her genealogy. At the same time that she obviates the need for her mother's confession—by proclaiming that she already knows "all about it,"—Ellen excises her white father, the subject of the incomplete confession, from her own family tree.[127] This move simultaneously acknowledges her biological relationship to him while also rewriting the terms of possible familial relation, remarking that her father is "nothing" to her, and that the full balance of her love has been rerouted to her mother. This control over inheritance and descent reclaims the historical tendency for white fathers to "disown" their Black children in the context of legal systems where it was also generally impossible for their Black children to inherit from them without their manumission and specific consent. Ellen establishes these questions of family belonging and inheritance as the domain of Black women and girls, changing the direction and temporality of descent so that she is able to reach back into her family history and strategically dispossess or divest herself from whiteness rather than being dispossessed by her father or the state.

Rather than understanding herself in relation to a white father, a white center, or a white world, Ellen instead begins and ends with her Blackness and her mother. It is also a clear expression of what Quashie calls her "right to be nothing to anyone but self,"[128] as she says, "I am nothing to my father, and he is nothing to me." That disavowal of relation and assertion of nothingness is, rather than dispossession, a site of liberation.[129] At this moment, within a chapter entitled "The Confession" where no confession has actually occurred, Ellen and her mother share a moment of intimacy that, once again, can be glimpsed but not fully accessed. It is confession twice removed; Linda's framing of confession elevates Ellen to a position of judging authority, and Ellen's refusal to hear the confession rewrites the logics of family relationship, kinship, and inheritance.

Thinking through the various confessions I have explored in this second chapter, it is no coincidence that Turner, Langston, and Jacobs all use confession's expected performance of surrender as a site of possibility for Black worldmaking. This shared rhetorical tradition suggests that superficially compliant engagements with law need not always be read solely through a lens of defeat, subjugation, or resistance; sometimes they index visionary worlds of Black innovation—worlds that claim their own forms of spiritual sovereignty, worlds that reclaim the status of the outlaw as a civic exemplar within Black-centered community, worlds where conceptions of familial relation can be reconfigured and reimagined. These writers leverage the potential of confession to embrace the distinction between guilty actions and a guilty mind—a distinction that also decouples the category of criminal action from the status as "criminal." As a legal site of permissible Black speech, confession retains the potential to reshape or remake the legal space and the forms of relation at work within it. Turner, Langston, and Jacobs all harness that potential in different ways, demonstrating that confession has the capacity to establish sovereign spiritual traditions, to obligate a person to break an unjust law, and even to restructure logics of familial relation. Like appeal and jurisdiction, confession reorders the textual world in which it arises, testing, at times in maddeningly fleeting ways, opportunities for elsewhere worlds and other logics of relation.

CHAPTER THREE

Jurisdiction

This chapter considers jurisdictional misdirection and experimentation as a technology of Black authorship that challenges place-bound constructions of sovereign power. As noted, this is the second of two chapters that consider how literary pro se advocacy uses legal form as a technology of Black sovereignty. While the first part of this chapter continues to read Jacobs's work in *Incidents in the Life of a Slave Girl* (1861) through the lens of jurisdiction, the second half of the chapter turns to the *Narrative of James Williams* (1838). In both texts, the protagonists'/narrators' staged disappearances paradoxically depend on their continued inhabitation of enslaving spaces. For Jacobs, this inhabitation occurs primarily through her seven-year secret confinement in a crawlspace, her so-called loophole of retreat. For Williams, who staged his disappearance in part by impersonating a waiter aboard a steamship, he effected a paradoxical absence-in-presence through overidentification with the expectations of servitude that attended his embodiment as a Black man. For both Jacobs and Williams, the counterintuitive occupation of enslaving spaces registers their exploitation of law's logics. Each person constructs a world beyond plantation jurisdiction—a system that gives enslavers absolute authority over the people and bodies within its borders. By removing their *legal persons* from this jurisdictional regime, even as their *bodies* remained within it, Jacobs and Williams theorize jurisdiction beyond place and instead as a form of human relation that they can create and revise. While Jacobs improvises place-bound logics as a means of writing herself into the rhetorical protection of law, Williams practices forms of radical personal fragmentation and reinvention as ways of avoiding personal jurisdiction over his body.

Before I turn to the two main figures of this chapter, Harriet Jacobs and James Williams, however, indulge me in a brief detour well outside the nineteenth-century parameters of this book, and linger for a moment with me in a wildly different narrative space, one that explicitly challenges us to think in terms of worldmaking, institutions, and what it means to be bound to a system of rules. In the opening scene of the 1999 film *The Matrix*, uniformed police in an unnamed city gather outside a rundown hotel. Several police cruisers block the street or alleyway, their lights flashing as perhaps a dozen officers mill around without any particular urgency. An unmarked car arrives, from which emerge three black-suited agents with earpieces and sunglasses despite the fact that the scene takes place well after dark. Though we later learn that these "men" are actually computer programs, they initially resemble federal agents—to a US audience, they could be from the Federal Bureau of Investigation or the National Security Agency. As they approach the scene, we hear the police officer mutter under his breath, "Oh, shit." The agent says, "Lieutenant, you were given specific orders," to which the officer replies: "Hey, I'm just doin' my job. You give me that juris my diction crap, you can cram it up your ass."[1]

Though neither the officers nor the agents have identified themselves as hailing from any particular place or government institution, the scene immediately makes legible this moment as a confrontation between two levels of power fighting for control of the people and events on-site. As a trope in crime and action films, this depiction is well worn; most viewers will immediately recognize what appears to be a conflict between state/local and federal power, where the presumably "federal" agents wield hierarchical power despite their relative lack of authoritative paraphernalia—their uniforms contain no badges, their car offers no sirens or flashing lights, and they wear identical generic suits that both are and are not immediately obvious as law enforcement uniforms.

There are subtle classed differences between these two groups as well. The agent speaks calmly and carefully, with the measured tones of a polished bureaucrat well-versed in the rhetorics of state power. The agents wear tailored suits and sunglasses that could be believable as high fashion in a different context. By contrast, the uniformed officer signifies membership in a blue-collar occupation and class status. He casually tosses vulgarities and, in an apparent refusal to conform to the visible hierarchies of power and class, he deliberately misuses the relevant legal term that governs this confrontation: jurisdiction. As he refers to "that juris my diction crap," the officer signals several things. First, he understands jurisdiction largely as a construct that allows federal agents to arrive and "steal" the power to arrest a criminal, prosecute a crime, and thus take credit for the governmental victory. The uniformed officer signals his awareness of, and disregard for, the *rhetoric* that enables that flex, unmasking jurisdiction as a literary or linguistic invention of bureaucratic architects.

This narrative about federal actors "stealing" control of a scene contains a subtext that the local police do the legwork, and the feds take the credit or cannibalize the most interesting cases for themselves, leaving their subordinates perpetually in the drudgery of police work. The further subtext is that jurisdiction is an invention deployed by federal actors as a prosthetic technology of authority, a rhetorical and ideological weapon that originates one type of power specifically for the purpose of displacing another.

But in rehearsing that trope, the officer in *The Matrix* also splits "jurisdiction" into its two Latin roots in a way that nuances and reworks its literal meaning—by inserting the word "my" between "juris" and "diction," he transforms the etymology of the word. It no longer simply means "the law speaks"; juris becomes a transitive verb that takes diction as its object. As (mis)spoken by the police officer, "juris my diction" is instead a command to, essentially, "suck my dick." This formulation, which attaches jurisdiction to both legal authority and male genitalia, collapses the concept of jurisdiction under the scene's signs of police power and federal bureaucracy. As clumsy as the pun is, it works precisely because it articulates a core truth about how jurisdiction operates in contemporary law enforcement as a command to subordinate oneself, to cede one's body to the discretionary whims of whomever occupies a position of greater authority, and how that subordination encodes a history of sexualized subjugation.

This framing of jurisdiction assumes at least some local authority over most conduct that occurs in a particular geopolitical space—a town, a city, a state—while acknowledging that federal authority governs certain specific types of conduct, or conduct that spans more than one local jurisdiction. In *The Matrix*, the uniformed officer names the gendered and sexualized dynamic that permeates this frictional relationship between different levels or types of jurisdictional authority. Jurisdiction over a particular place, over particular people, the scene tells us, can be wielded in a way that subjects not only civilians, but also local officials, to the dominance of a legal authority with the power to claim a sovereign right to discipline. As the uniformed police officer names this dynamic under the sign of male genitalia, he speaks back to that theory of sovereignty by expressing his own fantasy of using the claim of federal authority to sodomize the agent.

If it seems that we have traveled well afield from nineteenth-century Black literature, consider all that this scene from *The Matrix* contains. First, through this scene, we begin to see that jurisdiction can refer both to a place and to the power over that place. That capacity of jurisdiction, to be at once a site and the authority with control over that site, offers us a way into the concept of territorial jurisdiction as a logic of what I refer to as plantation jurisdiction, the logic that arranges the nineteenth-century "geographic domination" that Black feminist geographer Katherine McKittrick has theorized.[2] Under this logic, enslavers had nearly unqualified legal authority over the people they enslaved (and only slightly less authority over other Black people). As the classic example of jurisdictional authority in a plantation setting, the 1830 case *North Carolina v. Mann* infamously cosigned the use of physical force up to and including gunfire on an enslaved woman, Lydia, as she fled a brutal beating. In that case, Judge Ruffin offers the much-quoted holding that "the power of the master must be absolute, to render the submission of the slave perfect."[3] As Imani Perry has observed, Lydia's "will and wounds were not her own possessions; they belonged to whichever party had authority over her at the moment."[4] As it happens, Lydia had been "hired out" to a neighboring property; it was a man on this neighboring property who shot her. As the judicial holding demonstrates, the logic of plantation jurisdiction is so deeply embraced by the enslaving class that it was willing to protect that authority by temporarily ceding the master's "absolute" power to proxies, allowing enslavers to essentially deputize their territorial authority to others, even on land that they did not own, even over people who had been "leased" to other parties. The judicial opinion thus instantiated a particularly violent fantasy of place-bound white tyranny, essentially deeming a plantation a kingdom with no borders, a place where Black people and even their injuries belonged to an endless dynastic chain of white sovereigns.

Unlike a king, however, enslavers' authority derived not from their status as monarchs but through their property rights—a distinction that they used to justify transporting their methods of domination across geographic borders, extending the reach of authority that originates in place-bound logics. As McKittrick notes, "Geographically, in the most crude sense, the body is territorialized—it is publicly and financially claimed, owned, and controlled by an outsider."[5] This strategy of territorial jurisdiction was eventually federally sanctioned by the 1850 Fugitive Slave Act, which is discussed in chapter 2 and, after which, an enslaved person, once rendered property within the geographically bounded and delimited plantation space, could never—in this legal construction—get "off" the plantation, no matter where they traveled. With the passage of the 1850 Fugitive Slave Act, the entire United States was one big plantation, and there was no "outside" that offered absolute sanctuary.

Here it is helpful to turn to Shaunnagh Dorsett and Shaun McVeigh, who in their critical legal study of jurisdiction remind us that the word "territory" "was always connected to jurisdiction, but not to sovereignty. Sovereignty, in the form in which it existed in the classical world, had no explicit territorial link." But the word "territory"—as referring to "the district surrounding a city over which it had jurisdiction"—did have a secondary etymology according to Dorsett and McVeigh. In addition to deriving from the Latin noun *terra* (land/earth), "territory" also derives from the Latin verb *terrere* (to frighten).[6] This double descendancy, from the noun referring to land or earth and the verb to frighten, stitches together the combination of violent power and place on which territorial logics of jurisdiction rest. In the context of plantation slavery, the jurisdiction of enslavers derives precisely via this intersection of land ownership and terrorism.

Having sketched out the legal narratives of territorial jurisdiction and McKittrick's geographies of domination, it is also necessary to pause in consideration of how that seemingly all-encompassing legal narrative existed in tension with a deeply chaotic and constantly shifting landscape of hyperlocal legal rules, procedures, protocols, and customs. As I have described in the book's introduction and throughout the other chapters, the narratives in official legal documents, particularly at the federal level of government, establish theories of law and legal rule that are often contradicted or at least complicated by local customs (Hendrik Hartog, Laura Edwards), an unregulated and improvisational legal profession (M. H. Hoeflich), the inaccessibility or erasure of relevant records of Black legal culture (Saidiya Hartman, Dylan Penningroth), and, to borrow a medical metaphor, the "off-label" use of an available legal forum to sidestep other legal constraints on Black participation in litigation (Emily Owens, Thavolia Glymph, Kimberly Welch). I reiterate these material realities of Black litigants to demonstrate once more the gaps between "official" records and actual legal culture and also to underscore the pliability and amenability of legal culture to numerous creative purposes, strategies, and experiments. Even the federal geopolitical landscape in the first half of the nineteenth century was unstable, fluid, and somewhat fragile. New states were admitted to the union with some regularity, and before the passage of the 1850 Fugitive Slave Act, the state-by-state designations of "slave" or "free" meant that, for instance, crossing a river from Kentucky to Ohio could subject a traveler to vastly different legal worlds. In fact, as Laura Edwards and others have demonstrated, most legal enforcement was actually much more localized than the divisions visible at the state levels. Practical examples of the ad hoc nature of much antebellum legal culture include:

- the existence of "slave patrols," which I discuss in the preceding chapter in relation to Harriet Jacobs's depiction of these roaming bands of frequently disorderly white civilians;
- the temporary tribunal convened to try Nat Turner and other participants in the Southampton Rebellion (discussed in chapter 2); and
- the "court week" proceedings that took place in the antebellum period during designated weeks throughout the year and combined legal proceedings with open air markets and street fair entertainment.[7]

These examples of everyday legal culture are not arbitrarily chosen; each one is a well-documented site of Black legal participation or legal engagement, demonstrating the range of possibilities in legal regimes.

As with so much in the world, multiple things are often true at once. In antebellum legal culture, there was both (1) a range of improvisational, fluid, and robust Black legal participation that achieved wildly divergent outcomes in different places, for different people, often with great success and liberatory possibility; and (2) a determined, violent, anti-Black theory of legal authority that was equally unpredictable and varied. This theory of authority proceeded from the logics of domination and territorialization that are especially visible in plantation jurisdiction regimes and that steadily gathered steam and coherence in the decades leading up to the Civil War. Neither of these two truths can fully account, by itself, for the status of Black legal culture in the nineteenth century, but, held together, they suggest both the rich possibilities of legal culture during this period and the navigational difficulties this legal landscape posed. Moreover, as colonies achieved statehood and borders perpetually shifted, place-bound logics of jurisdiction gained power and visibility, particularly after the passage of the Fugitive Slave Act of 1850 and the related legislative package in the Compromise of 1850. For enslaved people, particularly in the Deep South, these place-bound logics posed particularly intense and powerful obstacles to movement and flight as viable liberation strategies.

The place-bound quality of jurisdiction has retained significance in the evolution of US common law, even in the areas of jurisdiction that refer to jurisdiction over people—as in, the ability of a court to adjudicate matters pertaining to specific individuals.[8] Until the 1878 case *Pennoyer v. Neff*, US constitutional law did not have any clear doctrine of personal jurisdiction, meaning the conditions that must be met to subject a specific person to litigation in a particular court; in 1878, *Pennoyer* established discrete geographical limits on personal jurisdiction, holding that states could only exercise jurisdiction over their own residents or nonresidents who were served with litigation while within the state's geographic borders.[9] That standard remained in effect—if chaotically applied—until as late as 1945, when the Supreme Court in *International Shoe Company v. Washington* modified the law of personal jurisdiction to allow its exercise on nonconsenting nonresidents who had "minimum contacts" in the relevant state.[10] I offer this brief legal history for two reasons: first, to demonstrate the hold of territorial logics on US constructions of personal jurisdiction well into the twentieth century, and second, to illustrate how the Fugitive Slave Act's exploitation of a gap in constitutional law allowed for frighteningly creative jurisdictional practice. Because enslaved people were not legal citizens or state residents, after the Fugitive Slave Law was enacted, there was no legal limit to the pursuit of so-called fugitive slaves beyond state borders.

Dorsett and McVeigh remind us how capacious jurisdiction is as a general matter, writing that "if jurisdiction inaugurates the law, it must also in some sense precede it."[11] Jurisdiction, as the thing that gives a legal actor or institution its "right" or "authority" to exercise legal power, is its own paradox—it is both the source of that legal authority and the instrument or technology of it. This paradox is terrifying and fertile. It suggests an elasticity inherent in jurisdictional logic, a potential for invention and innovation of the terms on which law gets named, asserted, and enforced. And though territorial jurisdiction is the most well-known example of jurisdictional logic, it is in fact just one of many ways of imagining structures of legal relation.

It is necessary to examine Harriet Jacobs's work across chapters 2 and 3 because, indeed, she uses the forms of both confession and jurisdiction in her text, and her use of jurisdiction does things that are not adequately addressed by her use of confession. Specifically, whereas Jacobs uses confession form to rearrange familial logics of relation and preserve sexual sovereignty, her use of jurisdiction rearranges place-bound logics of relation and authority to textually untether her from regimes of plantation jurisdiction. In addition to reading *Incidents* on jurisdiction, the second half of this chapter examines the *Narrative of James Williams* (1838). In examining the personae of "James Williams"—a name that I only use in these introductory pages out of convenience—I seek to explore the ways that his personal presences and absences rearrange concepts of personal jurisdiction in particular, not by frustrating logics of place but by pressing on questions like: Who or what is a person? Which person is which? Under scrutiny, and in the available archives, these personae tend to splinter, fragment, and detach from one another.

Rather than do the secondary violence of seeking to stitch these incommensurable identities into a unified whole, I have opted to let each persona punctuate the chapter. The personae appear suggestively, almost impressionistically, in a way that reproduces their ephemeral quality and unknowability in the archives where they have left traces. In so doing, this structure, along with the naming conventions I use for both him and Jacobs, may feel at times unwieldy for you as a reader. With my apologies in advance, this unwieldiness is quite deliberate. When not referring to one of his individual personae, I refer to "James Williams" in this text as Williams/Thornton/Wilkins (the surnames of the three personae discussed in this chapter). I am committed to the constant visual reminder of the ways in which Williams/Thornton/ Wilkins's jurisdictional experimentation disrupts language and the ways that one must labor to read, or speak, about him. I consider Williams/Thornton/ Wilkins to be the author of the (at least) three personae who refuse to be assembled into a single unified subject. These aliases and identities mark the intricate, contradictory, and largely unknowable terrain of what it meant to be Williams/Thornton/Wilkins.

Likewise, in discussing *Incidents in the Life of a Slave Girl*, I use the name Harriet Jacobs to refer to the author of that text; when discussing the narrator/character based on Jacobs within the text, I use Linda or Linda Brent, the pseudonym Jacobs used when she published the book in 1861. This distinction reminds us as well that even in the realm of autobiography, the narrator of *Incidents* is a persona, a version of the person named Harriet Jacobs and an example of what Uri McMillan describes as an "embodied avatar," a framing that reminds us that while we gain some access to the person known as Linda Brent within the text, we do not achieve or earn unrestricted access to Harriet Jacobs merely by reading her autobiography.[12] In the case of both Jacobs and Williams/Thornton/Wilkins, their disorienting inhabitations of this chapter leverage the affordances of jurisdiction and remind us of their vexed relationships to space and captivity, including on the page, such that their jurisdictional innovations materialize here as well.

AS ALREADY SUGGESTED by chapter 2, Harriet Jacobs's *Incidents in the Life of a Slave Girl* is practically a treatise on the many juridical principles and procedures that structured legalized slavery. Its opening page delineates her status as property ("merchandise," to quote her[13]), the book contains an entire chapter on the Fugitive Slave Act of 1850, and it persistently indexes both the nuance and illogic of legal rules governing property inheritance, contract, and, of particular interest to me here, jurisdiction. Bearing in mind the paradox of jurisdiction as both source and instrument of legal authority, this chapter considers several ways that Jacobs rehearses and reimagines jurisdictional logics: through her occupation of the so-called loophole of retreat, her use of jurisdictional misdirection in correspondence with her enslaver, and her brief imagination of an alternative structure to the nation-state as a source of feminine communal power.

What becomes possible if we read *Incidents* through a lens that is not solely circumscribed by fugitivity? What if we enter the narrative world of *Incidents* by assuming that the "loophole of retreat" is not merely incidentally or inadvertently invoking law but rather is one example among many in this text where Jacobs actively rearranges and reimagines the operative, and possible, legal principles? Specifically, I suggest that a reading of Jacobs as a jurisdictional theorist helps us see how she works with and against place-bound logics of authority. Her jurisdictional imagination and acts of misdirection both depend on and envision forms of Black sovereignty beyond the reach of territorial or plantation jurisdiction.

Apart from being tremendously well-versed in its forms and practice, Jacobs tends to think of law in terms of its capacity to protect rights-bearing choices, to sustain freedom practices, and to sanction forms of relation and kinship such as marriage.[14] This legal optimism can be surprising in a twenty-first-century context, where it is easier to regard these things as law's perpetually undelivered promises. But for Jacobs, law retains a certain fullness of possibility, particularly through a metaphor of the "shadow of law," to which she returns several times throughout the text. This phrase first appears in chapter 5 of the text, "The Trials of Girlhood," where Jacobs delineates the forms of sexual harassment and abuse she endures at the hand of her enslaver, Dr. Flint. She describes this treatment as an assault not only on her body but on her spirit and her virtue, writing, "He peopled my young mind with unclean images, such as only a vile monster could think of."[15] His relentless pursuit necessitated increasing forms of labor and strategy to evade him, as well as an escalating sense of desperation at the realization that there was nothing standing between her and Flint's prurient desires. But there is also a secondary irony here, wherein the language of personhood figures as an intrusion of Jacobs's subjectivity—the legal category of person or the plural "people" transforms from a noun to a verb to describe a form of transgression and sexual violation.

This sense of helplessness against a looming threat is one that Jacobs links immediately to her own status as legal *non*-person. She writes, "But where could I turn for protection? No matter whether the slave girl be as black as ebony or as fair as her mistress. In either case, there is no shadow of law to protect her from insult, from violence, or even from death; all these are inflicted by fiends who bear the shape of men."[16] For Jacobs, the "shadow of law" is not a fearful space, but rather a site of protection, an overhang beneath which one may seek shelter or sanctuary. At the same time, it is difficult to measure a shadow, which varies its shape over the course of the day, depending on the position of the sun; Jacobs's use of "shadow" here reminds the reader that, while law may be protective, it is also fickle, contingent, and frequently unpredictable.

In *Scenes of Subjection*, Saidiya Hartman takes up Jacobs's formulation of the "shadow of law" to think about nonconsent. She writes, "Outside the shadow of law, compulsion eclipses choice, as neither right nor protections secures the line between consent and nonconsent. Therefore, the effort to distinguish between being compelled to submit and 'giving oneself' relies on Flint's vile proposals and assaults in order to define choice by contradistinction. Nonetheless, the line between something akin to choice and nonconsent is permeable and uncertain because an absolute distinction between them cannot be sustained in the context of slave relations. This uncertainty expresses the dilemma of consent for the noncontractual subject."[17] For Hartman, a contract theory of law occupies the foreground, determining and producing Jacobs's repeated subjections. In a contract theory of law, Jacobs, as an enslaved woman, is unable to enter into contracts on her own behalf; by extension the inability to contract means an inability to consent or to withdraw consent, which is the unavoidable bind in Hartman's analysis.

While contract theory often holds appeal for those seeking to find autonomy, agency, and liberation in the right or ability to contract, Karla Holloway explains that a contract, as a legal promise, "may be the one area of law that most directly incorporates and composes complexities inherent in compelling narratives. A contract may even be judged as illusory. It has all the components of a fiction."[18] Holloway's theorization here demonstrates the limits of contract as a site of equity. Contract purports to establish an equal basis for negotiation, but that negotiating field is always already subject to various forms of power, coercion, and manipulation and crucially, as Gabrielle Foreman points out, there are "juridical consequences" for breaking the informal but oppressive social contract on which legalized slavery depends (while an enslaver failing to meet a promise is unenforceable, an enslaved woman who violates the norms of gender, race, and status becomes guilty of a "crime").[19]

The fact that Jacobs is "outside the shadow of law" helps explain why, in Saidiya Hartman's analysis, consent and contract models of legal relation will only reproduce Jacobs's subjection, at most trying to extract from her a consent to her own abuse. And yet, as Samantha Pinto reminds us, "When scholars such as Saidiya V. Hartman (1997) identify the coercion to consent to one's own brutalization and injury, they are identifying black subjects, particularly black women subjects, at the very heart of sovereignty rather than its antithesis."[20] This is in part because, as Pinto shows, sovereignty itself has a "dual distinction of being a key site of and for the enforcement of rights. It is also a key node of debate about the bureaucratic, cultural, and ideological perils of claiming 'autonomy' as the key virtue of a rights-bearing entity. As a synonym for autonomy and independence, but also power and authority, sovereignty is at the heart of the struggle over discussions of human rights and black freedoms."[21] Note the similarity here between Pinto's formulation of sovereignty and Dorsett and McVeigh's formulation of jurisdiction. In both cases, we return to forms of power that are place-bound and yet exceed place; power that grants rights and power that exercises rights; a site of independence that is simultaneously the right to exercise control over whomever or whatever exists at that site.

In adopting her own sovereign model, Jacobs herself rejects contract theory as the dominant frame for conceptualizing law, working from a jurisdictional theory of law instead. Jacobs is well aware that law is not written for her benefit—she says so quite plainly here as she describes the "shadow of law" and its unavailability to her, as well as throughout the text. Since she is not recognized as a contractual subject, she cannot realistically rely on contract remedies to save her—they will only, as Hartman shows, function as instruments of further subjection. Jacobs herself, however, threads this needle by thinking not contractually but jurisdictionally—a jurisdictional theory of law, because it does not depend on her enslaver's recognition of her right to nonconsent, affords Jacobs very different possibilities. In the loophole of retreat, beyond the gaze of her enslaver, Jacobs ruminates on, experiments with, and manifests her own jurisdictional logics. In imagining a "shadow" of law as a space of sanctuary, Jacobs suggests that law's surpluses—its overhangs, canopies, and cool corners—may be adapted for her own protection, even if that was not their intended purpose. It is in this ability to occupy the surplus or excess of legal forms that Jacobs consistently shows herself to be most nimble and innovative.

The Loophole of Retreat

The most well-known example of Jacobs's occupation of surplus space is of course her inhabitation of the so-called loophole of retreat, a tiny garret space above her grandmother's cottage. At once confined and liberated by the loophole of retreat, Jacobs spends seven years in what she describes as "the last place they thought of,"[22] just a few miles from the enslaver who had sexually abused her. The term "loophole" in this context refers both to the escape and respite offered by this space, as well as the tiny holes she bores into the exterior wall so that she may breathe limited fresh air and overhear passersby below. It might be tempting to read the use of "loophole," which has, according to the *Oxford English Dictionary*, retained a legal connotation of escape—often of a contract provision—since at least the seventeenth century, as evidence for a contract-based model of law within *Incidents*. However, given that this particular loophole is a tiny, practically uninhabitable space, right beneath Dr. Flint's nose, the connotation of "escape" in this context is far more complex than the liberation from an unfavorable contract provision; rather than flight or escape from plantation jurisdiction, the loophole of retreat effects something closer to an illicit occupation of that space—both in its physical parameters and its legal and geographic contexts.

The garret is one of several small spaces that Jacobs occupies in the text—her flight from Dr. Flint places her in other secret chambers, subterranean spaces, and, in one journey that marks a reframing of the Middle Passage, below deck on a northbound boat. But in particular, from this perch at her grandmother's cottage, and with the assistance of those few holes in the exterior wall, Jacobs achieves a space of privacy and a vantage point from which she reverses the panoptic gaze that had governed her enslavement. With a limited line of sight to the world below and the ability to overhear the conversations of passersby (including her children), Jacobs becomes a clandestine agent of her own liberation—or, in McKittrick's words, she "quietly critiques and undoes traditional geographies."[23] As a freedwoman, her grandmother enjoys a zone of qualified Black sovereignty in her cottage—a rare space of limited public Black authority that exists in fruitful contradiction to the regime of plantation jurisdiction that surrounds and surveils it. The cottage marks both the reach and the limits of whiteness against her grandmother's personal power—though the house remains subject to patrols and searches, there are certain forms of violence that simply may not be perpetrated there. It comes into view as an example of what Samantha Pinto urges when she asks us "to think of black women not as excluded from sovereignty but as the builders of alternative models and networks of sustained and sustainable vulnerability."[24]

While the forms of vulnerability demanded by this arrangement are difficult to perceive as "sustainable," the cottage nevertheless demonstrates the power and possibility of occupation as opposed to flight, of alternative models that leverage vulnerability toward something other than victimhood. Dr. Flint may visit the cottage, but her grandmother has the authority to cast him out, to name his crimes, to shame him, and to set limits on the violent acts he attempts there. Thinking jurisdictionally, the liminal nature of the cottage—outside the border of the plantation's territorial limits but within the geographic borders of a state where slavery is sanctioned—situates Jacobs in a space of qualified Black privacy, vulnerability, and self-determination that is submerged within several layers of juridical danger.

From within that vestibule—a reference to Hortense Spillers's formulation of "cultural vestibularity,"[25] also taken up by Imani Perry who references an enslaved person "left standing ... in the vestibule (as in the case of the slave, who is of the plantation household but not fully in it)"[26]—Linda also engages in a series of creative practices that facilitate her continued liberation and her eventual flight north.[27] It is within the loophole of retreat that she foments her final plans to leave; it is here that she sews clothing for her children's Christmas presents; here that she overhears crucial information that aids her in her fugitivity. Perhaps most critically, it is here, having never left the immediate region of Flint's plantation jurisdiction, that she steps into her own sovereignty and experiments with forms of jurisdictional misdirection.

Jurisdictional Misdirection

As discussed in chapter 2, Jacobs repeatedly asserts personal, sexual, and familial logics that refuse the seemingly operative legal jurisdictional regimes; by rearranging who counts as a moral authority and possible pardoner, and by reconfiguring familial histories, Jacobs experiments with various forms of jurisdictional thinking. One example of jurisdictional thinking that refuses to replicate place-based logics of authority is the misdirection Jacobs stages through Linda's letters to her enslaver. Throughout the text, while still concealed in the attic, Linda crafts or forges letters to Flint that friends mail from a variety of third locations, usually in the North. The postmarks on these letters authenticate them—and by extension Linda—as originating elsewhere. The goal here, which succeeds, is for Flint to assume that Linda has long since left the area and is in any number of possible Northern locations. In one particular letter, however, I suggest that this practice is more than a game of deception and evasion and instead demonstrates Jacobs's facility at occupying areas of law in unexpectedly fruitful ways that afford her forms of legal protection—it is a moment where Jacobs finds some sanctuary, if incomplete, in a "shadow of law."

At one point in the text, Linda dispatches a friend to mail a specific letter to Dr. Flint from New York. Within that letter, which will be postmarked from New York, she places a sealed second letter addressed to her grandmother, knowing that her enslaver will open and read it—he operates according to his own sense of his authority, in which she has no privacy, no right not to be overheard. In that second letter, she claims to be living on a specific street in Boston. This action is commonly read as a tactic of evasion, and of course it is. It is one of several strategically placed narratives of fugitivity in the text, several of which actually send Dr. Flint to the North in the hopes of recapturing her. However, in this instance, Jacobs takes care to note that her object was *not* to send Dr. Flint elsewhere. She writes: "If I had dated from New York, the old man would probably have made a journey to that city. But even in that dark region, where knowledge is so carefully excluded from the slave, I had heard enough about Massachusetts to come to the conclusion that slaveholders did not consider it a comfortable place to go in search of a runaway. That was before the Fugitive Slave Law was passed; before Massachusetts had consented to become a 'n****r hunter' for the south."[28]

First, note the way that Jacobs critiques purely place-bound jurisdictional logic in this passage, which initially appears to be deeply invested in the notion that place equals safety or sovereignty. On closer examination, she begins by identifying Massachusetts as a jurisdictional safe haven in contrast with the less abolitionist-oriented Northern state of New York, suggesting that the fiction of the North as a space of unqualified liberation is, at a minimum, overstated, fluid, and unreliable. She later confirms that suspicion of New York when chronicling how her employer eventually purchased her freedom, completing the sale in New York. As she processes the information that she has been sold, she says, "A human being *sold* in the free city of New York! The bill of sale is on record, and future generations will learn from it that women were articles of traffic in New York, late in the nineteenth century of the Christian religion."[29] There, the suspicion of New York comes full circle, as she realizes finally that its jurisdictional aura has ultimately been a myth.

But to return to this earlier passage, where she sends one letter inside another to Dr. Flint, Jacobs also signals that even Massachusetts, the supposed bastion of abolitionist spirit, offered that kind of jurisdictional shelter only temporarily before becoming, pursuant to the Fugitive Slave Act, "a n****r hunter." While Linda recognizes the immediate value of Massachusetts jurisdiction and mobilizes it to specific purposes, Jacobs—as the author writing with the benefit of retrospection—signals the limits of a jurisdictional model that is based purely in logics of place, pointing out that these logics essentially reproduce plantation jurisdiction at first in theory, and eventually in practice as well.

Another question looms, however. If Linda's object here was not to send Flint in false pursuit—as she takes care to say—what other purpose does this second letter accomplish? At this moment, prior to the passage of the Fugitive Slave Act, Linda gains something specific by locating herself in Massachusetts. Without having ever left North Carolina, Linda places herself under the protection, the "shadow" of Massachusetts law. In fact, the postmark on the outer envelope verifies her status in a way that would meet evidentiary standards of proof. It is legal protection that is obviously incomplete, but it is one of many examples from this text wherein Jacobs/Linda reconfigures jurisdictional logic to grant herself the privacy and the sovereignty of her own liberation and ultimately to imagine other forms of legal relation. Writing decades before constitutional law actually codified non-place-bound standards for personal jurisdiction, Linda imagines the protection of legal structures that do not cast her as a fugitive or as property, and she rearranges jurisdictional hierarchies to glimpse other possibilities for Black belonging, perhaps possibilities that ground her sovereignty in her shared life with her grandmother, or her ability to monitor her children from her hiding place. Perhaps these possibilities include her capacity to network and collaborate with her Black (and occasionally white) allies to sustain her liberation from Flint.

In studying examples of "infamous" Black women, Samantha Pinto writes that she considers "the ways that these infamous bodies reimagine the contours and content of the political in their own time, but most significantly beyond it, in the ways that they inhabit and transform the imaginable limits of political being and living in a patriarchal, antiblack world."[30] Though I would not classify Jacobs as infamous, per se, she too displays an ongoing propensity to live beyond the limits that should have applied to her occupation of a plantation space, an anti-Black world, and a seemingly inescapable jurisdictional prison. Jacobs's construction of her own sovereignty, formed in the course of her everyday life, and which becomes especially visible in her representation of this misdirectional correspondence, precedes the thing that is *supposed* to bestow sovereignty upon her—much the way that jurisdiction itself must at once precede and emanate from an imaginary original authority. Jacobs transforms herself into lawgiver, lawmaker, and law enforcer.

Imagined Alternatives and Elsewheres

In addition to rearranging the place-bound jurisdictional logics that would apply to her, Jacobs also offers glimpses of other possibilities for Black belonging. She does so through the use of counterfactual imagination, a technique discussed in chapter 2, but that has a tendency to surface throughout the entire book. As a form of a "what if?" line of thinking, counterfactuals, for Stephen Best, "constitute both a necessary feature of all literary and legal hermeneutics and a common component of historical and philosophical inquiry."[31] It is a mode of inquiry, a form of "subjunctive rhetoric,"[32] that invites speculation, revision, and other practices in worldmaking. As one of the ways that Jacobs improvises and reimagines jurisdictional logic, Jacobs rehearses a specific counterfactual thought experiment in chapter 8, "What Slaves Are Taught to Think of the North," where she once again tests the limits of place-bound forms of sovereignty.

Here, Jacobs writes about an enslaved woman whose husband "told her that the black people had sent word to the queen of 'Merica that they were all slaves; that she didn't believe it, and went to Washington city to see the president about it. They quarrelled, she drew her sword upon him, and swore that he should help her to make them all free." Jacobs continues, "That poor, ignorant woman thought that America was governed by a Queen, to whom the President was subordinate. I wish the President was subordinate to Queen Justice."[33] This textual moment formed the basis for both Lauren Berlant's conceptualization of "diva citizenship," as well as the title for her 1997 book, *The Queen of America Goes to Washington City: Essays on Sex and Citizenship*. For Berlant, "Diva Citizenship occurs when a person stages a dramatic coup in a public sphere in which she does not have privilege."[34] I have no investment in the figure of the diva in my analysis of Jacobs's jurisdictional imagination. However, Berlant's framing here in the language of "coup" does recall the tendency of a text like, for instance, David Walker's *Appeal*, or "Theresa, ___ a Haytien Tale," to, through the use of counterfactual, overturn a prevailing legal order from an apparently disempowered subject position.

In this passage from *Incidents*, the ostensible fantasy of a Queen of America comes not only from the imagination of a woman disempowered on account of her enslavement, but specifically from a woman Jacobs identifies as an exemplar of the forced or intentional forms of ignorance cultivated by enslavers. As Jacobs describes, these misapprehensions about government, current affairs, and so forth were incredibly common through a combination of intentional misinformation, literacy prohibitions, and the like. She describes how, when "the most ignorant" learned that she was able to read, "I was often asked if I had seen any thing in the newspapers about white folks over in the big north, who were trying to get their freedom for them. Some believe that the abolitionists have already made them free, and that it is established by law, but that their masters prevent the law from going into effect."[35] First, given that the Juneteenth holiday commemorates word finally making it to enslaved people in Texas—two full years after Emancipation—that they were legally free, some of these misapprehensions appear quite reasonable in retrospect.

But, crucially, her observations here also nod to forms of illicit freedom and practices of Black belonging that the text acknowledges in sidelong fashion. For instance, later in *Incidents*, as Linda drifts past the Snaky Swamp in a boat, her white captain says, "There is a slave territory that defies all the laws,"[36] an unmistakable reference to marronage that Jacobs follows up with a reference to the Great Dismal Swamp, the largest and most famous site of marronage in the United States. As it entered my analysis of the appeal form in chapter 1, marronage once again signals the possibility of alternative sites of Black belonging. An important feature of marronage—the thing that marks its paradoxical status—is the fact that maroon communities are literally spaces of autonomous Black life and community *within* a geographic entity where such a category purports to be unavailable. Like Linda's occupation of the attic space on the margins of a plantation jurisdiction scheme, marronage marks a mode of jurisdictional defiance, an absence in presence—or, in Neil Roberts's formulation, a freedom practice forged in flight.[37] Though I am reluctant to theorize Black subjectivity through fugitivity, Roberts's frame here emphasizes the "liminal and transitional" qualities of flight, which also speaks to what is liminal about Linda's occupation of spaces on the margins[38]—and indeed, her transit through the Snaky Swamp, an apparent avatar for the Great Dismal Swamp, the largest and best known site of marronage in the United States.

These counterintuitively (if incomplete) liberatory occupations of physical and legal space arise in *Incidents* as combinations of imagination and radicalism. Thus, when the enslaved woman suggests that a queen of 'Merica demanded freedom for the slaves at the end of her knifepoint on the President's neck, Jacobs carefully lingers on this moment in a way that satisfies the norms of her reading audience; in Pinto's words, she "strategically games the dictates of the politics of respectability,"[39] appearing to dismiss it as the ramblings of a "poor, ignorant woman."[40] However, even as she appears to dismiss this fantasy, Jacobs briefly claims it, envisioning a version of justice that rearranges national power—she works in a mode of speculative history that uses the counterfactual to suggest alternative futures. In expressing a wish, "I wish the President was subordinate to Queen Justice,"[41] Jacobs stops short of casting out the President—rather, in permitting him to remain, she has made him subordinate to a queen, reclaiming a logic of sovereignty for a form of belonging that safeguards Black liberation. In another version of the forms of overturning that continue to surface in antebellum Black literature, Jacobs revises the woman's "Queen of 'Merica," a jurisdictional logic of place, with "Queen Justice," a jurisdictional logic of moral or natural authority to stand above the President, or the leader of the nation-state. This substitution of justice for nation-state, female for male, relation for place, exemplifies Jacobs's jurisdictional praxis.

Moreover, although this counterfactual moves counter to fact—there is no "Queen of 'Merica"—it avoids the typical subjunctive construction.

In subjunctive formulation, Jacobs's statement would read "I wish the President *were* subordinate to Queen Justice," an expression of will that imagines an alternative history resulting in an ongoing relation of the President to Queen Justice. However, in saying "I wish the President *was* subordinate to Queen Justice," Jacobs's rumination actually seems to foreclose that possibility and say instead "I wish the President had been subordinate to Queen Justice." Both statements imply alternative histories, but Jacobs's past-tense construction in indicative mood reminds us that this apparent counterfactual actually asserts a factual condition. At the risk of making too much of this grammatical detail, I suggest that the distinction makes visible that this is an expression of alternative history, a version of what Uri McMillan describes as a trans- or polytemporal outcome produced through the performance of objecthood, a way for artists to "transmute their simulated identities into transhistorical figurations."[42] Rather than a straightforward hypothesis about future possibilities, Jacobs renders a vision of a queen who ruled at the tip of a sword and thus obliterated the world in which Jacobs then finds herself. If Queen Justice had reigned supreme, Jacobs seems to suggest, none of this would be necessary in the first place.

These transmutations of hypothesis into history and place-based logics into Black-centered ones unfold through the form of jurisdictional theory. By using a legal form that functions most commonly (or at least most visibly) as a structure of place, Jacobs cracks open its compartments and affordances, deploying it counterintuitively to both displace her embodied self from hostile territories and transmute those territories into sites of possible Black sanctuary. In the subsequent section, I examine how the man we typically refer to as "James Williams," the author of an immediately discredited 1838 freedom narrative, uses jurisdiction to effect apparent fragmentations of identity in order to exempt himself from hostile forms of personal jurisdiction.

Williams/Thornton/Wilkins

The man we call "James Williams"—the author of the 1838 freedom narrative *Narrative of James Williams, an American Slave, Who Was for Several Years a Driver on a Cotton Plantation in Alabama*[43]—entered the cultural imagination most famously as an accused impostor suspected of inventing a fictional autobiography. Almost as soon as it was published, his 1838 slave narrative was discredited as factually implausible or fraudulent, and scholarship on it has long focused on verification, on the question: was James Williams a "real" person? In his critical edition of the narrative, Hank Trent demonstrates that

"James Williams," the person I refer to here as Williams/Thornton/Wilkins, was in all likelihood a man born under the name Shadrach Wilkins, who used the names "James Williams" and "Jim Thornton" in various stages of his self-emancipation. These various personae—versions of James Williams who can't quite be dismissed as simple substitutes—appear in collateral texts ranging from fugitive advertisements to legal cases, where they persistently unsettle and destabilize their contexts.

Let me assert upfront that these various personae do *not* work as a collection of parts that can be assembled into a unified whole. This is not an act of reassembly. Different personae emerge and recede from view with unpredictability. As a result, it would be possible to acquiesce to law's pressures and to read the absences and incommensurability of these personae as some kind of failed or debilitated personhood. Instead, I suggest a version of fragmentary authorship and jurisdictional imagination that rests in its capacity to reiterate, reproduce, and generate multiple personae that disrupt and dislodge the logics of institutional power. Specifically, by practicing forms of radical self-fragmentation, Williams/Thornton/Wilkins made it impossible, and at points absurd, for courts to exercise personal jurisdiction over him—whereas Jacobs's use of jurisdictional form reimagines place-based jurisdiction in favor of a sovereign construction of self, Williams/Thornton/Wilkins's use of fragmentation makes it futile for jurisdiction to be applied to a "self" at all.

Over several years and using a variety of methods, which Hank Trent carefully traces in his 2013 edition of the *Narrative of James Williams*, Williams/Thornton/Wilkins made several unsuccessful attempts to flee from his owners until finally, in 1837, he stowed away on a northbound steamboat. Following his escape, his owner pursued legal remedies from the steamboat company for failing to secure his property—and the Louisiana courts gave the enslaver what he wanted. Shadrach Wilkins was declared lost property, and his owner recovered $1,600 as compensation for the loss.[44] However, as the courts and his enslaver well knew, Shadrach Wilkins hadn't simply vanished into thin air. He remained very much alive, having been last seen en route to a second steamboat. But for all practical purposes, the litigation that compensated his owner had declared Wilkins dead or destroyed or, simply, gone. This legal result should strike us as deeply strange, a rupture in the fictions of law that enabled legalized slavery in the first place—if Wilkins had not been a legal person to begin with, why should it matter to his owner whether Wilkins was dead or alive? To the owner, Wilkins was simply lost property, money out of the slaveholder's pocket.

In fact, not only was Shadrach Wilkins still alive, but while this lawsuit made its way through the Louisiana court system, Wilkins—by then traveling as James Williams—was in the process of publishing a freedom narrative. At the same time that the courts were reading him as fungible goods, he was writing himself in thoroughly different terms, asserting his personhood through a series of textual and extratextual performances that test the limits of what we typically recognize as Black authorship. In attending to these questions of authorship, fugitivity, and textual production, Xiomara Santamarina argues for reading the *Narrative of James Williams* as a novel, pointing out that such a reading would counteract the problematic politics of authorial suspicion that have accrued as already discussed around texts like *Incidents* and as noted by Santamarina (and which becomes relevant in chapter 4 of this book) around *The Bondwoman's Narrative*. For Santamarina, reading the *Narrative of James Williams* as a novel both honors what we know about the identities of Williams/Thornton/Wilkins while also attending to the intricacies of that text's use of fictionalization.[45] While I tend to push away from attachments to fugitivity as the dominant framework for Williams/Thornton/Wilkins, I find persuasive Santamarina's argument about the *Narrative of James Williams* as a novel, an argument that sensitively and productively addresses many of the theoretical questions my analysis engages here around genre, fictionalization, and literary innovation. Here again I find it useful to invoke Uri McMillan's formulation of an embodied avatar as the "artful embodiment" of objecthood,[46] a framing that helpfully links and distinguishes my analysis of Williams/Thornton/Wilkins and its resonances with both Santamarina and McMillan. While Santamarina focuses on innovation of the novel form and McMillan on the innovation of avant-garde art, my consideration of Williams/Thornton/Wilkins focuses on his uses of personae and fictionalization as literary innovations of jurisdictional logic.

As noted, the man most people refer to as James Williams was born under the name Shadrach Wilkins. Based on the archival research completed by Hank Trent, we know that he married an enslaved woman from a nearby plantation, but after being implicated in a plot to poison a nearby slaveholder, Shadrach Wilkins and his family were sold to a new enslaver in Alabama. While in Alabama, the Wilkins family made numerous attempts to flee together. They even spent a full month on the run in 1835 before being recaptured. At that point, Wilkins began attempting escape by himself. For six months, he traveled under the name "James Williams," working with a white man who posed as his owner—his ostensible owner would sell him to unwitting buyers and later surreptitiously "rescue" the slave so that they could repeat the routine in the next town. Using this scheme, the two men traveled from Alabama to Baltimore before Williams was recaptured and jailed—and thus returned to his identity as Shadrach Wilkins.

While incarcerated, he was sold to a slave trader who dispatched him to the New Orleans slave market in early 1837, where a hotel owner purchased him. Shortly after this sale, Wilkins fled by stowing away on a steamboat named the *Henry Clay*. Onboard, Wilkins now used the name Jim Thornton, as he avoided detection by posing as a waiter. His performance was so industrious, so convincing, that another steamboat offered Thornton a position. With his former owners in pursuit, Thornton traveled to Cincinnati, where he remained for several months (though it is unclear what name he assumed during that time). Toward the end of 1837, he traveled to New York, where he resurrected the identity of James Williams. In New York, James Williams encountered white abolitionists Emmor Kimber and Lewis Tappan, who interviewed him extensively and published his slave narrative in exchange for securing his passage to Liverpool. The narrative offered by James Williams omitted mention of his birth name or any of his other personae; it changed the names and locations of his previous owners; and it made other changes with respect to chronology, geography, and what we might call his history.[47]

The *Narrative*, which includes a preface by the poet and amanuensis John Greenleaf Whittier, became a touchstone and source of pride for the American Anti-Slavery Society (AASS), the institutional apparatus to which Kimber and Tappan belonged. Although several slave autobiographies had already been published in the United States, the antislavery press was just gaining traction in the late 1830s. While the James Williams *Narrative* marked the AASS's inaugural publication of a slave narrative, the society would not publish another one for seven years. That delay occurred in part because James Williams's *Narrative* was so mired in controversy. The circulation of the *Narrative* caught the disapproving attention of the *Alabama Beacon*, a newspaper that challenged the factual plausibility of Williams's *Narrative*. Ultimately, the controversy resulted in the formation of an investigative committee to adjudicate the accuracy of Williams's autobiography.[48] Unable to locate James Williams in England, the AASS had no means of verifying Williams's identity or background. The scant information available cast doubts on the *Narrative*'s authenticity and, by extension, Williams's reliability. In October 1838, the AASS announced a resolution discontinuing the sale of the Williams narrative. No one has ever been able to verify what later became of the man last known publicly as James Williams—once in Liverpool, records of him run cold. As mentioned, in the meantime, his former enslaver was proceeding with a lawsuit to recover damages for the loss of his living property.

In order to begin to grasp the context surrounding the slave known as James Williams, we must acknowledge his creation of at least three personae: James Williams, Jim Thornton, and Shadrach Wilkins. Using Hank Trent's archival research as a starting point, I have assembled this rough chronological summary of the various personae as a means of demonstrating why they do *not* work as a teleology or a sum. It is not simply the case that one alias gives way to the next—the personae evolve and resurface as needed, and they disappear when their presence becomes a liability. Moreover, there are long, unaccounted-for periods of time in which it is uncertain which persona(e) were in use at all.

In fact, each persona is maddeningly elusive, often disappearing precisely when an institution of power most "needs" him. Printed texts are in constant pursuit of the fugitive, a rhetorical posture that doubles the physical pursuit by former owners. Attempts to record the personae in print often operate as ineffectual "captures"—I argue that, in response to the personae's absences and refusals, legal and literary institutions eventually adopt a mimetic strategy of representation that replicate the personae's tactics of substitution and negation. The resulting tension—between the productive generation of personae on one hand and acts of textual suppression on the other—underscores that both law and white print culture relentlessly rely on figurations of enslaved people as dead or destroyed. As Stephen Best writes, "The law knows the fugitive as a nondescript."[49]

In fact, the recursive deployment of these various personae necessitates a messy circuit of creation and erasure, perhaps best exemplified in one of the relevant judicial texts that, unable to manage the appearance of multiple personae at once, represents the slave as "~~James~~ Shadrach."[50] I will return to this particular textual example later, but first I think it is useful to consider how the creation of the Jim Thornton persona demonstrates how Williams/Thornton/Wilkins manifested a richly complex version of personhood independent of the usual legal jurisdictional logics. Remember that Jim Thornton was the waiter aboard the *Henry Clay*, a diligent servant so dependable as to secure a second service position on another steamer. A strategic performance of servitude, claiming the identity of Jim Thornton was a conscious act of self-disappearance and refashioning. We come to know the Thornton persona mainly through the legal opinion *Slatter v. Holton*, a Louisiana court case in which Shadrach Wilkins's owner sought compensation for the property he lost when Wilkins fled north.[51] Because *Slatter v. Holton* ultimately litigates the status of Shadrach Wilkins, the persona of Jim Thornton enters the case record in glancing references. In the trial court opinion, the name Jim Thornton does not appear at all; that court merely held "that the Pltf's slave was on board the Henry Clay, the defendant's boat waiting at table."[52] By contrast, the appellate court, (the Supreme Court of Louisiana) tends to treat "Jim Thornton" as an alias, holding that witness testimony proved that Wilkins "was acting on board as one of the servants [on the *Henry Clay*] under the name of Jim Thornton."[53] That opinion also references the name Jim Thornton in three other instances. It refers to Wilkins as "the boy Shadrack, or Jim Thornton," and twice it describes a witness's identification of Thornton. The witness, Mr. Peterson, "instantly recognized Jim Thornton as [Wilkins]" and described him as "the boy passing by the name of Jim Thornton."[54]

In each of these examples, the persona of Jim Thornton appears as an alias or alter ego that merely substitutes for, or is interchangeable with, the name Shadrach Wilkins. The opinion's gloss on Jim Thornton, in particular, obscures a much richer portrait that emerges in the opinion's supporting materials—namely, interrogatory responses from witnesses and arguments offered by counsel. The witnesses who actually encountered Jim Thornton offered accounts that have much more to say about how Williams/Thornton/Wilkins refashioned himself in his fugitivity. For instance, William McBride (the pilot of the second ship where Thornton fled after leaving the *Henry Clay*) gave a deposition in which he offers this description of Jim Thornton: "rather tall . . . about 5 feet 9 or 10 of a copper color wore his hair well combed back from his face & was remarked on board the Wave for his neatness & activity in acting as a Waiter."[55] The description characterizes Thornton as respectable, a loaded term that evokes the tendency of white people to tolerate or reward performances of docile Blackness. McBride explicitly engages in this version of respectability politics, praising Thornton for the neatness of his hair and eagerness to please the passengers.

Compare this description with the fugitive slave advertisement that Shadrach Wilkins's owner placed in 1835: "SHADRICK, a yellow complected, likely fellow bold and impudent look, about 5 feet 10 inches high 26 years old, wears his hair roached, eyes of a yellowish cast, and wore a white hat."[56] This description obviously bears the bias of an enslaver whose property has vanished. Nevertheless, the difference in described physicality is stark. While the ad focuses on roached hair, yellowish eyes, and a "bold and impudent look," McBride describes a well-groomed and neat waiter whose execution of servitude apparently earned the admiration of the ship's passengers. Setting aside the expected pitfalls of discrepant eyewitness testimony, these two descriptions are largely incompatible—an example of the incommensurability of the various personae with each other. Based on the divergent descriptions, how unlike Shadrick is the polite waiter known as Jim Thornton.

The judicial fumblings around identification and alias expose a jurisdictional rupture—courts are only able to exercise personal jurisdiction over individual "people," but the framework of multiple personae that fragment a legal personality renders a theory of personal jurisdiction useless. It is tempting to conclude that Wilkins was such a gifted *performer* that his transformation into Jim Thornton merely reflects the effectiveness of his performances and disguises—and I do want to retain the performative lens that helps us see how, similar to McMillan's theory of embodied avatars, Williams/Thornton/Wilkins performs "Black objecthood... as a strategy rather than simply a primal site of injury."[57] Jim Thornton, however, was more than a series of garments or a change in hairstyle—the persona of Jim Thornton deftly navigated social codes that had trained others to encounter his body as one of labor and servitude. Thus, Shadrach Wilkins did not *transform* into Jim Thornton at all—rather, the persona of Jim Thornton was *deployed* when the need for him arose. Williams/Thornton/Wilkins pursued liberty not merely through self-representation, but through the creation of Jim Thornton.

To deploy the persona of Jim Thornton, it was necessary only to present a public identity that would align with the social expectations projected onto his body. This creation of personae recalls Marisa Fuentes's formulation of enslaved Caribbean women's creation of "alternative selves" who subvert, from a position of fugitivity, "the very paradigm of enslavement—immobility, disembodiment, violation."[58] This tension of public persona versus the pressure to render a single individual entity returns us to the realm of sovereignty, where Williams/Thornton/Wilkins's proliferation of personae undoes the possibility of personal jurisdiction easily exercised by the state. However, he also transmutes those paradigms of slavery, particularly immobility and disembodiment, leaning into their possibilities for jurisdictional rearrangement—a disembodied, fragmented, or proliferated subject creates very serious problems indeed for state structures that depend on theories of personal jurisdiction that understand state authority as operating over individuals. Never mind the problems created when one persona is the subject of litigation and his connected persona has been declared legally dead.

The man who called himself Jim Thornton "passed" for a waiter, trading forced labor for voluntary service, deploying the persona of Jim Thornton as an authorial strategy of personhood—the descriptions of Thornton as "passing" here obviously conjure associations with other fugitive practices that are impossible to ignore and obviously critical to thinking of these personae and their jurisdictional mystification as, ultimately, a survival practice. Captain Spalding (*Wave*) testified: "There was a coloured boy that passed by the name of Jim Thornton from steamboat Henry Clay.... This Jim Thornton being very active about the table and my Steward being sick at the time I let him work his passage above Flint Island, where I discharged him."[59] The double use of "passed" and "passage" draws discursive connections between Thornton's specific persona and the more general terrain of jurisdictional personhood. As a strategy of survival, a so-called fugitive must "pass" for a member of a group to which—according to prevailing legal and cultural narratives—the fugitive ought not belong. The successful "passing" as a waiter then ensures several other passages: from one steamboat to another, from South to North, from slavery to freedom.

For the fugitive, however, the project of "passing" is never truly complete and as passing is also a transitory, liminal status, Thornton's passing practice once again recalls Neil Roberts's framing of freedom (flight) as marronage.[60] The fugitive slave laws during the antebellum period, which frequently authorized recapture even from free jurisdictions, recast passing not as a temporary strategy, but as a permanent condition of fugitivity.[61] What jurisdictional form offers that fugitivity does not, however, is theorization of Black legal innovation from a zone slightly less entangled with—if not completely independent of—constructions of criminality. Moreover, jurisdictional innovation elucidates the ways that Williams/Thornton/Wilkins's personae interfered with the logics that animated the pursuit of fugitives: by deploying personae that proliferate, rather than conceal, identities, personal jurisdiction is difficult if not impossible for enslavers and patrollers to exercise over a pursued person.

Thornton's hypervisibility on the steamboat thus exploited the various categories of personhood that hovered around his body. Only in certain narrow contexts did his Blackness render him legible and, paradoxically, thus safely *invisible*. Apart from depicting Thornton as highly "active," the testimony in *Slatter v. Holton* is notable for *where* it depicts him—at table. The persona of Jim Thornton was thus legible specifically (and exclusively) in the context of servitude. He must have taken breaks, spoken to other crew members, and so forth. But there are no descriptions of him elsewhere aboard the boat, nor any accounts of him engaged in any other activity. It is impossible to know what happened to Jim Thornton during moments away from the labor he performed as a crew member. It is tempting to ask, where did he *go*? The legal record is unable to answer that question.

Thornton's ability to hide in plain sight among the passengers offers a counterpoint to the elusiveness of Shadrach Wilkins from the judicial record. Wilkins was absent or lost during a time of his enslaver's need and again when the white institution litigating his disappearance had need of his whereabouts; by contrast, Thornton was exceptionally *present* for the white passengers on the ship. Thornton's presence in this context was safe precisely because the need he filled, while also in service of white supremacist customs, did not depend on his specific persona and was in fact completely fungible—any other waiter could have easily replaced him. And in any case, his readiness to be of service ensured that he always appeared *before* his presence could be called into question. In Jim Thornton's case, his servitude is reinvented through rituals that appear to manage both his status as legal slave and his claim to a civil body. The performance of Jim Thornton's persona, and the claim to that name, suggest an evacuation of Shadrach Wilkins—a disavowal of the legal slave, Wilkins, in favor of a claim to Thornton's civil body. The birth of Jim Thornton thus occurs in concert, or at least in tension, with the social death or negative personhood of Shadrach Wilkins.

It is no surprise, then, that *Slatter v. Holton* expends little effort to plumb the depths of "Jim Thornton." That litigation has no interest in Thornton, who merely haunts the case materials to interrupt the trajectory of Shadrach Wilkins, slave and property. Just as Jim Thornton jettisons Shadrach Wilkins in order to avoid jurisdictional claims over his body, the legal opinion must jettison Thornton's presence by "returning" him to classification as Wilkins. In the very first sentence of the opinion, the trial court holds "that the testimony produced by the plaintiff clearly establishes the fact that the Pltf's slave was on board the Henry Clay, the defendant's boat waiting at table."[62] In fact, this holding completely contradicts the testimony, which almost universally identifies Jim Thornton—and not Wilkins—as having been onboard. By holding that Shadrach Wilkins was on board the *Henry Clay*, the court collapses Thornton and Wilkins together in order to produce a legally readable personality: the slave.

The opinion thus produces a strange result wherein Thornton's existence constitutes the erasure of Wilkins, an erasure that entitles a slave owner to damages for lost property. In reaching this result, the court makes the slave owner whole by ordering that he be compensated for Wilkins's value, rendering the disappearance of Shadrach Wilkins a matter of law. This legal fiction operates despite the court's knowledge that the man known as Jim Thornton walked off the ship and presumably was then living elsewhere under that or another name. Lacking a framework of discourse or compensation that would recognize Thornton's existence or exercise jurisdiction over him, law can only adjudicate the person known as Shadrach Wilkins who is declared dead or destroyed. The judgment is a bizarre form of emancipation that uncouples Wilkins from his enslaver, though there is no available legal language to describe it in those terms—nor does law have any interest in framing it accordingly. Moreover, the only persona over whom the court exercises any jurisdiction is Shadrach Wilkins, and then only to codify his death.

Is there a living persona in the Williams/Thornton/Wilkins nexus who remains vulnerable to state theories of personal jurisdiction? The persona of James Williams is perhaps the most difficult to parse, as it initially promises—through his self-authored slave narrative—coherent, self-realized subjectivity. Having authored the *Narrative* with the mediation of abolitionists including John Greenleaf Whittier and Lewis Tappan, James Williams offers readers the fantasy of that text as a more authentic rendering of his personhood as a fugitive. The slave narrative as a genre purports to document the conditions of slavery, and it supplies a tantalizing textual metaphor for the slave's deliverance from slavery into a kind of literary emancipation—a popular, and convincing, account of the slave narrative is that it was the medium through which formerly enslaved people wrote themselves into history, personhood, and freedom. Indeed, the slave narrative did do these things in various ways, and to varying degrees.

However, as scholars have increasingly noted, the location of the slave narrative within structures of white abolitionism also presents complex and vexed questions about the agency and creative control of the enslaved people under whose names these narratives were published. These questions are particularly urgent in the case of James Williams's slave narrative. Santamarina's reframing of the *Narrative of James Williams* offers one way of helping us read this text with more nuance that the slave narrative as a genre seems to afford. Reading this narrative through a jurisdictional lens offers another way to productively complicate that text, by taking seriously the *Narrative* as one of several connected, but ultimately ephemeral and incommensurable, performances that undo and rearrange jurisdictional logic.

Since 1838, a single question has consistently preoccupied literary critics and historians of this *Narrative*: Was James Williams a "real" person? The *Narrative* itself even constructs Williams around the terms of that question. It is replete with data points that appear to verify the world from which he fled: names of people and places, timelines, and other details that document the existence of a person within various bureaucratic and geographical boundaries. The *Narrative* marshals the ephemera of James Williams's history to produce a legible telos that begins with his trustworthiness and the injustice of his enslavement and ends with his freedom—precisely the telos that abolitionists were interested in consuming and peddling, and, it has to be said, the telos that his enslaver(s) and pursuers were equally interested in capturing.

What the *Narrative* explicitly does *not* do is afford access to the subjectivity or selfhood of the man who created the James Williams persona. Instead, it denies any connection whatsoever to that man, much less to the other personae associated with him. Like Jacobs, the jurisdictional authority of Williams/Thornton/Wilkins both appears to precede and follow an imagined "original" figure who is *supposed* to bestow sovereignty—whether personal or authorial—upon him. He persistently frustrates operative logics of state jurisdiction by refusing to make himself legible as the object of personal jurisdiction; at the same time, this ability, like jurisdiction itself, like sovereignty itself, is a paradox. Even as I have, in this chapter, used a tripartite formulation to refer to him, I remind myself and my reader again that this formulation never takes us back to a coherent, whole, single individual. Even within the *Narrative of James Williams*, Williams uses polyvocality to assign insurrectionary liability across multiple subjects. Like Jacobs, Williams references Turner's rebellion, but he discusses it by ventriloquizing his brother, a preacher who has secretly learned to read and write. Williams writes that, when a local church routinely removed Black worshippers from their seats to make room for white churchgoers, his twin brother "on one occasion preached a sermon from a text, showing that all are of one blood. Some of the whites who heard it said that such preaching would raise an insurrection among the negroes." Williams later says, "Since the insurrection of Nat. Turner [his brother] has not been allowed to preach at all."[63] By deploying the story about his brother, the literate preacher silenced by a white audience, Williams frames the *Narrative* as occupying the razor's edge between language and silence, absence and presence. First by substituting his brother for himself, and then by referencing the white tendency to equate Black speech with insurrection, Williams displaces his own subjectivity and explicitly tests the politics of the white abolitionists recording his story.

In his *Narrative*, "James Williams" claims to have a twin brother named Meshech [Meshach].[64] Given that Williams's birth name was Shadrach Wilkins, this naming is significant, as the figures of Shadrach and Meshach appear together in a story from the Book of Daniel. In that story, Shadrach and Meshach refuse to worship an idol, and the Babylonian king Nebuchadnezzar orders them cast into a massive furnace to be burned alive. In light of their faith, God delivers them unharmed; a stunned Nebuchadnezzar sees them walking about in the fire, calls them out of the furnace, and promotes them to esteemed positions in Babylon.[65]

That Shadrach was a character in a story of biblical deliverance is at the least an uncanny foreshadowing of Wilkins's later freedom—and it may simply reflect the longing of a mother to see her newborn children be delivered from the earthly misery of slavery. Through naming her children after these particular biblical figures, Williams's (or Wilkins's) mother called her sons explicitly into deliverance. However, in naming two boys Shadrach and Meshach, their mother not only speaks them into that narrative but also registers the absence of at least one other person. In Daniel, the Babylonian deliverance saves not two, but three men: Shadrach, Meshach, and Abednego. Moreover, when Nebuchadnezzar peers into the furnace, he also sees a fourth unnamed figure, saying, "Did not we cast three men bound into the midst of the fire?" When his guards affirm the question, Nebuchadnezzar exclaims, "Lo, I see four men loose, walking in the midst of the fire, and they have no hurt; and the form of the fourth is like the Son of God!"[66] Despite the appearance of a fourth form, only the three named men emerge from the fire, and there is no other mention in Daniel of that fourth figure.

This biblical tale depicts three recipients of deliverance—Shadrach, Meshach, and Abednego—even as a fourth unnamed figure haunts the story as an uncertain member of their group. The act of naming twins after two of these figures therefore makes visible the absence of the third and fourth members, without whom the tale of deliverance is less complete (though not altogether unreadable)—another example of "under-erasure." Williams/Thornton/Wilkins's birth as Shadrach thus locates him immediately in an apparatus that depends both on multiplicity and conspicuous absences, a jurisdictional reframing. His very name acts as a sign for multiple iterations, alter egos, and shadow figures. This mode of being appears to inflect a strategic praxis that permeates his textual, quotidian, and juridical appearances as Wilkins, Thornton, and Williams, respectively.

As a complete text, the *Narrative* largely refuses readerly access to a formulation of Williams's interiority, offering a series of substitutions and metonyms that contradicts the traditional conventions of the slave narrative as a genre and supports Santamarina's reframing of the text as a novel. On one hand, this metonymic engagement is an effective literary device that suggests the endless and ceaseless routine inherent in slavery. On the other hand, it is a convenient means of refusing details that might endanger Shadrach Wilkins and jeopardize James Williams's chance at securing passage to Liverpool.

These acts of self-disappearance are actually most visible as disruptions of personal jurisdiction in an 1835 court opinion that predates the *Narrative* by several years. Remember that, during one attempted escape from his Alabama owner, "James Williams" was also the name he used when traveling from town to town with an accomplice who repeatedly sold him to unsuspecting marks. When he was finally captured in Baltimore, his "actual" owner submitted an affidavit accusing Williams's accomplice "of stealing from [his] possession ... his negro man, ~~James~~ Shadrach."[67] The judicial strikethrough, reminiscent of Jacques Derrida's "sous rature" or "under-erasure" is, as Gayatri Spivak has written, "the mark of the absence of a presence."[68] It is also useful to consider the strikethrough as described by Calvin Warren as a sign of "metaphysical nothing, the terror of metaphysics, in an antiblack world."[69] The strikethrough is a visual representation of how crowded texts become, how one persona is excised to make room for another, but not without leaving behind a surplus or remainder that in turn shapes our reading of both and makes it impossible to extend normative (white) constructions of personal jurisdiction.

Here, the proliferation of personae instead produces a series of under-erasures that nevertheless leave the remaining personae visible in their absence. In affirming the presence of Shadrach's persona, the court thus permits the residue of James to continue inhabiting the text. This process of striking and rewriting personae is a mimetic replication of the process that Williams/Thornton/Wilkins repeatedly enacts. Just as Shadrach Wilkins disappears in order to make room for Jim Thornton, so does the court strike out the name James in order to accommodate Shadrach. Confronted by a fugitive who repeatedly erases and rewrites himself, the court adopts an identical rhetorical strategy—the effect of which, however, leaves a visual and textual trace that isn't easily absorbed into a single coherent subject. Not only has Williams/Thornton/Wilkins frustrated the court's logic of personal jurisdiction, but he has actually reshaped it, coercing the court into adopting *his* jurisdictional logics.

This 1836 textual appearance of the Williams persona stifles any temptation to read Williams/Thornton/Wilkins as the mere sum of his personae. James Williams's emergence in 1835 predates the emergence of Jim Thornton aboard the *Henry Clay*, suggesting that these personae were deployed, abandoned, and recycled as their contexts made necessary and appropriate. Therefore, one act of vanishing does not preclude the vanished persona from returning in future. At the most, the discursive representations of each persona appear as versions of the strikethrough—vanished for now, but perhaps more accurately described as "dormant."

This jurisdictional reframing requires us to accept the unknowability and incoherence of Williams/Thornton/Wilkins, and to accept each separate persona both as a fully realized subject *and* as uncontainable within then-existing frameworks of personal jurisdiction. The proliferation of personae does not mark the inadequacy or incompleteness of a subject—instead, it records the subjective space that neither law nor text can fully represent. Faced with that failure of representation, Williams/Thornton/Wilkins mobilizes the legal form of jurisdiction and its capacious possibilities for thinking spatially. Leveraging jurisdiction as a strategy of radical self-making, Williams/Thorton/Wilkins deterritorializes or perhaps reterritorializes his own body and persona, and he literally embodies jurisdictional possibility.

CHAPTER FOUR

Precedent

Precedent is about authority. Similar to its colloquial usage, legal precedent refers to a set of rules that must be applied in a given situation. At law, it generally refers to a specific kind of authority: judicial opinions. Precedent evolves and accumulates over time, but it always aims to preserve a unified narrative about the current state of the law based on how courts (judges) have ruled in the past. If you need to know what the relevant precedent is for a particular legal rule, you must look at what the courts in your jurisdiction have said about it most recently—an example of the ways that this form is intertwined with the jurisdictional form taken up in chapter 3. Thus, precedent is *narrative*. It is the story that a court tells about what the law means, a story that compels other, future courts to follow suit. Its status as narrative warrants my methodology of engaging it via literary analysis, which helps us see how precedential narrative meaning arises through intertextuality or citation. To quote Karla Holloway on this shared point of contact with fiction, "Like legal precedent, literature retains its connection to some notion of a scripted past through allusion."[1]

This chapter reads two such narrative forms together—specific trial records on the one hand and a fictionalized autobiography on the other hand—to demonstrate how the nineteenth-century writer Hannah Crafts reimagined the operation of legal precedent by locating it within her literary text and rearranging its assumed logics of temporal continuity. I develop this reading of Crafts's authorial strategies by close reading her novel, *The Bondwoman's Narrative*, in dialogue with the legal testimonial records of a woman named Jane Johnson, who is covertly referenced in Crafts's text. It is beyond the scope of this chapter to undertake a biographical or historiographical study of either author; my energies as a literary scholar and lawyer maintain pressure on the texts themselves as opposed to the biographies of the people who produced them, though of course I consider how these texts make meaning in their historical and historicized contexts. Gregg Hecimovich's 2023 volume *The Life and Times of Hannah Crafts* marks an important tract on her life; I hope that my readings of Jane Johnson's testimonial records in particular will productively suggest to historians, philosophers, and social scientists other points of entry for additional research into her life as well.

In 1855, a set of Philadelphia legal proceedings captured the public's attention: several well-known abolitionists, both white and Black, stood trial for assisting in the emancipation of an enslaved woman named Jane Johnson. The trials were newspaper fodder in part because of the high profiles of the opposing parties. Johnson's enslaver was a well-connected politician and diplomat, whereas the white abolitionist who assisted her became a minor celebrity when he spent several months in prison for failing to deliver Johnson to the authorities. Johnson's public appearances were strategic and limited; with the Fugitive Slave Act of 1850 in effect, Johnson's fugitivity demanded that she remain mostly hidden to avoid being captured and re-enslaved, but she participated in the litigation surrounding her escape via testimonial documents and one dramatic in-person court appearance.

Johnson's highly publicized testimonial presence underscores again the importance of testimony and witnessing as crucial sites where formerly enslaved and free African Americans could literally and metaphorically inhabit and claim rights of citizenship, freedom, and even privacy. As I traced in the introduction, the slave narrative/freedom narrative genre arose in part to claim a site where Black testimony could circulate publicly in print, albeit often mediated or shaped by white and Black abolitionist networks. Johnson's participation in legal proceedings offers an important archive of her testimonial presence, even as the records of her testimonial participation are deeply unsatisfying as artifacts of her biography or personality. And as she is not known to have published a freedom narrative, her visible authorial identity resides primarily in these few surviving documents. Where Johnson does briefly appear, however, is in another enslaved woman's autobiographical novel: Hannah Crafts's *The Bondwoman's Narrative* (2002).[2] As the final chapter in this volume about antebellum Black authorship, chapter 4 examines Crafts's experimentation with the legal form of precedent. The connection between the legal record from Jane Johnson's case and the autobiographical fiction in *The Bondwoman's Narrative* offers a unique site in which to explore the affordances of legal precedent as a literary form. Like the other legal forms explored in this book, legal precedent opens up possibilities for literary experimentation along spatiotemporal axes, situating speculative worldmaking as an understudied feature of antebellum Black literature and legal form as a constitutive authorial strategy among antebellum Black writers.

A recurring affordance among the legal forms in this volume is retrospective review and revision as a futurist mode of Black fictionalization. Precedent is the legal form that most potently mobilizes temporal authority and capacity in service of this literary mode. While other chapters in this book have examined, at times, both legal records and literary works, this chapter offers a detailed study of a literary work that documents and fictionalizes a specific legal record, rendering it a rich site of examination from which to observe Black authorship's relationship to legal form. Each chapter in this book has acknowledged the ways that, on one hand, Black litigants creatively accessed and improvised varied forms of legal participation, while, on the other hand, Black writers imported lawyerly imagination into their autobiography, pamphlets, and fiction. While this book's central object of inquiry is antebellum Black literature and its relationship to legal culture, I have endeavored throughout to contextualize these literary practices in light of the many other social, institutional, and sometimes carceral engagements with law undertaken by Black Americans during this period. My goal has been to attend to the ways that Black writers imaginatively confronted legal regimes and literary networks that were sometimes friendly, sometimes violently prohibitive. This book has thus analyzed methods of legal and literary innovation that Black writers developed and refined over these decades before the Civil War, showing how an investment in legal form both collaborated with specific rights-oriented policy projects and, additionally, leveraged legal form as an imaginative and deeply creative literary device in service of Black world-making more generally.

Precedent in the Nineteenth-Century Common Law Tradition

In the common law tradition, courts attempt to bring consistency and coherence to legal rules through precedent. Like the appeal form, institutional investments in precedent present law as stable, efficient, and predictable (which of course it cannot be, or litigation would never be necessary, and which is exposed in abrupt departures from precedential continuity, as in the 2022 overturning of *Roe v. Wade* by *Dobbs v. Jackson Women's Health Organization*[3]). In a precedential common law framework, previously adjudicated cases, once cited, stand in as metonyms for the legal rules established in them. Take, for instance, the 1857 Supreme Court opinion from *Scott v. Sandford* (the Dred Scott decision).[4] That case, one of the most famous cases in nineteenth-century US jurisprudence, held that African American people were categorically disqualified from US citizenship. The underlying case was a freedom suit, an action brought by a plaintiff alleging unjust enslavement (in this case on the basis that Scott's enslaver had temporarily transported him to a free jurisdiction and thus had no right to re-enslave him).

I have considerably condensed this immense case into a few key bullet points here in order to demonstrate how precedent functions. A precedential citation to *Scott v. Sandford* metonymically encodes all of the legal principles and fact patterns in that litigation; *Scott v. Sandford* then becomes shorthand for a range of intricate narratives held together by the opinion's unifying and operative logic, in this case its holding that African Americans were constitutionally barred from achieving citizenship status. A reference to *Scott v. Sandford* references this legal holding; it references the other cases cited within that opinion; it references Dred Scott the person; and it also references the entire *line* of subsequent cases and statutes that reappropriate, resist, and ultimately overturn (via the ratification of the Fourteenth Amendment) the 1857 Supreme Court decision that we reference merely by mentioning "Dred Scott."

In terms of precedent, cases decided after *Scott v. Sandford* were subject to the rule of law established in that decision until either the Supreme Court decided to overturn itself—a highly uncommon and judicially disfavored outcome for the most part, absent massive social change or a significant ideological change to the makeup of the court—or, in this case, until a constitutional amendment overturned the precedent. In general, courts prefer to preserve the appearance of precedential continuity by leaving existing holdings undisturbed (the well known principle of stare decisis) and using factual, or circumstantial, difference to justify reaching different outcomes in subsequent cases. It cannot be overstated that stare decisis favors, first and foremost, the *appearance* of judicial stability, whether or not it actually applies the same standards to subsequent litigations.

To return to the example of *Scott v. Sandford*, under the principles and practice of stare decisis and precedential continuity, litigants bringing freedom suits in 1860 (before *Scott* was overturned) could reasonably expect to meet the same fate as Scott and his wife—provided that those subsequent litigants were subject to similar factual circumstances as those in Scott's freedom suit. That final caveat—the requirement for factual approximation—leaves room for wide variation in subsequent trial outcomes even as precedent appears, facially, to remain undisturbed. Because stare decisis only "works" for cases with substantially similar fact patterns, one obvious way around unfavorable precedent is to press a claim that the facts of a new case differ meaningfully from those in the operative precedent. In this way, stare decisis permits a narrative that preserves the "stability" of the original underlying precedent while branching off into exceptions, modifications, and subrules for cases where the fact patterns differ. Importantly, this stability is constructed, even fictional; through processes of selective inclusion and exclusion, it is relatively easy to present an opinion in a way that makes it appear consistent with existing precedent. One accomplishes this veneer of consistency merely by narrating the facts in a way that sounds as close as possible to the fact pattern of the underlying case.

In addition to favoring the appearance of judicial stability, precedent also promotes the appearance of judicial teleology. The production of precedent assumes a relatively linear temporality; precedent technically only moves in one direction, in other words: forward. As speech act, the holding of a judicial decision always unfolds in present tense; for example, "This court holds that . . ." or "The decision of the lower court is hereby overturned." Textually, this language functions analogously to the literary present, but with unnervingly polytemporal implications. The present tense holding in an opinion preserves each judicial action in a frozen "present" that nevertheless arises out of the "past" narrative world as described in the opinion and determines the operative rule for "future" cases that will rely on the present-tense case as precedent. The very nature of precedent assumes a before-and-after or cause-and-effect relationship that moves teleologically and with the assumption that the state of the law at any given moment is the most "complete" that it has ever been.

And yet, it is also constantly falling out of date and into obsolescence; not to mention the overturning of precedent renders its permanent present tense disorienting and misleading unless you know with certainty that the opinion is "good law" (that it hasn't been overturned)—in which case, the persistent present tense of the overturned precedent or "bad law" is even more disorienting to read. This accumulation and obsolescence of previous case law is relentless and unending; a case that ceases to be "good" precedent is never erased from the legal record (an echo of the strikethrough observed in my discussion of Williams/Thornton/Wilkins in chapter 3). This accumulation of precedent means that the many intertwined narratives within the common law case system continue to circulate as ghostly aftereffects even when their specific legal rulings are no longer mandatory nor reliable. And even binding precedent is never *really* fixed in the present. The present tense of the holding may conceal the case genealogies contained within the full opinion, but it does not erase them. And even though it figures itself as a present-tense construction, every judicial holding becomes both legal history and futurist case law the moment it issues; it modifies what came before, and it prescriptively anticipates what will follow. In this way, precedent's temporal qualities correspond with what I have called retrospective futurity throughout this book.

We can see, then, how a citation to the Dred Scott judicial opinion encodes a vast world of legal narratives that both include and exceed the specific ruling in that decision: narratives that stretch all the way back to Roman law, Norman law, and British law; narratives of the Three-Fifths Compromise; narratives of US citizenship as a primarily white-embodied category; narratives of the United States as a nation-state capable of determining which types of persons count among its subjects and citizens and which do not; and narratives of slavery as generating and sustaining quasi-persons whose legal status as property contradicts their actual status as human beings. Precedent, while a crucially important narrative device, is nevertheless just one of many strategies by which law constructs, manipulates, and produces narrative structure. As Simon Stern writes in a discussion of legal fictions and their relationship to literary fiction, "narrative logic is an essential and commonplace feature in law." Stern further points out that "legal language varies in the means and degrees by which it exhibits its own artifice"; while legal fictions frequently call attention to what is "artificial" about them, precedent works within a different metric. In legal precedent, the construction of narrative logic may, in Stern's words, "conceal its imaginative origins," but the artifice is there all the same.[5] Rather than calling attention to its fictional dimensions, legal precedent builds meaning by encoding its component parts and creating narrative through implication, analogy, juxtaposition, and affiliation—citation.

As a final pass around precedent before returning to Crafts and Johnson, I offer an excerpt from an untitled document in Mary Ann Shadd Cary's papers at Howard University, where she trained as a lawyer in the 1870s. Shadd Cary, who was a prolific journalist, publisher, and teacher in addition to a lawyer, presumably drafted this document herself; as it lacks a caption or other identifying material, I think it unlikely that she prepared it in connection with an actual legal case. Rather, the undated document, which is styled as a "Brief," is, in my best estimation after consultation with several other scholars, something she produced as an exercise or debate while she was a law student.[6] In it, Shadd Cary appears to be debating a proposal to eliminate precedent in favor of statutory law and offers numerous defenses of precedent, including this one: "So numerous and so comprehensive are precedents that to conced[e] to them other than the highest consideration would be to render them valueless, as would be all legal authority, whether statutory or from custom . . . [and] would evidently suggest a relapse into barbarism, or to say the least, lawlessness."[7] Shadd Cary's somewhat surprisingly full-throated defense of precedent is one of the reasons that I suspect this document was part of a school assignment, so I approach this text with some skepticism.

However, I include it here because it historicizes the status of precedent for legal professionals at roughly the midpoint in the nineteenth century, demonstrating the centrality of precedent to the legal profession's collective identity and also highlighting the extent to which Shadd Cary clearly locates law not just as a site of possibility but also perhaps as a prerequisite for civic life—by characterizing precedent as a mainstay against violence and barbarism, Shadd Cary, like Jacobs, theorizes law as a source of protection. This question of law's protective capacity surfaces once more in considering the relationship between *The Bondwoman's Narrative* and the legal proceedings involving Jane Johnson.

Encrypted Citations

Close reading of *The Bondwoman's Narrative* alongside the legal documents from Jane Johnson's self-emancipation reveals how Crafts's novel reformulated and innovated legal precedent by encoding and encrypting references to a history that both is and is not a "true" account of Johnson's escape. Encoding is a process that puts information in a readily accessible format that is legible precisely because it follows a set of knowable and stable rules. Encryption, by contrast, *conceals* information so that it only becomes accessible if one is in possession of the appropriate decrypting knowledge or key. These two terms help us understand how Crafts uses legal precedent to both encode knowable and readily accessible history and themes in her text while also encrypting information that more fully reveals itself when read alongside other documents—in this case, when read alongside the legal records of Jane Johnson's escape. Here again, we see echoes of Harriet Jacobs's strategic disclosures and concealments, as well as Williams/Thornton/Wilkins's tension between absence and presence, and Nat Turner's use of insurrectionary revelation as an instrument of spiritual sovereignty. I compare Crafts's encrypted citations to the formation of legal precedent in order to show how her legal strategies worked on two levels in her literary text: first, as a means of countering violent legal narratives and, second, as a way of generating new literary forms that fall somewhere between the poles of what we would typically call fiction and nonfiction, literary forms that experiment with narrative practices such as speculation and fabulation and are more commonly associated with later Black literature and speculative fiction.

I read Crafts's embedding of narratives as a citational practice that encodes legal precedent and legal testimony in service of Black worldmaking. By innovating legal citational form within the novel, Crafts encrypts her text with additional meaning that only emerges when read alongside the legal record—although it also refuses to be bound by that legal record. As I close read Crafts's text in the rest of this chapter, I show how Crafts both makes Jane Johnson's story legible and encrypts Johnson's legal narratives by altering key details. Crafts may have encrypted references to Johnson's escape in part to protect Johnson and anyone who assisted her, but the encryptions also permit Crafts to reimagine Johnson's biography and the legal/political landscape in which her subsequent fugitivity unfolded. In other contexts, the word "encryption" might suggest the existence of a decipherable, pure original. I use the term here to show how Crafts's citational practices expose the malleable affordances of precedent as a legal form and how her innovations of that form continually reshape legal and literary narratives. This practice of encryption does not protect or safeguard a mythical, recoverable "original," nor does any crypto key unlock the encryptions to give us direct access to Jane Johnson. Rather, I read Crafts's work while bearing in mind Marisa Fuentes's provocations in *Dispossessed Lives*, her study of archives of enslaved Caribbean women: "How do we narrate the fleeting glimpses of enslaved subjects in the archives and meet the disciplinary demands of history that requires us to construct unbiased accounts from these very documents? How do we construct a coherent historical accounting out of that which defies coherence and representability? How do we critically confront or reproduce these accounts to open up possibilities for historicizing, mourning, remembering, and listening to the condition of enslaved women?"[8] Like Saidiya Hartman and other scholars of slavery's archives, Fuentes presses us toward reading practices that grapple with the limitations of archive and honor enslaved women's lives through forms of readerly restraint and reluctance to make coherent narratives out of incoherent fragments. With these provocations in mind, I attend to Crafts's own engagement with legal archives, demonstrating how she encrypts precedent rather than deferring to it. I argue that her literary engagement with legal archives anticipates and rehearses many of the same critical reading and narrative practices advocated by Fuentes and Hartman in particular. Through her engagement with legal archives, Crafts innovates precedent to transform "fact" into "narrative" and imagine entirely new legal or literary worlds.

Encryption in *The Bondwoman's Narrative*

The Bondwoman's Narrative captured the immediate interest of literary scholars and historians in 2002, when Henry Louis Gates Jr. released his edition of this previously unpublished novel. Gates and other scholars contended in the early 2000s over both the authenticity of the text and the identity of the author, whom the manuscript identified as Hannah Crafts. Although Gates was unable to definitively identify Hannah Crafts, he and other scholars were able to identify many of the people referenced in the text, including John Hill Wheeler, her enslaver in Washington, DC, and North Carolina during the 1850s. Much of the ensuing scholarship concerned authorial identity and the truthfulness of the events the text represents.[9]

In 2013, Gregg Hecimovich identified Hannah Crafts as Hannah Bond, an enslaved woman who escaped from Wheeler's North Carolina plantation around 1857 and ultimately resettled in New Jersey.[10] Hecimovich's conclusion has been reviewed and accepted by a number of scholars, including Gates, although ambiguity lingers about genre and how best to taxonomize *The Bondwoman's Narrative*. The discourse surrounding the text—its authorship, the people represented in it—has always been freighted. A pseudonym, after all, is a means of concealing an author's identity, as are many of the other practices used throughout the text. Concealment of identity was, on one hand, a common Black survival practice in the nineteenth century, and one that this book has already taken up in relation to Harriet Jacobs's pseudonym and Williams/Thornton/Wilkins's proliferation of personae. Despite the fact of concealment as a common nineteenth-century strategy of Black survival, much of the twenty-first-century scholarship on *The Bondwoman's Narrative* has remained preoccupied with revelation and unmasking, with much of that scholarly energy focused on identifying the author's identity.

In fairness, some of this scholarly focus is to be expected for an unpublished text by a previously unknown author. And one of the main strategies for unmasking Hannah Crafts's identity had to do, ironically, with the citational practices of *The Bondwoman's Narrative*. As critics identified similarities between Crafts's work and nineteenth-century British literature, the scholarly conversation around *The Bondwoman's Narrative* has increasingly attended to the text's relationship to other geographies and genres outside antebellum African American literature.[11] While the vast majority of this critical conversation has thought about Crafts in relation to other authors of literary fiction, at least one work, Bridget Marshall's *The Transatlantic Gothic Novel and the Law, 1790–1860* (2011), has sought to treat legal history as a lens for nineteenth-century novels, including *The Bondwoman's Narrative*. In addition, or perhaps antecedent to, the multiyear quest to identify "Hannah Crafts" and her relationship to Anglophone literature more broadly, there has also simmered the question of how best to classify *The Bondwoman's*

Narrative generically. As suggested by trends in the scholarship, this question of generic labeling animates related questions about where to situate Crafts's text—is it best classified as a novel, a slave narrative, or, as Tess Chakkalakal suggests, a "slave fiction"?[12] Many of these questions also haunted Harriet Jacobs's *Incidents in the Life of a Slave Girl* (1861), hinting at the ways that Black women at the midcentury had begun to push at the generic limitations of the freedom narrative, particularly when self-publishing or attempting to self-publish their work.

Though we do not know why the text was never published during the nineteenth century, the refusal to hew more closely to the generic constraints of the slave narrative form likely would not have helped her publication prospects at the time, at least within white abolitionist printing networks, despite the text's immense readability and similarity to other popular fiction genres, particularly serialized British popular fiction. But as *The Bondwoman's Narrative* shuns the constraints of the slave narrative genre and embraces aspects of popular fiction, it also rehearses a deep facility with legal culture and imagines, through precedential counterfactual, other worlds of being and alternative collective histories. I read this complex engagement with legal form as the reimagining of existing legal logics of authority and community, a reimagining that opens out onto capacious questions of what alternatives to the nation-state might have arisen in place of the United States.

The Bondwoman's Narrative does retain certain similarities to a freedom narrative, in that it claims in the preface to be a "record of plain unvarnished facts," and Crafts identifies herself on the title page as "A Fugitive Slave Recently Escaped From North Carolina."[13] Like most slave narratives, *The Bondwoman's Narrative* offers an autobiography of Crafts's life in slavery, opening with a description of the narrator's childhood that mirrors the genealogical absences typical of self-emancipated authors: "No one seemed to care for me till I was able to work, and then it was Hannah do this and Hannah do that.... Of my relatives I knew nothing. No one ever spoke of my father or mother, but I soon learned what a curse was attached to my race, soon learned that the African blood in my veins would forever exclude me from the higher walks of life."[14] Crafts thus opens her text in a format reminiscent of a slave narrative, acknowledging her fugitivity, claiming a truthfulness in the "unvarnished facts" of her story, and establishing her origin story within enslavement through the language of familial separation.

Despite these affinities with generic markers of slave narratives, *The Bondwoman's Narrative* then departs from the genre in several important respects. First, unlike most of the slave narratives published by white abolitionist societies, *The Bondwoman's Narrative* lacks an amanuensis.[15] This detachment from abolitionist infrastructure also means that Crafts's manuscript was not subject to the political aims and proprieties of a white abolitionist culture that frequently privileged its own institutional survival and publicity over its concern for the enslaved writers whose narratives it commodified, though it was nevertheless subjected to an editorial schema when published by Henry Louis Gates Jr. in 2002.[16] And commodification of the literary text may have simply been an unrealized goal of Crafts; as Sandra Pacquet has considered in relation to Mary Prince in particular, and enslaved women more generally, literary publication was also a pragmatic and available economic strategy for women who needed to earn money to buy their freedom, as was the case for Prince.[17]

The professionalization and monetization of publishing, while sometimes obscured by the politics of respectability at work, is also visible in narratives like *The History of the Carolina Twins*, the autobiography of the conjoined McKoy twins, who acknowledge their economic interest in publishing and underscore their deliberate commodification of autobiography when they write, "We might, could we feel disposed, tell many anecdotes of our travels, but we think a simple narrative of ourselves is all that at present those of our patrons who buy our little book will require."[18] We do not know whether Hannah Crafts intended to publish her novel or where, much less the extent to which the writing of it was part of an effort to monetize her skill as a writer. We can say, however, that because the novel was not published by white abolitionist networks, it appears to have maintained at least the appearance of independence from that specific publishing regime, an independence that is supported in part by the fact that it does not take great pains to reproduce that genre's features, despite its other elaborate forms of textual citation and engagement, particularly its use of features more commonly associated with fiction and the novel in particular. Well-documented intertexts such as Charles Dickens's *Bleak House* (1852) permeate *The Bondwoman's Narrative*,[19] and scholars have also noted Crafts's use of gothic tropes such as the linden tree, whose ominous creaks portend death and doom.[20] These discursive citations to fiction suggest that Crafts located her text within that general category despite how rooted it apparently also was in the details of her own life.

It has been necessary to sift through these questions of authorial identity and generic classification as a means of situating this text and understanding how it recasts what we know about the emergence of the African American novel and of Black women writers in the nineteenth century. Yet the critical focus on authenticity and autobiography have perhaps circumscribed the conversations on Crafts such that other aspects of the work remain unexplored, including its relationship to legal history and legal citational practices and the sort of model it offers for how we might read other nineteenth-century African American writers. *The Bondwoman's Narrative* encrypts and encodes legal narratives within its fictionalized accounts of verifiable "factual" or "historical" events, including Jane Johnson's escape. It is impossible to say how many other verifiable events are encoded within the text, which persistently cedes narrative space to other enslaved figures beyond Crafts.[21] In fact, Crafts's text virtually bursts at the seams with the many biographies and narratives contained within it. The result is a text that looks a good deal more like Harriet Beecher Stowe's *Uncle Tom's Cabin* (1852) than the *Narrative of the Life of Frederick Douglass, an American Slave* (1845).[22] Often, a glancing reference in the text actually cites, encodes, and abridges another biography that could have, on its own, served as the framing structure for an entirely separate novel.

The final chapter, "In Freedom," offers an example of this textual pregnancy, in which *The Bondwoman's Narrative* seems always on the verge of giving birth to another narrative world. In this chapter, Crafts writes of her life after slavery and her life in the North, including her unlikely reunion with her own mother:

> Can you guess who lives with me? You never could—my own dear mother, aged and venerable, yet so smart and lively and active, and Oh: so fond of me. There was a hand of Providence in our meeting as we did. I am sure of it. Her history is most affecting and eventful. During my infancy she was transferred from Lindendale to the owner of a plantation in Mississippi, yet she never forgot me nor certain marks on my body, by which I might be identified in after years. She found a hard master, but he soon died, and she became the property of his daughter who dwelt in Maryland, and thither she was removed. Here she became acquainted with a free mulatto from New Jersey, who persuaded her to escape to his native state with him, where they might be married and live in freedom and happiness. She consented. . . . We met accidentally, where or how it matters not. I thought it strange, but my heart yearned towards her with a deep intense feeling it had never known before.[23]

In this passage, Crafts condenses what might have been her own mother's autobiography or slave narrative into a brief summary, narrating her mother's separation from her and her journey into freedom. Crucially, Crafts supplies a number of geographical details, such as specific states of residence, but minimizes the moment that might bear the greatest narrative fruit. She writes of their initial reunion: "We met accidentally, where or how it matters not." Although she proceeds later to tell of their tearful realization of their connection to each other, Crafts glosses over this first meeting, denying the reader any narrative suspense or drama associated with the details or "providential" happenings that actually brought these two women face to face against unimaginable odds. Although Crafts *appears* to supply a short biography of her mother's life after slavery, this summary is more cipher than elaboration—a glimpse of the forms of Black life that linger just out of view, and a preservation of Black privacy even within the ostensible publicness of the text as a whole. Crafts offers enough details to make her mother's story legible, but she also withholds enough information that the reader has the feeling of having reached merely the tip of the iceberg.

These literary excesses—in which the novel generates a surplus of narratives that threaten to burst through the central plot—in addition to signaling the forms of Black interiority and privacy imagined by Kevin Quashie, resemble what Nicole Aljoe describes as "embedded slave narratives."[24] In *Creole Testimonies: Slave Narratives from the British West Indies, 1709–1838* (2012), Aljoe builds on Saidiya Hartman's formulation of "critical fabulation," archival engagement employed "not to *give voice* to the slave, but rather to imagine what cannot be verified... and to reckon with the precarious lives which are visible only in the moment of their disappearance."[25] In echoes of Fuentes, Aljoe uses a practice of "strategic reading and creative hearing" to recover slave narratives that have been embedded elsewhere, often in fragmentary form in genres such as "travel narratives, diaries, and journals or... in records kept by legal, medical, and religious institutions."[26] For Aljoe, regardless of the slave narrative's generic legibility, these instances of fragmented narratives have one thing in common: testimony about the experiences of enslavement. This testimonial capacity of slave narratives is, for Aljoe, a central aspect of a reparative reading of unexpected archives. Aljoe's theorization of embedded narratives is especially formative to my consideration of *The Bondwoman's Narrative*—reading Crafts's text through Aljoe's framework helps me construe the novel as an archive that is capable of containing multiple embedded archives within it.

At the same time, Crafts is not necessarily so invested as Aljoe in the testimonial as the "re-presentation" that Hartman urges in her critical fabulation methodology—whereas the testimonial is ultimately evidentiary, the practice of re-presentation innovates legal precedent and citational practice. While Crafts cedes narrative space to many other people, including Jane

Johnson, she does not ventriloquize them nor reproduce their testimony. Rather, somewhat more like Hartman, Crafts herself practices a version of critical fabulation, "a history written with and against the archive" that raises questions and generates a "counter-history" without speaking in the voice of those whom her text references.[27] In gathering and "re-presenting the sequence of events in divergent stories and from contested points of view," Crafts assumes the role of critical fabulist, archivist, and autotheorist.[28] She accomplishes this re-presentation by not only rearranging the "facts" of the stories she presents but also by linking them in visible, but clandestine, ways to other archives, much the way that precedent links together disparate litigants; where Jane Johnson does not speak for herself in *The Bondwoman's Narrative*, for instance, Hannah Crafts leaves open the suggestive relationship to places where Johnson *did* offer testimony, in court. This relegation of testimony to that space also bolsters my claim that the freedom narrative as a genre was evolving in ways that increasingly reached beyond the testimonial and toward the other affordances of autobiography and even fiction.

I do not make these connections between precedent and *The Bondwoman's Narrative* haphazardly or anecdotally. Other contemporaneous African American texts likewise cite and encode legal narratives in a range of forms and for various purposes. The 1860 slave narrative *Running a Thousand Miles for Freedom* by William and Ellen Craft periodically interrupts their autobiography with extracts from legal cases and statutes, dramatizing for the reader the relationship between their escape—a performance that encrypted Ellen Craft's race and gender to avoid detection—and the legal narratives that structured their life in and after slavery. Their references to specific legal histories further built a meta-argument into their slave narrative, forming a palimpsest of autobiography and legal precedent that encode each other and collaborate to create what resembles an encyclopedia of slavery laws. On the other hand, William Wells Brown's 1853 novel *Clotel; or, the President's Daughter* repeatedly appropriates legal records and news stories to structure that novel's central plot. In that text, which is obviously participating in some of the forms of counterfactual worldmaking that I have chronicled in this book, the text becomes so crowded with visible references to well-known and rumored events that it eventually feels like a strained effort to coax a single narrative out of slavery's wide-ranging, complex, and vast legal terrain. However, Brown also famously said, "Slavery has never been represented; slavery never can be represented," suggesting that perhaps that novel was less about representing slavery than re-presenting it, to return to Hartman's formulation, or about demonstrating the failures of representation.[29]

The formal and substantive qualities of *The Bondwoman's Narrative*, however, make that text a particularly hospitable case study in how antebellum African American literature rehearses encryption as a literary and legal strategy. *The Bondwoman's Narrative* contains a rich set of references and terms that suggest Crafts's self-conscious engagement with legal rhetoric and practice as a general matter. Whether through the character of Trappe, an unscrupulous lawyer who blackmails light-skinned women passing for white; references to legal terms of art such as "chain of evidence";[30] or even direct addresses to lawmakers, the novel is thick with law. Jane Johnson, referred to simply as "Jane" in the novel, serves as a specific intersection between the novel's quasi-fictional world and the so-called real world of the legal system that regulated and terrorized fugitives from slavery.

In *The Bondwoman's Narrative*, the narrator Hannah travels from her original station at the Lindendale plantation to a series of other locations on her way to ultimate freedom in New Jersey. Her initial escape from Lindendale occurs in cooperation with her so-called mistress, a white-passing woman enslaved at birth and under threat of exposure by Trappe, who is blackmailing her. When the two women are captured, her companion ultimately hemorrhages and dies; Trappe then sells Hannah to a slave trader. During transport, however, their carriage overturns, killing the slave trader and leaving Hannah in a precarious position of unsettled ownership. The local Henry family takes Hannah into their service while communicating with the next of kin of her last living enslaver. Hannah's prospects are thus already imbued with legal meaning and legal tension. Laws of inheritance determine who has an enforceable claim of ownership over her body, and the uncertainty of her ownership becomes a torturous condition, as Hannah begs the relatively kind Henrys to buy her and save her from the devil she doesn't know. Rather than buying her themselves, however, the Henrys arrange for the sale of Hannah to the Wheelers, distant relatives in North Carolina. It is through Hannah's intersection with the Wheelers that *The Bondwoman's Narrative* encodes not merely Hannah's legal narrative, but also that of Jane Johnson.

In the novel, Mrs. Wheeler purchases Hannah to be her new "lady's maid" because her previous maid, "Jane," has disappeared. This unassuming reference introduces an encrypted literary version of Jane Johnson. For sake of ease, this essay uses "Jane" to refer to the character in the novel and "Jane Johnson" to refer to the historical figure. The novel contains few details of Jane's disappearance, with Mrs. Wheeler initially saying merely that "Jane ran off." Displeased with Hannah's efforts to comb her hair, Mrs. Wheeler elaborates: "Jane was very handy at almost everything.... You will seldom find a slave so handy, but she grew discontented and dissatisfied with her condition, thought she could do better in a land of freedom, and such like I watched her closely you may depend." In between Hannah's pulls on her snarled hair, Mrs. Wheeler continues, "Oh dear, this is what I have to endure from losing Jane, but she'll have to suffer more, probably. I didn't much like the idea of bringing her to Washington. It was all Mr Wheeler's fault. He wanted me to come, and I couldn't think of doing without her in my feeble health."[31] This introduction to Jane, appearing almost casually in the text amid Mrs. Wheeler's pleas for Hannah to be gentle with her hair, underscores the extent to which intense questions of legal personhood and slavery suffuse the most prosaic and intimate aspects of daily life in the antebellum South. Reading the subtext of Mrs. Wheeler's characterization that Jane "grew discontented and dissatisfied with her condition," it seems clear enough that Jane self-liberated.

By suggesting that Jane simply changed her status on becoming dissatisfied, Mrs. Wheeler's euphemistic description affords Jane an agency that obscures the obvious legal and personal risks associated with fugitivity. Hinting merely that Jane will "suffer more, probably," Mrs. Wheeler gestures toward the possibility of recapture and punishment without naming it, choosing instead to frame Jane's absence as a matter of intense personal inconvenience. Jane's interchangeability with another slave comes into focus when Mrs. Wheeler says of Hannah, "She could fill the place of Jane so exactly."[32] Jane is not a person in this characterization but a space to fill—a space that fits exactly the shape of another enslaved woman and a characterization Crafts might have taken from Hortense Spillers's work on fungibility had her novel not preceded the 1987 essay "Mama's Baby, Papa's Maybe: An American Grammar Book" by more than a century. While the reader never obtains access to Jane's own words, Jane's narrative is a wheel within the wheel of Crafts's larger novel, and her evacuation from the Wheeler home and the novel is an invitation for the narrator, Hannah, to enter and occupy both spaces.

Despite the reader's inability to hear from Jane directly, the novel's backstory on Jane also cites as precedent, and subsequently encodes, a legal drama that unfolded in Pennsylvania in 1855—and the record of that legal drama does offer Jane's firsthand testimony. The Wheelers described in *The Bondwoman's Narrative* are thought to be John Hill Wheeler, state legislator and federal appointee, and his family.[33] The circumstances surrounding Jane Johnson's escape from the Wheelers received considerable media attention, especially in the Philadelphia area, where it took place.[34] Crafts is ambiguous about the geographical specifics of Jane's escape but suggests, including through Mrs. Wheeler's comment that the mistress "didn't much like the idea of bringing [Jane] to Washington,"[35] that Jane fled while in the nation's capital.

The Legal World of Jane Johnson

To fully understand the nature and effect of Crafts's encryption of law, it is necessary to spend some time in the legal and journalistic record of Jane Johnson's escape.[36] In "reality," Johnson fled not in Washington but in Philadelphia, where the Wheelers stopped en route to New York and then Nicaragua, where Colonel John Hill Wheeler was to begin a diplomatic position. On July 18, 1855, accompanying the Wheeler family, Jane Johnson arrived in Philadelphia along with her sons, Daniel and Isaiah, who are unnamed in and completely absent from *The Bondwoman's Narrative*. Here, with the assistance of several abolitionists, Johnson escaped, taking her children with her.[37] In an effort to effect Johnson's return, Colonel Wheeler filed a petition for a writ of habeas corpus in the Eastern District of Pennsylvania, a federal district court. In that petition, Colonel Wheeler urged the court to compel white abolitionist Passmore Williamson to produce Jane Johnson and her children. Judge John Kane granted Wheeler's petition and ordered Williamson to produce Johnson and her children. Williamson declined to do so, and on July 27, 1855, Judge Kane imprisoned Williamson in Moyamensing Prison on a charge of contempt;[38] he would remain there for nearly four months until his eventual release in November 1855.[39]

Despite Johnson's evasion of Wheeler, however, she offered her own written and oral testimony in connection with Williamson's imprisonment. First, Jane Johnson submitted an affidavit in an attempt to exonerate Williamson during his habeas and contempt proceedings; Judge Kane refused to acknowledge Johnson's standing in the court, however, and denied the affidavit. Meanwhile, William Still, an African American abolitionist, faced criminal charges in the Court of Quarter Sessions in Philadelphia, a state court. Jane Johnson appeared in person to testify in that trial, in which Still and most of his codefendants were acquitted.[40]

The trials of Williamson and Still, and in particular Williamson's imprisonment, generated considerable attention in an era of fraught politics regarding fugitive slaves. Pennsylvania, a free state, had long been a site for legal posturing regarding self-emancipated individuals. In the 1842 case *Prigg v. Pennsylvania*, the United States Supreme Court had essentially voided a state law that prohibited the transport of free persons out of Pennsylvania and into slavery.[41] The Court held that the state law, widely regarded as an obstacle for enslavers, could not supersede the (federal) Fugitive Slave Act of 1793, which was then in force. With the passage of the Fugitive Slave Act of 1850, the rights of enslavers further expanded, allowing state and local authorities to be compelled to assist in the recovery and return of fugitives, even in free jurisdictions.

Against this backdrop of geographical and ideological division, the abolitionist press paid close attention to litigation surrounding fugitives from slavery. Jeannine DeLombard's compelling account of the "trial" of slavery both in actual courts and the court of public opinion demonstrates the salience of legal battles in the public consciousness during the nineteenth century. As DeLombard notes, roughly 500 people visited Passmore Williamson during his imprisonment.[42] Media coverage of the Jane Johnson escape and subsequent litigations ranged across and beyond the abolitionist press, achieving notoriety in publications such as *The National Era, The Philadelphia Bulletin,* and *Frederick Douglass' Paper*.[43] Such far-reaching media coverage makes it possible, even where the legal records themselves may be sparse or missing, to locate corroborating coverage in other contemporary documents.[44] Indeed, a number of media accounts and legal records corroborate Johnson's participation in both the Williamson and Still proceedings.

Johnson's participation in these proceedings took two very different forms—written affidavit and recorded testimony—each of which yields different information and presents different problems for critical consideration. However, the particular status of the documents within the legal realm does offer a certain amount of documentary reliability, as rules of procedure require the authentication of documents entered into evidence. Though these legal documents and appearances present their own questions of authenticity and authorship, theorizing them is not so different from theorizing more traditional slave narratives, where similar questions also arise in the context of slave testimony.

In the Williamson litigation, Johnson attempted to offer a written affidavit into the record. Johnson's sworn affidavit to Judge Kane stated that Passmore Williamson had not abducted her. Johnson signed the affidavit with an "X" and the notation "Her mark";[45] there is no indication that Johnson could read or write, and the X in place of her name seems to confirm her lack of formal education. This X is also a reminder of her fraught status as a quasi-legal personality by virtue of her enslavement and fugitivity—the substitution of her name with an X enacts on one hand a denial of her subjectivity and individuality while on the other hand claiming her right to submit the affidavit and be heard by the court.[46] In addition to the X, there are other indicators that she did not personally draft the content of the affidavit. For instance, throughout the affidavit, references to Johnson herself appear as references to "your petitioner" (Johnson, as the affiant, submitted the affidavit as a petition to Judge Kane). These linguistic and stylistic features counsel in favor of an attorney or other legal expert having drafted the affidavit on Johnson's behalf.[47]

Though this revelation somewhat complicates the question of authorship, it is of course customary for attorneys to draft affidavits on behalf of clients and witnesses. Moreover, in the traditional generic slave narrative, an amanuensis frequently acted as the scrivener for a formerly enslaved person's narration. In such cases, the freedom narrative was also mediated through a third party, and the question of authorship presents a similarly fraught scenario. Therefore, the question of authorship in the Johnson affidavit is not so far afield from the same questions of authorship frequently present in a traditional slave narrative. The fact that Johnson signed the affidavit, and that it was sworn under oath, both authenticate the document and support its credibility, at least in the eyes of the law. These authenticating gestures are of a piece with authentication of other, more traditional slave narratives, where the marks on a formerly enslaved person's body might authenticate claims of physical abuse. These similarities with the slave narrative genre situate Johnson's narrative in this legal document in a manner consistent with Aljoe's theorization of embedded narratives. This particular narrative, however, is not only embedded within the affidavit but also reinscribed and encrypted in *The Bondwoman's Narrative*.

The content of Johnson's testimonial narrative offers an elaboration on her brief appearance in Crafts's novel. In the affidavit, Johnson asserts that she "was very desirous of procuring the freedom of herself and her children" and that "she did wish to be free." Johnson repeatedly affirms her own agency and her desire to escape from Colonel Wheeler—in describing her flight, Johnson casts her freedom as the product of *her* desire and *her* "[wish] to be free." Throughout the affidavit, Johnson repeatedly makes similar assertions, including a claim that none of the abolitionists ever restrained or coerced her in any way. In fact, Johnson states that the free Black people who assisted her "took her children with her consent."[48] By establishing herself as someone entitled to, and capable of, offering her consent, Johnson asserts not only that she was a free person but also that she was *already* free when she left Colonel Wheeler in Philadelphia. The capacity to consent, like the capacity to contract, is a privilege of free personhood; the right to withhold consent was unavailable to enslaved persons. As Saidiya Hartman writes in her discussion of

Harriet Jacobs's *Incidents in the Life of a Slave Girl* (1861), "Outside the shadow of law, compulsion eclipses choice, as neither right nor protection secures the line between consent and nonconsent."[49]

Johnson's affidavit does not contain details about her life as an enslaved woman—in fact, based on Crafts's descriptions of life with the Wheelers, the novel promises more information about what Johnson's daily life must have been like at the side of Mrs. Wheeler, a conniving and manipulative woman preoccupied with her own vanity and quest for status. Even without any elaboration on her daily life as an enslaved woman, the affidavit explicitly expresses Johnson's desire to escape from slavery and her insistence on herself as an agent of her liberty. This testimonial narrative embedded in the legal affidavit, in combination with Crafts's factual alterations in *The Bondwoman's Narrative*, act together as a corrective to the erasure of "Jane" by Mrs. Wheeler in the novel. The affidavit refutes and explains Mrs. Wheeler's statements in the novel; the novel in turn contextualizes Johnson's statements in the legal affidavit, nuancing daily life at the hands of Mrs. Wheeler in a way that the affidavit cannot do by itself.

In the legal proceedings, Judge Kane ultimately refused to admit the affidavit into evidence, using a host of dubious justifications for the exclusion. In a particularly suspicious moment of legal reasoning, Kane claimed to be unable to confirm that Jane Johnson was the same person referred to in Wheeler's petition, noting that the latter document referred only to "Jane" and omitted a surname.[50] Kane conceded that Johnson's testimony might have been properly admissible had she been either a party to the litigation or a witness called to testify in court. His general holding, however, was that Johnson lacked "status" in the court, a move that technically referred to the fact that she was not a party to the litigation but obliquely called attention to the fraught nature of Johnson's status as a full legal "person."[51] In Pennsylvania, she had personhood; in North Carolina, she was Colonel Wheeler's property.

Despite Johnson's claims to her own agency, Judge Kane's reasoning demonstrates the extent to which law's institutional weight pushed against an enslaved person's desire for freedom even after self-liberation. Without explicitly saying so, what Kane actually denied Johnson was a recognition of her status as a person entitled to testify in court. Judge Kane gestures toward the unique and ambiguous status Johnson occupied—formerly enslaved, ostensibly free, her agency and identity were at the heart of the trial of a white abolitionist. Kane writes, "The very name of the person who authenticates the paper is a stranger to any proceeding that is or has been before me. She asks no judicial action for herself, and does not profess to have any right to solicit action in behalf of another: on the contrary, her counsel here assure me expressly, that Mr. Williamson has not sanctioned her application. She has therefore no status whatever in this Court."[52]

By casting Johnson as a "stranger" to the court proceedings, Judge Kane emphasizes that the legal proceedings revolved not around Jane Johnson herself but Passmore Williamson, the white abolitionist accused of helping her escape. More than simply calling her a stranger in the sense of someone who is not a party to the litigation, Kane's language calls attention to the strangeness of Johnson as a legal personality—indeed, she is the body, or *corpus*, being sought by Wheeler's petition for a writ of habeas corpus. Yet despite her intimate connection to the case, Johnson remained a "stranger" to the litigation of her own freedom. At this point, Johnson is neither wholly enslaved nor wholly free. As Judge Kane points out, Johnson "has therefore no status whatever in this Court"—her lack of status refers to the fact that she is not a named party to the litigation, but it also underscores the many broader ways in which Johnson could be said to be status-less. She lacks standing to bring a lawsuit of her own. She lacks status as a citizen entitled to the rights and privileges of other free persons, and given that "status" and "state" share the same Latin root, Kane's severe language reminds the reader that Johnson lacks any meaningful belonging in either Pennsylvania or the United States as a nation-state.

Despite Judge Kane's exclusion of Johnson's affidavit from evidence, it nevertheless appears in its entirety as part of the decision in the Williamson litigation.[53] In this way, Johnson's affidavit—although not admitted—remains hidden in plain sight, inscribed within the legal archive of the Williamson litigation and also reprinted in the *Narrative of Facts in the Case of Passmore Williamson* (1855), and *Case of Passmore Williamson: Report of the Proceedings on the Writ of Habeas Corpus, Issued by the Hon. John K. Kane, Judge of the District Court of the United States for the Eastern District of Pennsylvania, in the Case of the United States of America ex rel. John H. Wheeler vs. Passmore Williamson, Including the Several Opinions Delivered, and the Arguments of Counsel* (1856), two pamphlets that documented Passmore Williamson's lengthy legal battle. Although Johnson was not a party to the litigation, and although this case was not a freedom suit of the sort in which one would expect to encounter documents such as the Johnson affidavit, Johnson's story is yet a part of the legal record. In this context, her story offers more insight into law's treatment of enslaved people, even in free jurisdictions, than it does about Johnson's personal experience as the property of the Wheelers.

Whereas Johnson submitted a written affidavit in the Williamson litigation, her in-court appearance at William Still's trial proved to be her most dramatic participation in the legal actions surrounding her emancipation. Still and several codefendants faced criminal charges in the Court of Quarter Sessions in Philadelphia for assault and riot-related charges. On August 29, 1855, Johnson appeared in court at Still's trial.[54] What Johnson's written affidavit lacks in data about her life in slavery, her oral testimony compensates for with greater detail. As Johnson spoke of her escape from Colonel Wheeler, she first identified herself and her children.[55] In a turn familiar from traditional slave narratives, Johnson betrayed her lack of verifiable genealogy, stating, "I can't tell my exact age; I guess I am about 25; I was born in Washington City."[56] She also spoke of a third, estranged child, a boy living in Richmond, Virginia: "I have not seen him for about two years; never expect to see him again."[57] The opening of her oral testimony thus mimics the traditional introductions to slave narratives and indeed the opening of the fictional narrative offered in *The Bondwoman's Narrative*. Johnson, like Crafts, characterizes herself through a series of negatives. Whereas Crafts's novel opens with her assertions of "no training, no cultivation" and her claim that "of my relatives I knew nothing,"[58] Johnson commences her testimony unable to tell her "exact age" and certain that she "never expected" to see her third son again. For both women, these evacuations of history and familial connection operate as a kind of authentication of the autobiographies that follow. In both the slave narrative genre and legal testimony, the establishment of gaps in personal and familial histories verify the witness as enslaved (or formerly enslaved) and implicitly testify to slavery's theft of this autobiographical and ancestral knowledge, establishing an "injury" that forms the basis for the witness's accusations.

In her oral testimony, Johnson continues by describing her journey with Colonel Wheeler en route to Nicaragua, noting that while they were in Philadelphia, "Mr. Wheeler kept his eye on me all the time except when he was at dinner."[59] This documentation of Wheeler's constant surveillance establishes Johnson's incarceration, a claim that becomes even more visible when she describes Wheeler's limitations on what she might disclose about herself to those she met during the journey. According to Johnson's testimony, Wheeler had admonished her "not to talk to colored persons; to tell everybody I was traveling with a minister going to Nicaragua; he seemed to think I might be led off."[60] Johnson's testimony again underscores her self-characterization as an agent. Although she relays Wheeler's instructions to her, she maintains an awareness of his intentions, as when she says, "he seemed to think I might be led off."

Johnson thus reveals herself as a keen judge of character. This moment captures not only her awareness of Wheeler's fears about her possible escape but also her awareness of his relation to her as one of subjugation. The phrase "might be led off" is a grammatical construction that casts her as disabled or subhuman; rather than worrying that she might run away of her own volition, she understands Wheeler's fear to be one of, essentially, misappropriation—that someone else might "steal" her. Johnson testified that, on hearing that freedom was hers for the taking if she desired it, she left Wheeler immediately. Addressing any argument that she had been persuaded or otherwise coaxed to leave, she says, "I did not say I did not want my freedom; I have always wanted it; I did not say I wanted to go with my master; I went very willingly to the carriage, I was very glad to go."[61]

Johnson's oral testimony unswervingly asserts her agency. Her habit of starting each sentence and clause with "I" offers a grammatical reinforcement of her insistence on her subjectivity; her description of her departure exonerates Williamson and Still, but it also refuses to give them any credit for her escape. Whether or not this refusal was an intentional effort to assist the abolitionists, Johnson's oral testimony persistently demands that her listeners encounter her as a fully realized subject and that they respect her capacity to consent. Essentially, Johnson testified not as a fugitive but as a free person. The distinction is critical because Johnson, rather than proving that her otherwise illegal flight from an owner was justified, instead argued that she existed *legally* as a free person who had *legally* exercised her free will in leaving Wheeler.[62]

Two Narrative Worlds Touching Each Other

In William Still's account of Jane Johnson's in-court appearance, he notes that Johnson arrived in court "veiled, and of course was not known by the crowd, as pains had been taken to keep the public in ignorance of the fact, that she was to be brought on to bear witness."[63] This description evokes and erodes the similar "white envelope" associated with traditional slave narratives that are mediated by the labor of white amanuenses. Johnson was cloaked in court literally by her veil and also by the phalanx of abolitionists who escorted her to the courtroom. What her testimony offers, however, is a moment of revelation—a lifting of the literal and metaphorical veils that hung between Johnson and her audience.

While self-authored accounts of her experience may inhabit the legal archive surrounding Williamson and Still, it is more appropriate to say that it is the *legal* narrative, rather than the personal or slave narrative, of Jane Johnson that inhabits *The Bondwoman's Narrative*. This re-presentation of the legal archive demonstrates again how Crafts's engagement with the Johnson litigation rehearses a version of the critical fabulation practice that Saidiya Hartman has advocated as an ethic of archival encounter. Mrs. Wheeler's descriptions of "Jane" in the novel make much less sense when decoupled from the legal narratives that offer context for Jane's escape. While the novel suggests to the reader that Jane was "discontented and dissatisfied with her condition," Johnson never actually appears in the novel except through the dubious and brief narration of Mrs. Wheeler, whose manipulations to purchase Hannah (among other things) cast doubt on her reliability as a truth teller.[64]

In fact, the novel offers yet another explanation for Johnson's flight; an enslaved boy reports that Jane had been in correspondence with a servant of "the 'Hio man," who is, in Mrs. Wheeler's description, "The Senator from Ohio . . . who professed a great regard for slaves and negroes. . . . [His servant] was thought to have his master's concurrence in persuading servants to abandon their masters; it was even suspected that the grave senator assisted in spiriting them away." In contradiction of the legal record, when pressed by Hannah on whether the Wheelers took efforts to recover Jane, Mrs. Wheeler replies, "Oh, no: Mr Wheeler said that it would be of no use, and then he disliked making a hue and cry about a slave at the Federal Capital, so we said little as possible about it."[65] A reader familiar with Johnson's escape would immediately recognize Mrs. Wheeler's dishonesty, a moment where the novel's encryption of the legal record exposes Mrs. Wheeler's treachery without requiring Hannah (or Hannah Crafts, for that matter) to endanger herself by making accusations. That encryption works within the novel, as well, where Hannah's silence affirms Mrs. Wheeler's (false) belief in her ability to remake "truth" and "history" with impunity.

The novel's factual alterations—re-presentations that refuse to speak in Jane's voice, and thus perform a proto-version of critical fabulation—call attention to the relevant legal narrative and recast its terms. In Hartman's language, the effect is that it "jeopardize[s] the status of the event, to displace the received or authorized account."[66] While Crafts's novel makes an intimate connection between Johnson's escape and the federal government, Johnson's real-life testimonial performance further complicates her relationship to the federal government. During her in-court testimony and cross-examination at

William Still's trial—where she arrived dramatically in the aforementioned veil[67]—Johnson testified that she did not know her exact age but had been born in Washington, DC, "about the time the British burnt the Capitol."[68]

By staging Jane's escape in Washington, DC, instead of Philadelphia, the novel returns the character of Jane to the scene of Jane Johnson's birth—an event that Johnson's own testimony links to the US national peril during the burning of the Capitol in the War of 1812 (which I note also featured obliquely in chapter 1 in relation to David Walker's *Appeal to the Coloured Citizens of the World*). That single narrative move—establishing Washington, DC, as the site of Jane's escape—introduces a counterfactual that recenters Johnson's self-emancipation around the place of her birth, her self-proclaimed hometown; and that geographic change represents the capital/Capitol not as the seat of an infallible nation-state but as a contested zone of power. Even Mrs. Wheeler's (mendacious) claim that Mr. Wheeler thought pursuit would be useless inscribes the terminology of federal government: "[H]e disliked making a hue and cry about a slave at the Federal Capital, so we said little as possible about it."[69]

Why, the reader might wonder, would it be unseemly to pursue a fugitive from slavery in the District of Columbia? Although the novel's chronology is somewhat uncertain, it is generally accepted to have been written in the 1850s. Johnson's flight and the ensuing legal actions took place in 1855, suggesting that, regardless of when the novel took place, it was written sometime after 1855. In the 1850s, Washington, DC, was at the heart of the slavery debate, both literally and symbolically. Although slave trading was banned in the District in 1850, slaveholding was still legal there until 1862, and the city had sizable populations of both enslaved and free African Americans. Mrs. Wheeler fails to elaborate on this peculiar claim about their unwillingness to "make a hue and cry" about Johnson's escape, but her comment calls attention to the symbolic weight of the District of Columbia in questions of slavery's legality. To "make a hue and cry" about their fugitive slave in the "Federal Capital" of all places would throw into controversy the legality of slavery in a concrete and visible manner. Given the intense legislative battles around the Compromise of 1850 and the Fugitive Slave Act of 1850 in particular, the novel's recasting of Johnson's escape thus places slavery, quite literally, at the federal government's doorstep. The introduction of foreign diplomats into this equation further exposes a tension between the notion of the United States as a "civilized" international state and an image of the United States as unable to manage its own domestic affairs or to keep the peace between slaveholding and non-slaveholding jurisdictions.

These departures mark the novel's reference to the legal record and precedent not merely as citational but also as encrypted. It is obviously impossible to say with any certainty whether Crafts's changes were attempts to protect her identity or that of Johnson, though her retention of the Wheeler family name certainly makes it less likely that these editorial changes were tactics of evasion (especially since the text was not published during her lifetime). The novel's treatment of "Jane" therefore reveals as much about the Wheeler family and about various legal narratives surrounding slavery as it does about Jane Johnson, reinforcing that it is not merely Johnson's personal story embedded within *The Bondwoman's Narrative* but a much thornier legal and cultural narrative—a narrative for which the literary character of "Jane" is a cipher. If Johnson's in-court veil is symbolic of her remove from the legal system in which she speaks, she is doubly veiled in the novel, where the reader can only come to know her through inference and absence. Moreover, the novel's fictionalization of Jane—whether that fictionalization occurs solely at the hands of Hannah Crafts or by virtue of Mrs. Wheeler's deception—establishes the intersection of Jane Johnson's legal personhood and her literary personhood as a character in a work of fiction. Her literary self and her legal personality can certainly be read together, but these various selves cannot coalesce into a single, coherent whole by merely placing the texts alongside one another any more than the personae of Shadrach Wilkins, Jim Thornton, and James Williams could combine into a single being.

In addition to the specific departures that *The Bondwoman's Narrative* makes from the "real-life" events in Jane Johnson's life, the novel repeatedly engages other strategies of encrypting and encoding legal narratives through plot, characterization, and occasional addresses directly to the reader. In other words, it is not solely through the fictionalization of Jane Johnson that *The Bondwoman's Narrative* encrypts and recasts law. In a novel that seems always on the verge of erupting into yet another enslaved person's biography, the law lingers at the margins and in the depths of what we are urged to read as the autobiography of Hannah Crafts. I have already alluded to some of the ways that legal language and theme permeate the text, as with the character of Trappe and the persistent use of legal terms of art. In one such example, as the narrator hesitates to write Mrs. Wheeler's false account of her character, Hannah confesses, "No one can doubt that I hesitated to pen such a libel on myself," once more infusing plot with (accurate) legal conclusions.[70] But in particular, one of the novel's peripheral characters demonstrates how Crafts's literary strategies engage explicitly with legal personhood. In chapter 14, "Lizzy's Story," the narrator makes plain how these capsule narratives are more than mere flourish—and in particular how what is embedded within these narratives is not only firsthand testimony but also the author's commentary on the laws of slavery.

Lizzy is an enslaved woman whom Hannah first meets at Lindendale, the plantation on which the novel opens. While still in Washington, DC, Hannah has a chance encounter with Lizzy while she runs errands for Mrs. Wheeler. In another example of the novel's use of nested narrative architecture, "Lizzy's Story" is not the story of Lizzy's experiences but rather a story about the current "master" and "mistress" of Lindendale, as told to Lizzy by yet another enslaved woman named Lilly. This relentless layering of levels of remove demonstrates that the novel takes great pains in *refusing* to claim that it is an anthology of individual slave narratives. Given the multiple tiers of narration, "Lizzy's Story" cannot reasonably be read as containing embedded *testimony*—instead, it is encrypted here for its narrative significance rather than embedded for its testimonial *truth*.

In Lizzy's account, the mistress at Lindendale has recently discovered that her husband, Cosgrove, has fathered several children of enslaved women on the estate; in her rage, she demands that the women and children be sold out of state entirely. What begins as an entirely too familiar plantation drama explicitly engages law in its framing. When confronted by his wife, the enslaver first says, "And I say . . . that there is law in this country for the slave as well as the free, and if you attempt to injur[e] them you will find it so to your sorrow. Proud as you are, and rich as you think you be, the key of the prison door has been turned on richer and nobler people times without number."[71] His implication is clear: that, should his wife attempt to interfere with his property, he will ensure that she suffers the *legal* consequences for the property damage or loss. Perversely, his declaration begins with the claim "that there is law in this country for the slave as well as the free," suggesting that enslaved people themselves actually benefit from laws regarding their treatment. In fact, as his monologue becomes visible as a threat, it is evident that his reference to "law for the slave" actually refers to law for the *enslaver*. Whether his threat to his wife is the product of some obscene "affection" for the enslaved women is, of course, immaterial—their status as his property is the lever across which he intimidates his wife with the threat of incarceration for property interference.

The presence of slavery law thus frames the encounter between husband and wife to expose how the legal narrative of slavery enables Cosgrove's power struggle with his white wife and her complicity in the deadly consequences that follow for the Black women they have enslaved. Several days after this marital dispute, a slave trader arrives at Lindendale to examine and purchase the women and children in question. When an enslaved child calls his owner "Pa" and implores his father not to sell him, the child's mother takes unimaginable action against her other child, an infant in her arms: "with a motion so sudden that no one could prevent it, she snatched a sharp knife which a servant had carelessly left after cutting butcher's meat, and stabbing the infant threw it with one toss into the arms of its father. Before he had time to recover from his astonishment she had run the knife into her own body, and fell at his feet bathing them in her blood. She lived only long enough to say that she prayed God to forgive her for an act dictated by the wildest despair."[72]

This gruesome scene takes advantage of specific imagery to unmistakably interrogate the enslaved woman's status as living property. In this rapid murder and suicide, the mother butchers her child and herself, gesturing toward the oft-repeated comparisons between the legal status of enslaved people and animals (and livestock in particular).[73] She tosses the dead infant into its father's arms, and her own dead flesh literally lands at his feet. By heaping these enslaved bodies onto the enslaver—who is not only the father of the dead baby but the rapist of the mother—the narrative repeats the trope first suggested in Mrs. Wheeler's description of Jane's flight. In that earlier example, the specter of a fugitive from slavery in the nation's capital would cast an uncomfortable shadow on any myths of benevolent slaveholding. Similarly, Cosgrove is left to contend with the obscenity of his own actions—his hands are literally full, and his feet are drenched from the corpses of the mother and child. By the scene's end, the woman and her baby are meat.

In the aftermath, Cosgrove's threat to his wife about property interference hovers with renewed force. The dead bodies at his feet, the property in question, have effectively violated the law of slavery that Cosgrove previously deployed against his wife. This upsetting of legal norms—in which the ostensibly objectified slave becomes the agent of her own destruction—is a radical recasting of the law that Cosgrove cites. In this account, the property dies, testing the borders of ownership but also of what it means to be owned. Cosgrove's ownership of this woman, despite his posturing to his wife, turns out to be far from absolute. The dead woman, unnamed in the novel, thus echoes Jane Johnson's claim that she "had rather die than go back [to Wheeler]."[74]

The narration of this scene, however, contains another invocation of law that offers an even more direct example of how the novel encrypts and recasts legal narratives. After Lizzy's story of Lindendale concludes, the narrator's voice intrudes in a striking address directly to imagined readers. Here is the narrator's commentary on the scene Lizzy has described, with the dead mother at Cosgrove's feet: "She smiled faintly, turned her eyes to the child which had breathed its last. A slight spasm, a convulsive shudder and she was dead. Dead, your Excellency, the President of this Republic. Dead, grave senators who grow eloquent over pensions and army wrongs. Dead ministers of religion, who prate because poor men without a moment[']s leisure on other days presume to read the newspapers on Sunday, yet who wink at, or approve of laws that occasion such scenes as this."[75] The abrupt narrative turn, from the inward-facing world of the scene just described to the outermost reaches of possible audience, marks a shift from literary fiction to legal protest. The subjects of the address range from the President to senators to religious ministers, all of whom are made responsible for the young woman's death.

The moment of actual death is almost unremarkable, "a slight spasm, a convulsive shudder"[76] preceding the nothingness of an unnamed woman's death. The lightness of the death and the anonymity of the enslaved woman stand in stark contrast with the weight of those whose hypocrisy the narrator exposes. The narrator specifically addresses both lawmakers and religious leaders who approve of brutal slavery laws while obsessing over trivial matters, explicitly making the enslaved woman's death a matter of law. Specifically, the address recasts the death as a *crime*, for which the lawmakers—and not the woman herself, or even her enslaver—are responsible. Note here the resonances with David Walker in chapter 1, naming slavery as the crime and Black people of the world as judge and jury, and Charles Langston in chapter 3, whose identification as a citizen-outlaw obligates him as a lawbreaker in the face of laws that violate natural rights. And think as well about the mysterious repetition in the Black press throughout the 1830s and 1840s, the return to the verse from Ezekiel in which a prophecy promises a tripled overturning. In each of these examples, and in this moment from *The Bondwoman's Narrative*, legal forms turn law inside out and upside down, reversing the order of time, laying waste to the very legal systems and institutions being addressed.

And as in Thomas Ruffin Gray's transcript of Nat Turner's criminal sentencing, this passage in *The Bondwoman's Narrative* also triples the woman's death to peculiar effect. Although it reminds its audience of the woman's death, the tripling of "dead" in the novel works to enliven rather than destroy or purge the body it describes. Each deployment of "dead" figuratively places her body at the feet of a different audience. Beginning with the President himself, whom the narrator sarcastically refers to as "your Excellency," the dead body first rests before "the Republic." This move again insists on the connection between legal slavery and the nation-state, troubling the myth of the United States as a civilized nation and instead littering the ultimate seat of power with corpses. The narrator then addresses senators, ensuring that the legislative branch of government—and, specifically, representatives of individual states—also bear responsibility for this woman's death. There is no distinction here between senators from different jurisdictions, suggesting that the existence of legalized slavery anywhere has corrupted the legislative process everywhere. To underscore the pervasiveness of law's hypocrisy, the address ends with religious ministers who "wink at, or approve of laws that occasion such scenes as this."[77] The tripling thus unites all three audiences in a conspiratorial network of complicity in the enterprise of slavery. Here, the fact that the woman appears to die three times in succession demonstrates how the legally sanctioned violence is excessive, wasteful, and obscene.

By bookending this scene in legal language—first with Cosgrove's assertion of law and later with the address to lawmakers—the novel embeds law within its own narrative, seizing on law as an appropriate frame and then turning the law back onto itself, while also signaling this legal context for the reader. As a result, the novel absorbs law but reimagines it in subtle yet radical ways. Like David Walker, who reappropriates the structure of the Declaration of Independence in order to argue against the constitutionality of legalized slavery, Crafts borrows from legal norms and principles to expose the intense *culpability* of lawmakers for the violence carried out by individual enslavers. As Crafts writes, "The Constitution that asserts the right of freedom and equality to all mankind is a sealed book to [slaves]."[78] Her citation of the Constitution both verifies her own legal consciousness—she is acutely aware of the Constitution's guarantees—and claims that, in the hands of lawmakers, that same document is unable to deliver on its promises.

It is evident that Crafts not only understands the rhetorical power of law to transform "facts" into enduring narratives, but she also uses this feature of law to transform legal narratives into literary fiction—the same process through which precedent establishes narratives of legal continuity. More than a compendium of fictionalized slave narratives, the novel innovates precedent as a form by acting as a cipher for various legal narratives and ultimately for a set of legal arguments about the failures and injustices of slavery. It encodes specific legal narratives of actual enslaved people, as in the case of Jane Johnson—an encryption that, first, places the novel in relation to the legal documents containing Johnson's testimony and, second, critiques the prevailing law that applied to Johnson's fugitivity.

The novel also encodes more general legal narratives that are decoupled from official legal records. As in the case of the enslaved woman who kills herself and her baby, the novel uses law as a framing device for plot lines and then subsequently uses the plot lines to upset and rewrite the expected legal outcomes. Literary fiction—as distinguished from the individual slave narrative genre as understood by white abolitionist publishers—thus emerges as a technology to expose and reimagine various legal fictions and legal theories.

Law is present at every turn in *The Bondwoman's Narrative*, and the fog of law that hangs over the entire novel reminds us that we are never firmly outside of law or wholly inside fiction. Pressing on the borders of the slave narrative genre by using overtly fictionalized accounts of numerous enslaved individuals, the text also exceeds this literary genre as an available forum for the endlessly concentric narratives encoded within it. In defying or transforming existing literary taxonomies, Crafts also presses on the supposed authority of law and the US nation-state as a source of higher law, opening space to imagine alternative legal histories altogether—a legal history, for instance, in which Jane Johnson is permitted to return to the place of her birth to emancipate herself and reinscribe her personal history alongside a reimagined US national history. How might the world look different, the novel seems to be asking in yet another counterfactual, if Jane Johnson had grown up in Washington, DC, as a free woman? One of the silent companion questions, then, is how might the world look different to Jane Johnson if the nation's capital had kept burning in 1814? At least in the narrative world of *The Bondwoman's Narrative*, these encryptions contain the possibility of restorative justice through the demolition of the US nation-state, which begs the question: what other forms of Black belonging might have arisen in its place?

Coda
African American Literary Futures and Law's Possibilities

"We wish to plead our own cause. Too long have others spoken for us."[1] At the end of this book, I find myself back at its beginning, making a fourth pass around these lines from the 1827 inaugural issue of *Freedom's Journal*. It is not that I want to retrace my steps, exactly, but that I now want to explore what lingers in these lines that might help us move *beyond* the nineteenth century. For example, once we recognize antebellum Black writers' innovative engagement with law, how does this shape our understanding of the African American literary tradition more broadly? Specifically, what are the stakes of legal thinking in the twenty-first century, with the benefit of decades' worth of critical race theory and Black feminist theory in particular, both of which—for good reason and in different ways—often urge us to pursue liberatory and abolitionist ends by *letting go* of attachments to legal logics and legal systems?[2] Is there such a thing as freedom in law? As I reread those two sentences by John Russwurm and Samuel Cornish, I see inherent in their words the seed of the retrospective futurism that I have elaborated over the course of the past four chapters. Notice now how their claim to a posture of pro se advocacy is the expression of a "wish"—an inherently futurist posture and a desire for a specific future world that does not yet exist. And yet, this futurist imagination also explicitly stakes itself on the past, noting that it has been "too long" that others have spoken on their behalf.

As I now sit in a posture of review, looking back at the preceding chapters, I see that this orientation—retrospection—is a feature of each text in this volume. In many ways, this book about law and legal writing is persistently a book about different ways of thinking space and, especially, time. The writers in this book use legal form to reimagine logics of power, and their literary experimentation with legal form persistently practices futurist thinking through return to the past—whether in freedom narratives' documentation of past abuse and emancipation, in litigation of or confession to alleged past "crimes," or in works of fiction that use counterfactuals to suggest alternative futures. In particular, I want to highlight here the specific counterfactuals that practice forms of retrospective fictionalization by rewriting the historical past: the fantasy of a Haitian teenage girl who rescues Toussaint L'Ouverture during the Haitian Revolution and possibly saves his life in the short story "Theresa, _____ a Haytien Tale" (chapter 1); the fantasy that arises in several different texts about the British setting the Capitol on fire in 1814 and the implicit curiosity about the entire thing going up in flames (David Walker's *Appeal* in chapter 1 and the trial testimony of Jane Johnson in chapter 4); Harriet Jacobs's brief wish for a sword-wielding queen of America (chapter 3); and so forth. Sitting with these counterfactuals brings into sharper focus the way that legal form facilitates bidirectional or nonlinear time and speculative possibility.

This relationship to time aligns with Tao Leigh Goffe's assertion that "Black temporality is a refusal to labor within the limits of history."[3] In thinking about Black time as operating "in contrast to imperial time," Goffe considers the ways that Black storytellers, whose time was stolen from them and who "stole away" time in return, have turned to speculative fiction, itself "a political battleground for the future existence of people of color."[4] Likewise, Justin Mann identifies speculation as both a response to state violence and the "false promises" of securitization,[5] and he traces a practice of "pessimistic futurism" in contemporary Black speculative fiction that "couches the prospects of tomorrow in the uncertainties conditioned by the past and present."[6] In examining Octavia Butler's 1987 novel *Dawn*, Mann points to the ways that the context of Reagan-era nuclear threat "reveals an orientation to the future that synthesizes the events of the past to propose an alternative horizon."[7]

Notice the similarity here to the alternative histories identified in this book—retellings of the Haitian Revolution, the British burning of the US Capitol, even David Walker's reimagination of the Declaration of Independence. Each of these projects also turns to the past as a means of imagining alternative futures. Their creative labor thus indexes historical violence while refusing, in Goffe's terms, to be constrained by "the limits of history."[8] Nineteenth-century Black writers, like contemporary authors of Black speculative fiction, tend to decouple time from history, an anti-colonial practice that unsettles several disciplines at once: it challenges white narratives of progress, teleology, and history, and it exposes the ways that literature and literary genres often participate in these projects. The twentieth- and twenty-first-century works of speculative fiction that Goffe and Mann turn to thus find common ground with the nineteenth-century counterfactuals and alternative histories explored in this book.

While Mann theorizes pessimistic futurism and Goffe theorizes "Maroon time,"[9] both formulations address futurist modes of Black temporality grounded in speculative storytelling. In proliferating new genres of literature, writers like Harriet Jacobs, Hannah Crafts, and Victor Séjour use legal form for textual experiments that process the violence of "the past" (Mann) while mobilizing critiques that reimagine both "present" and "future" (Goffe). In particular, the appeal form, a legal process premised on reviewing and undoing, performs a looking backward that has the capacity to overturn, revise, and remake. It is not merely coincidental that both Séjour and S., the author of "Theresa, _____ a Haytien Tale," draw on that form in their reimaginations of the Haitian Revolution—an event that itself overturned colonial rule and resulted in the creation of a Black state. Revolution, like appeal, has a temporal quality; its Latin root word, *revolvere*, literally means "to roll back," a reminder that while revolution often signifies culturally as a futurist project or a new chapter, it encompasses a rolling back of another regime or unjust action. Even in the sense of planetary orbit, revolution is often measured not only in distance traveled but in time, namely the time it takes to complete one full circle around a fixed object. A completed revolution thus returns a planet to its point of origin, which, as a point on a circle, is an arbitrary fiction of origination that cannot really signal anything like "past" or "future" except through the narrative we apply to its trajectory.

Of course, appeal is not the only legal form that permits this nonlinear temporal orientation—the presence of counterfactual across this book speaks, rather, to law's temporal capacity. As it happens, the ability to bend or loop time can do or undo actions, it can change definitions applied to a person or a place, and, as narrated by recent formulations of the so-called multiverse, nonlinear temporality can generate countless possible "futures" that have both not yet happened and are already occurring. Confession, as a review of past "crimes," is generally intended to absolve or at least to mitigate, as preparation for rehabilitation and/or punishment—though the writers in this book mobilize confession as a means of reframing the operative legal worlds, crafting new possibilities for citizenship, and imagining new structures of kinship in the family sphere. Jurisdiction, as both a place or context and the authority to adjudicate matters in that place or context, creates its own temporal paradox: it cannot exist without a preceding jurisdictional authority, a contradiction that scrambles the utility of time. And precedent only exists by maintaining simultaneous backward- and forward-looking language, by using the present tense formulation of judicial holdings to (1) identify the operative previous cases whose rules are relevant in the current case (backward-looking) and (2) anticipate an opinion's afterlife as controlling authority for future cases (forward-looking). For most laypeople, law is not an obvious site of possibility for nonlinear temporality—or Black freedom. But given these surprisingly nimble and nonlinear temporal possibilities, and given how well versed nineteenth-century Black writers were in legal thought, it is no wonder that these authors would seize on law's affordances as containers for Black narratives.

Nor is it surprising that this use of legal form would confound and remake existing literary genres, such that taxonomic divisions even between fiction and nonfiction become very difficult to parse in antebellum Black literature. In surveying Black and Indigenous storytelling traditions, Goffe describes Black temporality as follows: "A politics and aesthetics of shapeshifting and mutability, defying genre, Black temporality cyclically emerges as a resource for Black people but also influences the fate and story of the world, as Du Bois prophesied."[10] What I want to press here, which Goffe also presses, is that the use of nonlinear temporality as a genre breaker and maker, while now enjoying a twenty-first-century flourish, is by no means a new or recent invention. Rather, it is intrinsic to Black ways of thinking and theorizing time and place, and especially to modes of Black storytelling.

Goffe's and Mann's formulations of the speculative remind us that futurity in Black storytelling is more than futuristic aesthetics; it is a form of worldbuilding that addresses, and perhaps redresses, histories, a posture that also recalls the sankofa bird in Akan culture. This bird, whose literal name translates roughly to "go back and get it," stands with its head turned back to face the past while its feet face the future—the sankofa bird is associated with a proverb which Appiah Kwartang summarizes as "Always remember the past, for therein lies the future, if forgotten we are destined to repeat it."[11] One of the through lines of this book has been to chart nonlinear temporality as a resource that legal form offered to nineteenth-century Black writers, who often practiced futurity by constructing counter*histories*—a narrative orientation to futurity that embraces the nonlinear and the speculative at once. Tracking this nineteenth-century relationship to temporality inflects our understanding of the African American literary tradition in broad terms and especially movements and genres that are often classified in the contemporary as Afrofuturist.

"Afrofuturism" is the term coined by Mark Dery to describe "speculative fiction that treats African-American themes and addresses African-American concerns in the context of twentieth-century technoculture—and, more generally, African-American signification that appropriates images of technology and a prosthetically enhanced future."[12] Given Dery's definition, which emphasizes technoculture, and which typically refers to contemporary cultural productions, it would be temporally and historically strange to describe nineteenth-century writers as deliberately participating in "Afrofuturist" projects. But in theorizing Afrofuturism as a Black feminist mode, scholars like Ytasha Womack have taken a more capacious view of Afrofuturism's scope, with Womack characterizing Afrofuturism as "a free space for women, a door ajar, arms wide open, a literal and figurative space for black women to be themselves," a space where it is possible to "dig behind societal reminders of blackness and womanhood to express a deeper identity and ... to define blackness, womanhood, or any other identifier in whatever form their imagination allows."[13] And while Womack nevertheless retains a focus on technoculture in Afrofuturism, Bennett Capers observes generally that a "mainstay of Afrofuturism is a commitment to the disruption of hierarchies based on race, gender, sexuality, and class"[14] and notes that "[a] recurring theme in Afrofuturism is reclaiming the identities and perspectives that were lost as a result of the slave trade and colonialism."[15] By decoupling Afrofuturism from technoculture and focusing on its tendency to unsettle and remake oppressive paradigms, these framings theorize Afrofuturism as a mode of imagining and enacting liberation. Having a broader context for this imaginative mode also permits deeper engagement with and connections to forms of literature and culture that might otherwise be assumed to fall outside Afrofuturism's perimeters.

For example, as this book has demonstrated, nineteenth-century Black writers frequently deployed speculative storytelling models, but this creative labor obviously did not operate within the specific cultural project that Dery attached to twentieth-century engagements with technoculture.[16] Even so, scholars like Capers consider texts as early as Martin Delany's *Blake, or the Huts of America* (1857) to be Afrofuturist, largely on the basis of that text's "alternative history" of Black revolution in Cuba and the United States.[17] But of course, texts like "Theresa, _____ a Haytien Tale," "The Mulatto," and *The Bondwoman's Narrative* also deploy alternative histories, suggesting that the speculative/counterfactual roots of Afrofuturism were present in the very earliest works of African American fiction. Likewise, Kelly Ross reads both *The Bondwoman's Narrative* and *Incidents in the Life of a Slave Girl* as speculation fiction, emphasizing that while these texts—which I have read through jurisdiction, confession, and precedent—are "not engaged with the scientific topoi of speculative fiction," they nevertheless imagine futurity by deploying speculation via spying and "financial risk-taking."[18] And without using the language of Afrofuturism specifically, Britt Rusert theorizes "fugitive science" in nineteenth-century Black literature—including *Blake*—as a fugitive form of worlding that is rooted in scientific experimentation and functions as an "itinerant" freedom practice.[19] These engagements with multiple valences of speculation are informed by, and should also inform, scholarship on more recent examples of speculative fiction. Increasingly, in ways that productively complicate our sense of "when" Afrofuturism or Black speculative fiction "began," scholars of nineteenth-century Black culture are excavating the speculative in literature, finance, and science; this book adds law to that list.

With this addition of law, and bearing in mind the nonlinear qualities of Black temporality, I suggest that, rather than turning back the clock toward an "origin point" for Afrofuturism, we instead regard the speculative and specifically the legal as formative features of the African American literary tradition; I further suggest including law, like science/technoculture, as a constitutive context for Afrofuturism in particular. One of the things that I hope this book has illuminated is the pliability of legal form in the hands of nineteenth-century Black writers, who mobilized it as an experimental, public form of narrative advocacy and imagination. To borrow from critical race theory, in their analysis of Hurricane Katrina's narrative framing, Cheryl Harris and Devon Carbado remind us that frames are "interpretational structures that, consciously and unconsciously, shape what we see and how we see it."[20] In Harris and Carbado's formulation, frames—if you're a literary scholar, you might prefer "narratives"—give shape and meaning to facts. "We do not believe that facts speak for themselves," they write.[21]

For nineteenth-century Black writers, framing via legal form was a way not only to give persuasive meaning to the material realities of slavery and racial oppression (the facts) but also to imagine new worlds by "dislodg[ing] the normativity" of the existing legal regime.[22] Normativity, in Robert Cover's formulation, also helps explain law's simultaneously oppressive and fertile terrain. Like Harris and Carbado, Cover identifies narrative as the linchpin in normativity's power: "Once understood in the context of the narratives that give it meaning, law becomes not merely a system of rules to be observed, but a world in which we live."[23] The indefinite article in "a world" is significant here. As Cover recognizes law as a site of worldmaking, he identifies the multiplicity inherent in any worldbuilding project. There is no single, inevitable world governed by law, only "a world"—one world that one set of rules has constructed, a world that may differ in large or small ways from other possible worlds governed by other rules and different norms. That world is far more fragile than it claims to be.

In fact, in addressing Euro-modern law as a normative technology designed to perpetuate colonial violence and racial injustice, Foluke Adebisi writes,

"To question the presumptions upon which the world-making of Euro-modern legal knowledge is based, the tools adopted must have the capacity to bend the rules of law's assumed 'naturals' with impunity. Science fiction provides us with just such a prospect, as it has the potential to . . . 'imagine alternative worlds' and 'imagine radical alternatives.'"[24] For Adebisi, law as a "colonial discipline" that serves property and capital is unavailable as a site of possibility, but the narrative power of science fiction has the capacity to undo the things that law has naturalized and normalized. Adebisi is obviously and absolutely correct in the assessment of law as an instrument of colonial violence—my only question here is why we still tend to place the realms of science and science fiction on the "outside" of an imagined lawscape. Like law, it is increasingly impossible to construe Euro-modern science as anti-colonial, and yet science fiction remains one of the most visible and accepted sites of radical Black possibility. What if we identified Black radical possibility not only through science fiction but also through legal fiction or legal narrative?

Like science, law's contingency on narrative vests actual material world-making power in storytellers, who wield presumed authority whether as scientists, legal experts, or artists. Black writers in the nineteenth century—who were steeped in legal knowledge and legal culture—were in fact much *better* poised to engage with law than many twenty-first-century laypeople, for whom access to legal discourse has largely disappeared behind paywalls, legal reporter subscriptions, and billable hours. In the nineteenth century, legal texts circulated rather more freely and publicly, and as some of the most precarious legal persons at the time, Black readers and writers became, as a matter of common sense and practical survival, legal experts. We literary scholars should be attending much more closely to the legal dimensions of Black writing during this period, and we should better account for the work that cultural and legal historians have done on that front, work that establishes a record of robust and complex nineteenth-century Black legal participation. There is real danger in fetishizing "literature" as a category that exists outside or in opposition to other forms of textual production. Legal imagination is inextricable from creative literary imagination in nineteenth-century Black literature, and legal form would have been readily visible to nineteenth-century Black audiences— certainly more visible than it is to many twenty-first-century literary scholars and laypeople. But even beyond the nineteenth-century context of this book, is there room to read more recent Black literature as legal fiction or legal experimentation? Is it possible to do so as a means of deepening and enlarging our sense of that literature and not as a practice of limiting or enclosing it in hostile terrain?

Perhaps more specifically, is it possible for Black literature, in something akin to Afrolegalism, to perform legal thinking without resorting to "the master's tools" that Audre Lorde rebuked?[25] One way that legal scholar Angi Porter has anticipated or answered this question is to propose what she calls "Africana Legal Studies," an approach that would center African ways of knowing and acknowledge African models of governance.[26] One of the ways that Porter seeks to avoid Lorde's problem of "the master's tools" is to use the term "protocol" to (1) refer to "the body of African systems of governance, rules for Social Living. Protocol is not Law but something else with which Law interacts"[27] and (2) to make visible that references to "Law" tend to import a Eurocentric model and worldview such that even a modified term like "African Law" refers to "the European-derived systems of law that exist in Africa because of colonialism."[28] I find Porter's formulation compelling, and I am in agreement about her desire to extend the methodology of Africana studies to a legal context. When I use the term "Afrolegalism" here, I am aiming to make a move similar to Porter's. By using "legalism" rather than "law," my goal is to decentralize institutions and instead think about legalism as a habit of mind, a way of thinking and organizing the world. But rather than treating it as a descendant of Eurocentric legalism, I mean to nod toward an Afrodiasporic legalism that, like Afrofuturism, identifies global Black ways of envisioning the future while leaving space for those visions to branch in various directions according to the specific local customs, cultures, and ideologies that form around the diaspora.

As I queried in the beginning of this coda, is freedom possible in law? Another way of asking this question is to revisit Jennifer Nash's provocation: "What if the disavowed deathly archive of law is reimagined as a home for black feminism's loving practice? How might we reimagine black feminist feelings toward intersectionality by reengaging its largely forgotten connections with law and its fundamental commitment to remaking law in unfamiliar and productive ways?"[29] Like Porter, like Nash, like the writers I have studied in this book, I both recognize the dangers and the violence that law poses for Black subjectivity *and* I note that it nevertheless retains certain affordances that Black writers have persistently indexed as sites of possibility for various freedom practices. This tension prompts the further question: what then does a Black legal world look like, whether we approach it through Africana legal studies, Afrolegalism, or intersectionality and Black feminism?

As Adebisi urges, and I think as confirmed by Justin Mann's scholarship on securitization and world-breaking and Simone Browne's scholarship on surveillance, in order to promote Black liberation, legal thinking must operate on a world-level scale that unsettles and rewrites existing legal regimes.[30] A radical Black legal world might imagine rules of relation and community using terms untethered from the nation-state or even the nuclear family, perhaps creating spaces of Black privacy and intimacy that respond to an historically anti-Black world by remaking the terms of Black life, as in Christina Sharpe's theorization of "the hold."[31] A radical Black legal world might theorize personhood in ways that transcend altogether the white supremacist ideals of wholeness, ability, and singularity, favoring forms of shared consciousness and communal rights-bearing models—tropes seen as early as the nineteenth-century pamphlet *The History of the Carolina Twins* by Millie-Christine McKoy (18—) and across contemporary Black diasporic texts ranging from Toni Morrison's *Beloved* (1987) to Erna Brodber's *Louisiana* (1994) and Nnedi Okorafor's short story "Hello, Moto" (2011).[32] Afrolegalism, if we look for it not just in but beyond the works in this book, would overturn and unsettle normative universes that existing legal regimes treat as natural, inevitable, permanent, and inescapable.

Rather than framing law as an instrument of capital, of white supremacy, or of incarceration, Black legal thinking might productively and radically extend Harriet Jacobs's framing of law as a protective overhang, a shield against violence, and an instrument of rights for all, and especially the oppressed—it might create a habitable version of the world that Emily Owens cites as having been unavailable to nineteenth-century Black women in Louisiana: "a world in which their consent [is] a meaningful expression of autonomous life unmoored from contract, subjugation, captivity, and confinement."[33] Black legal thinking might establish for Black women and Black queer people a doctrinal imaginary that Owens identifies as having belonged to nineteenth-century enslavers, space to "imagine their ideal society and attempt [] to bring it into existence."[34] It might move to the center what have been the "liminal spaces" that Alejandro de la Fuente and Ariela Gross have examined, spaces in which Black women "could claim freedom for themselves and their loved ones and create communities that challenged slaveholders' efforts to align blackness with enslavement."[35]

Black legal thinking might norm authority and power in entirely different ways, organizing sites of belonging that foreground a "nonhierarchical distribution of power" in the Combahee River Collective's "vision of a revolutionary society."[36] It might, in borrowing from Neil Roberts's theorization of marronage as a freedom practice, organize communities of belonging according to logics that cannot be imagined, much less mapped, on or in white cartographies and geopolitical systems.[37] And Black legal thinking would certainly incorporate Angi Porter's assertion that "one cannot fully understand the thoughts or attitudes of African Americans about U.S. Law without first understanding the unique world-senses and Protocol of their African ancestors."[38] For this reason, Black legal thinking also requires more case studies like Porter's of the Bamana people of eighteenth-century Louisiana, which makes visible how ancestral knowledge and oral traditions, for example, infused both daily life and the Bamana taxonomies and cosmologies that structured their legal theories.[39] This type of history/memory work brings to the fore African ways of knowing that have shaped centuries of legal culture within and beyond state legal institutions, and it prompts us to think of legal culture in more expansive terms.

Afrolegalism, as an ally and coconspirator of Afrofuturism, therefore holds potential to deepen our study of how Black writers have historically understood and engaged law; it also has the potential to help us link, with nuance, some of the earliest Black fiction and literature with artifacts of contemporary Black culture. And it may even, as a technology of worldmaking, be an unexpected site of possibility for imagining and materializing pathways to Black liberation. This potential of law to make manifest contextualizes Patricia Williams's gravitation toward the language of alchemy and mythology in her meditation on how, in the 1990s, the field of critical legal studies might mobilize law as a device of freedom. In describing the labor of "unmasking ... rights mythology in liberal America," Williams writes: "The task ... is not to discard rights but to see through or past them ... so that privacy is turned from exclusion based on self-regard into regard for another's fragile, mysterious autonomy; and so that property regains its ancient connotation of being a reflection of the universal self."[40] Here Williams frames the work of law—and its "unmasking"—as mysterious, tracing an ancient, sacred, and liberatory frame for property, one of the primary legal drivers of anti-Black oppression. This unmasking—like revolution, appeal, and counterfactual—is not mere disposal but undoing plus remaking. Williams does not advocate doing away with rights altogether as a framework for social and political relation; rather, she urges that we proliferate rights in places where they have not historically resided or reached: "Unlock them from reification by giving them to slaves. Give them to trees. Give them to cows. Give them to history. Give them to rivers and rocks. Give to all of society's objects and untouchables the rights of privacy, integrity, and self-assertion; give them distance and respect. Flood them with the animating spirit that rights mythology fires in this country's most oppressed psyches, and wash away the shrouds of inanimate-object status, so that we may say not that we own gold but that a luminous golden spirit owns us."[41]

Williams's formulation reorganizes the hierarchies wrought by a model of relation founded on property and replaces it with a vision of sociality that Jennifer Nash reads as one of networked vulnerability.[42] Without necessarily overidentifying with vulnerability as a frame—despite its material accuracy—Williams's extension of rights signals a relation of interdependence and, very materially, community. It at once dispenses with hierarchical taxonomies and brings people into new intimacy not only with each other but also with the texture of the physical world in which they live. This rights-bearing and rights-proliferating model—which must have sounded a bit like science fiction when Williams published this provocation in 1991—has found embrace in conservation and sustainability networks, as well as Indigenous sovereignty movements, where personhood status is now frequently sought for rivers and other geographic features. In 2017, when New Zealand granted personhood status to the Whanganui River, that determination occurred in connection with a settlement with a Māori nation, and other Indigenous nations have sought similar personhood declarations for rivers around the globe.[43] These movements have exploited the legal fiction of, for example, corporate personhood and productively extended it into a technology of sustainability.

Indeed, in a world where legal rights have historically operated as a currency of the powerful and a means of white supremacist exclusion, this example suggests that visions for liberation need not necessarily relinquish the legal altogether—despite its undeniable historical violence and carceral logics—so much as dismantle and remake it, and then as Patricia Williams suggests, give it away. There may be room yet to work with law in a framework other than mastery. Perhaps by approaching law from a sideways view, overidentifying with its rights-bearing promises, and taking advantage of its temporal unfixity. Perhaps by mobilizing law's worldmaking possibility to, in Kevin Quashie's provocation, "imagine a black world."[44] We find these same strategies in the ways that Harriet Jacobs, Hannah Crafts, David Walker, and others gave breath to their legal imagination in the nineteenth century, the ways that they envisioned Black futurity and alchemized it on the tips of their pens.

Notes

Introduction

1. John Russwurm and Samuel Cornish ("The Editors"), "To Our Patrons," *Freedom's Journal* (New York), March 16, 1827.
2. Russwurm and Cornish, "To Our Patrons."
3. Russwurm and Cornish, "To Our Patrons."
4. Ross, *Witnessing & Testifying*, 15.
5. Holloway, *Legal Fictions*, x.
6. Hartman, *Scenes of Subjection*, 3.
7. Hartman, *Scenes of Subjection*, 5.
8. Nash, *Black Feminism Reimagined*, 119.
9. I am thinking here, as always, of Kevin Quashie's question, "What . . . would a concept of expressiveness look like if it were not tethered to publicness?" Quashie, *The Sovereignty of Quiet*, 20.
10. Russwurm and Cornish, "To Our Patrons."
11. Russwurm and Cornish, "To Our Patrons."
12. Thank you to Shoniqua Roach for this language of critical reorientation through corrective testimony.
13. I alternate between the terms "freedom narrative" and "slave narrative," which I regard as largely interchangeable. The choice to vary my description is grounded in a politics of visibility that acknowledges the violence experienced by these authors and also seeks, in emphasizing their survival and self-emancipation, to honor their humanity rather than dwelling exclusively in their dehumanization. This variation also marks my engagement with scholarly works that specifically use the language of the former while moving toward a practice of adopting the latter in alignment with the language practices outlined in P. Gabrielle Foreman, et al. "Writing about Slavery/Teaching About Slavery: This Might Help" community-sourced document, accessed September 8, 2024, https://docs.google.com/document/d/1A4TEdDgYslX-hlKezLodMIM71My3KTNozxRvoIQTOQs/mobilebasic.
14. Justice Taney's decision in *Scott v. Sandford*, 60 US 393 (1857), famously foreclosed African American citizenship in a standard that lasted until the ratification of the Fourteenth Amendment in 1868; the Fugitive Slave Act of 1850, 9 Stat. 462 (1850), contained prohibitions on testimony by people merely *accused* of being fugitives from slavery. While these federal legal standards are among the most frequently discussed, one of the greatest challenges in navigating the laws of slavery arose out of their variety, nuance, and difference across different jurisdictions. Justin Simard has observed in "Slavery's Legalism" that "slavery did not exist in the common law" (577) and that, as a general matter, "law differed, sometimes substantially, from state to state" (584).
15. Fuentes, *Dispossessed Lives*, 76.
16. Jacobs, *Incidents in the Life of a Slave Girl*, 40–42.

17. Russwurm and Cornish, "To Our Patrons."
18. See generally Walker, *Walker's Appeal*.
19. Davis and Gates, "Introduction," xv.
20. See Jefferson, "Query XIV," *Notes on the State of Virginia*, 138–59.
21. See Equiano, *The Interesting Narrative of the Life of Olaudah Equiano*; Smith, *A Narrative of the Life and Adventures of Venture, a Native of Africa*; and Cugoano, *Narrative of the Enslavement of Ottobah Cugoano*.
22. See Prince, *The History of Mary Prince*.
23. See Douglass, *Narrative of the Life of Frederick Douglass*.
24. "North American Slave Narratives: Chronological List of Autobiographies," Documenting the American South, University Library, University of North Carolina at Chapel Hill, accessed September 8, 2024, https://docsouth.unc.edu/neh/chronautobio.html.
25. See Goddu, *Selling Antislavery*, for a deeper discussion of the corporatization and commercialization of the genre by white abolitionist networks.
26. The first three waves of this trajectory are reflected in the organization of Davis and Gates's volume, *The Slave's Narrative*, which consists of, first, an anthology of primary source narratives from 1750 to 1861; second, a critical section entitled "The Slave Narratives as History"; and third, a critical section entitled "The Slave Narratives as Literature." See Davis and Gates, *The Slave's Narrative*, ix–x. Davis and Gates's 1985 volume marked what purported to be a shift away from focusing purely on the "documentary" nature of the genre and offered an indictment of literary studies for failing to treat these narratives as works of literature. They write, "But rarely has a volume attempted to analyze these texts as narrative discourses as important to criticism for their form and structure as they are important to historiography for the 'truths' they reveal about the complex workings of what [John] Blassingame calls 'the slave community.'" Davis and Gates, *The Slave's Narrative*, xii.
27. See Andrews, *To Tell a Free Story*; Carby, *Reconstructing Womanhood*; Smith, *Self-Discovery and Authority in Afro-American Narrative*; and Andrews, *African American Autobiography*.
28. Polley, *Echoes of Emerson*, 3.
29. Polley, *Echoes of Emerson*, 78.
30. Goddu, *Gothic America*, 145. Though *Black Pro Se* does not engage poetry, it bears noting that Matt Sandler has traced a tradition of Black romanticism among abolitionist poets in *The Black Romantic Revolution: Abolitionist Poets at the End of Slavery*. Sandler's attention to the prophetic in particular has greater bearing on the early works of fiction discussed in chapter 1 than to the genre of the freedom narrative per se. However, his work in *The Black Romantic Revolution* underscores the ways that Black writing in the nineteenth century is susceptible to reading through a variety of the dominant literary modes of that century, including romanticism, gothic romance, realism, and sentimentalism.
31. Windell, *Transamerican Sentimentalism*, 172.
32. Windell, *Transamerican Sentimentalism*, 139.
33. Moody, *Sentimental Confessions*, 2.
34. Samuels, "Introduction," 6.
35. McDowell, "In the First Place," 36.
36. McDowell, "In the First Place," 58.
37. See Gardner, *Unexpected Places*; and Aljoe, *Creole Testimonies*.

38. See Snorton, *Black on Both Sides*, 55–98; and McKittrick, *Demonic Grounds*, 37–64.
39. See, for example, DeLombard, *Slavery on Trial*.
40. Barrett, "Self-Knowledge, Law, and African American Autobiography," 154.
41. Nyong'o, *The Amalgamation Waltz*, 12–13.
42. Barrett, "Self-Knowledge, Law, and African American Autobiography," 154.
43. As an example, *People v. Hall*, 4 Cal. 399, 399 (1854) (citing the 1850 California statute that provided, "No Black or mulatto person, or Indian, shall be allowed to give evidence in favor of, or against a white man").
44. McBride, *Impossible Witnesses*, 5–6.
45. McBride, *Impossible Witnesses*, 5.
46. See generally Hartman, *Scenes of Subjection*.
47. For other work on circulation and African American networks of print culture, see Spires, *The Practice of Citizenship*, and Sinche, *Published by the Author*.
48. See Crenshaw, "Demarginalizing the Intersection of Race and Sex," 139–67.
49. Reichman, "Law's Affective Thickets," 109.
50. Simard, "Slavery's Legalism," 584.
51. See Levine, *Forms*, 3–11.
52. See Hartman, *Scenes of Subjection* and "Venus in Two Acts."
53. See Owens, *Consent in the Presence of Force*.
54. Fuentes, *Dispossessed Lives*, 3.
55. McMillan, *Embodied Avatars*, 9.
56. Russwurm and Cornish, "To Our Patrons."
57. Harris and Carbado, "Loot or Find? Fact or Frame?" 91.
58. Judiciary Act of 1789, 1 Stat. 73, ch. 20 § 35 (1789).
59. Swank, "The Pro Se Phenomenon," 374 (internal citations omitted).
60. Swank, "The Pro Se Phenomenon," 375 (internal citations omitted).
61. Swank, "The Pro Se Phenomenon," 376 (internal citation omitted).
62. Shepherd and Hening, *Statutes at Large of Virginia*, 1: 364.
63. As late as 2013, an American Bar Foundation study found that pro se representations for employment discrimination claims were more than two and a half times as likely among African American plaintiffs as they were among white plaintiffs. Debra Cassens Weiss, "More Blacks than whites eschew lawyers in job bias suits; are attorney weeding procedures to blame?" Daily News, *ABA Journal*, https://www.abajournal.com/news/article/Blacks_are_more_likely_to_file_job_bias_suits_without_a_lawyer_are_lawyer_w.
64. See Russwurm and Cornish, "To Our Patrons."
65. Here again Jeannine DeLombard's formulation (*Slavery on Trial*) contextualizes print as a site for staging adjudication outside the courtroom.
66. "Brother Ray," *The Colored American* (New York), July 4, 1840.
67. De Stefano, "*Persona Ficta*: Frederick Douglass," 785.
68. De Stefano, "*Persona Ficta*: Frederick Douglass," 794.
69. De Stefano, "*Persona Ficta*: Frederick Douglass," 793.
70. Hartman, "Venus in Two Acts," 11.
71. For an example of how the field is increasingly deepening its engagement with studies of race, ethnicity, and sexuality, see Anker and Meyler, *New Directions in Law and Literature*.

72. "Slave Code for the District of Columbia," *Slavery and the Judiciary, 1740–1860*, Library of Congress, accessed September 8, 2024, https://www.loc.gov/collections/slavery-and-the-judiciary-from-1740-to-1860/articles-and-essays/slave-code-for-the-district-of-columbia/.

73. Edwards, "The Forgotten Legal World of Thomas Ruffin," 859.

74. Hartog, "Pigs and Positivism," 900.

75. Kennington, *In the Shadow of Dred Scott*.

76. See, for example, Owens's account of Delphine, *Consent in the Presence of Force*, 29–55.

77. Welch, *Black Litigants in the Antebellum South*, 13.

78. Penningroth, "Law as Redemption," 793.

79. Penningroth, "Law as Redemption," 794 (discussing Ari Bryen's work on legal interpretation in Roman Egypt).

80. Welch, *Black Litigants in the Antebellum South*, 29–31.

81. Penningroth, "African American Divorce," 22.

82. Spires, *The Practice of Citizenship*.

83. Spires, *The Practice of Citizenship*, 2–3.

84. See generally Jones, *Birthright Citizens*; and Mitchell, *From Slave Cabins to the White House*.

85. Hyde, *Civic Longing*, 7.

86. Hyde, *Civic Longing*, 8.

87. Welch, *Black Litigants in the Antebellum South*, 42.

88. In particular, Welch describes courtroom storytelling "as an attempt to interpret and organize the world in which the teller . . . lived . . . [by] imagining and then signaling the narrator's *own* interpretation of how the world should function and how the parties involved should repair a break in normal relations." *Black Litigants in the Antebellum South*, 63 (emphasis in original).

89. Williams, *The Alchemy of Race and Rights*, 1.

90. Hoeflich, *Legal Publishing in Antebellum America*, 7.

91. Hoeflich, *Legal Publishing in Antebellum America*, 6–7.

92. Hoeflich, *Legal Publishing in Antebellum America*, 10–12.

93. Russwurm and Cornish, "To Our Patrons."

94. Nash, *Black Feminism Reimagined*, 130. Emphasis in original.

95. Dayan, *The Law Is a White Dog*, 12.

96. Cover, "Nomos and Narrative," 5.

97. Cover, "Violence and the Word," 1604.

98. Welch, *Black Litigants in the Antebellum South*, 63.

99. Mann, "Black Insecurity at the End of the World," 11.

100. See Russwurm and Cornish, "To Our Patrons."

101. Frederick Douglass, "The Constitution and Slavery," *The North Star* (Rochester, NY), March 16, 1849.

102. Barrett, "Self-Knowledge, Law, and African American Autobiography," 154.

103. Williams, *The Alchemy of Race and Rights*, 1.

104. Philip, *Zong!*, 196.

105. Philip, *Zong!*, 196.

106. *Gregson v. Gilbert*, 99 E.R. 629 (1783).

107. Philip, *Zong!*, 201.
108. Holloway, *Legal Fictions*, 5.
109. Langston, "Charles Langston's Speech at the Cuyahoga Courthouse."
110. Holloway, *Legal Fictions*, 17.

Chapter One

1. For discussions of sentimentalism and sympathy, see Samuels, "Introduction," 3–8, and Moody, *Sentimental Confessions*.
2. "Appeal to the Friends of Liberty," *The Colored American* (New York), September 14, 1839.
3. "Appeal to the Friends of Liberty."
4. "Appeal to the Friends of Liberty."
5. "Appeal to the Friends of Liberty."
6. See *U.S. v. Schooner Amistad*, 40 U.S. 518 (1841).
7. Of course, in the *Amistad* case, the captives were not African Americans, but West Africans who had been kidnapped in Sierra Leone and were being transported to Cuba when they staged their shipboard insurrection.
8. In *Selling Antislavery*, Teresa Goddu charts the ways that white abolitionist networks manufactured much of this urgency and drama through their use of mass media strategies and circulation of slave narratives.
9. I pause to note both the irresistible impulse to use the word "appealing" here and the equally powerful instinct to avoid it. More than a symptom of my own writerly state of mind, the vexed availability of the word "appeal" in so many different contexts speaks seriously to the ways that its colloquial meaning has been hollowed out over time.
10. Powell, *The Law of Appellate Proceedings*, 3.
11. Powell, *The Law of Appellate Proceedings*, 28. Note that this logic also warrants reliance on precedent, which is the focus of chapter 4.
12. Spires, *The Practice of Citizenship*, 163.
13. See Owens's discussion of Delphine in *Consent in the Presence of Force*, 29–55. For Glymph's discussion of archives that document refugee status, see "'She Wears the Flag of Our Country,'" 316–17.
14. Jacobs, *Incidents in the Life of a Slave Girl*, 27.
15. Bilder, "The Origin of the Appeal in America," 914.
16. Bilder, "The Origin of the Appeal in America," 915.
17. See "Varieties," *Freedom's Journal* (New York), October 26, 1827. This column lists the following joke under the heading "The Pocket Better than the Head": "A barrister, who was making a large oration for his client, happening to forget himself in one of his references, in order to refresh his memory, took Blackstone out of his pocket, when one of his colleagues, with a smile, remarked, 'That he had more law in his *pocket* than he had in his *head*.'" This item reflects both a familiarity with legal training and reading but also suggests how ubiquitous and portable Blackstone's *Commentaries* were.
18. We do sometimes refer to "pressing charges" in contemporary terms to refer to the filing of necessary police reports and making formal allegations that could then trigger a criminal prosecution by the relevant local, state, or federal attorney. The decision to

prosecute ultimately falls to the prosecutor, but they are far less likely to pursue an indictment where a victim is not willing to cooperate as a witness.

19. Blackstone, *Commentaries on the Laws of England*, 308.

20. Blackstone, *Commentaries on the Laws of England*, 310–12.

21. "Appeal," *Black's Law Dictionary*, 2020, accessed September 8, 2024, https://thelawdictionary.com/appeal/. See also "Appeal," *Oxford English Dictionary* (Oxford University Press, 2020), which includes the following definition of "appeal, v.": "to accuse of a heinous crime whereby the accuser has received personal injury or wrong, for which he or she demands reparation."

22. Walker, *Walker's Appeal*. See Hinks's introduction to the *Appeal* at xlv.

23. Hinks, *To Awaken My Afflicted Brethren*, 124. Here Hinks notes that Elijah Burritt, the publisher of the *Statesman & Patriot*, reprinted a *Boston Centinel* column that included excerpts from *Walker's Appeal*. As Hinks notes, "Such excerpting of the *Appeal* was extremely rare in the South primarily because it could contribute to the circulation of the ideas among African Americans."

24. Hinks, *To Awaken My Afflicted Brethren*, 116–172.

25. M'Baye, "Radical and Nationalist Resistance," 113–43.

26. Hubbard, "David Walker's *Appeal* and the American Puritan Jeremiadic Tradition," 331–46.

27. Spires, *The Practice of Citizenship*, 90 et seq.

28. Jefferson, *Notes on the State of Virginia*.

29. Nyong'o, *The Amalgamation Waltz*, 89.

30. See frontispiece to the 1830 edition.

31. Walker, *Walker's Appeal*, 35.

32. See "Document III, David Walker Mails the *Appeal* to Virginia 1829" in Hinks, *David Walker's Appeal*, 92.

33. Spires, *The Practice of Citizenship*, 4.

34. Spires, *The Practice of Citizenship*, 112.

35. Walker, *Walker's Appeal*, 72.

36. Nyong'o, "Race, Reenactment, and the 'Natural Born Citizen,'" 97.

37. Walker, *Walker's Appeal*, 47 et seq.

38. M'Baye, "Radical and Nationalist Resistance," 127.

39. Michael E. Grass, "British Burned D.C. 196 Years Ago Today," *Washington City Paper* (Washington, DC), August 24, 2010.

40. Walker, *Walker's Appeal*, 53.

41. These unconventional occupations of space within the text resonate with the experimentations of presence and absence that appear in my study of James Williams in chapter 3.

42. Walker, *Walker's Appeal*, 54.

43. Walker, *Walker's Appeal*, 44.

44. Bhabha, *The Location of Culture*, 128.

45. Quashie, *The Sovereignty of Quiet*, 22–23.

46. Walker, *Walker's Appeal*, 80.

47. Sandler, *The Black Romantic Revolution*.

48. Mann, "Figuring Black Lives," 636.

49. See Pelletier, *Apocalyptic Sentimentalism*.

50. Sulzener, "Night of Death, Morning of Rebirth," 623.
51. "WHIG TRIUMPH," *The Colored American* (New York), November 18, 1837.
52. "Ezekiel 21:27," Bible Hub, accessed May 19, 2024, https://biblehub.com/ezekiel/21-27.htm.
53. Mann, "Black Insecurity at the End of the World," 11.
54. "Reorganization of Society," *The Liberator* (Boston), August 9, 1844.
55. See, for example, "PREAMBLE," *The Liberator* (Boston), November 1, 1834; "CONTRAST," *The Colored American* (New York), July 29, 1837; and "THE COURSE WE HAVE RUN," *The Liberator* (Boston), January 3, 1835.
56. Powell, *The Law of Appellate Proceedings*, 3–4.
57. Thank you to Petal Samuel for the many conversations we had about this text during our writing sessions. While I had a difficult time isolating and anchoring a citational praxis to specific claims in this section, your general presence and community in thinking with me about this text nevertheless demand citational visibility here.
58. Cover, *Justice Accused*, 119.
59. Séjour, "The Mulatto," 304.
60. Séjour, "The Mulatto," 305.
61. Séjour, "The Mulatto," 305.
62. See Roberts, *Freedom as Marronage*.
63. In chapter 3, I take up questions of geographic jurisdiction; in some ways, this book remains haunted by marronage in each chapter.
64. Séjour, "The Mulatto," 306.
65. See S., "Theresa, _____ a Haytien Tale"; Turner, *The Confessions of Nat Turner*; Delany, *Blake, or the Huts of America*; and Jacobs, *Incidents in the Life of a Slave Girl*.
66. Séjour, "The Mulatto," 306.
67. Brown, "Seditious Prose," 176.
68. Séjour, "The Mulatto," 307–8.
69. Hartman, *Scenes of Subjection*, 132.
70. Séjour, "The Mulatto," 307.
71. Séjour, "The Mulatto," 308.
72. Séjour, "The Mulatto," 298.
73. S., "Theresa, _____ a Haytien Tale," 639–45.
74. S., "Theresa, _____ a Haytien Tale," 644.
75. S., "Theresa, _____ a Haytien Tale," 644.
76. Albanese, "Caribbean Visions," 575.
77. Albanese, "Caribbean Visions," 575.
78. Albanese, "Caribbean Visions," 576.
79. Albanese, "Caribbean Visions," 579.
80. Philip, *Zong!*, 196.
81. Williams, *The Alchemy of Race and Rights*, 1.

Chapter Two

1. Moody, *Sentimental Confessions*, 4.
2. Edwards, "The Forgotten Legal World of Thomas Ruffin," 859.

3. For a discussion of the informal nature of Southern law, see generally Edwards, *The People and Their Peace*, and Welch, *Black Litigants in the Antebellum South*. See also my discussion of plantation jurisdiction in chapter 3 for a fuller discussion of the territorial logics of abuse that governed plantation rule, and through which enslavers often sought to extract confessions.

4. Thomas and Leo, *Confessions of Guilt*, 71–73.

5. "LYNCH-LAW CONFESSIONS," *The National Era* (Washington, DC), January 6, 1859.

6. "A Ghostly Witness," *Provincial Freeman* (Chatham, Canada West), February 16, 1856 (reprinting Sir Erskine Perry, "A Bird's-eye View of India").

7. "NEGRO INSURRECTION," *Douglass' Monthly* (Rochester, NY), November 1860.

8. "CONFESSION UNDER TORTURE," *The North Star* (Rochester, NY), April 10, 1851.

9. Edwards, *The People and Their Peace*, 83–84.

10. Welch, *Black Litigants in the Antebellum South*, 121.

11. See generally Owens, *Consent in the Presence of Force*.

12. DeLombard, *In the Shadow of the Gallows*, 14 (citing Andrews, *To Tell a Free Story*, 43, 44).

13. DeLombard, *In the Shadow of the Gallows*, 15.

14. DeLombard, *In the Shadow of the Gallows*, 15.

15. Pinto, *Infamous Bodies*, 177.

16. Perry, *Vexy Thing*, 21.

17. Perry, *Vexy Thing*, 16.

18. Pinto, *Infamous Bodies*, 182.

19. Perry, *Vexy Thing*, 21.

20. Pinto, *Infamous Bodies*, 182–83.

21. Owens, *Consent in the Presence of Force*, 14.

22. Pinto, *Infamous Bodies*, 183.

23. Pinto, *Infamous Bodies*, 183.

24. I am grateful to Petal Samuel for her assistance in crafting this hybrid term.

25. *Miranda v. Arizona*, 384 US 436 (1966).

26. Thomas and Leo, *Confessions of Guilt*, 69.

27. Thomas and Leo, *Confessions of Guilt*, 75.

28. Thomas and Leo, *Confessions of Guilt*, 71 (internal citation omitted).

29. Thomas and Leo, *Confessions of Guilt*, 72.

30. See notes 5 through 8 and accompanying text.

31. Hartman, "Venus in Two Acts," 11.

32. Hartman, "Venus in Two Acts," 12.

33. Styron, *The Confessions of Nat Turner*.

34. Quashie, *The Sovereignty of Quiet*, 22.

35. Hartman, "Venus in Two Acts," 12.

36. Tomlins, *In the Matter of Nat Turner*, 27.

37. Turner, *The Confessions of Nat Turner*.

38. Tomlins, *In the Matter of Nat Turner*, 43.

39. See Tomlins, *In the Matter of Nat Turner*, 32–34; Smith, *The Oracle and the Curse*, 157–59; Sundquist, *To Wake the Nations*, 37–38; and DeLombard, *In the Shadow of the Gallows*, 164–76. I pause to note here, as I did in the book's introduction, the capacity of Black text to be claimed by multiple genres and movements. I do not make this observation as a critique of these scholars, each of whom offers a sensitive and nuanced reading of

Turner; rather I offer this observation as a reminder of the general inhospitability of white generic taxonomy for Black writing.

40. Tomlins, *In the Matter of Nat Turner*, 44 (citing Turner, *The Confessions of Nat Turner*, 18).
41. Turner, *The Confessions of Nat Turner*, 12; 9.
42. Turner, *The Confessions of Nat Turner*, 2.
43. Turner, *The Confessions of Nat Turner*, 4.
44. Prince, *The History of Mary Prince*, i.
45. Jacobs, *Incidents in the Life of a Slave Girl*, 6.
46. See Goddu, *Selling Antislavery*.
47. Turner, *The Confessions of Nat Turner*, 7.
48. Turner, *The Confessions of Nat Turner*, 20.
49. Turner, *The Confessions of Nat Turner*, 10.
50. Turner, *The Confessions of Nat Turner*, 11.
51. Tomlins, *In the Matter of Nat Turner*, 43.
52. Akinyela, "Battling the Serpent," 256.
53. Akinyela, "Battling the Serpent," 269.
54. Turner, *The Confessions of Nat Turner*, 8–9.
55. Turner, *The Confessions of Nat Turner*, 9.
56. Akinyela identifies in particular Turner's experiments at making paper and gunpowder as signifiers of rootwork and conjure practices. "Battling the Serpent," 272.
57. Akinyela, "Battling the Serpent," 275.
58. Turner, *The Confessions of Nat Turner*, 20.
59. Roane, "Plotting the Black Commons," 249.
60. Turner, *The Confessions of Nat Turner*, 12–13.
61. Sundquist, *To Wake the Nations*, 70.
62. Turner, *The Confessions of Nat Turner*, 14.
63. The tribunal, a deity, his coconspirators, Gray, and the presumably white reading audience targeted by Gray's pamphlet are all potential audiences for Turner, and each audience/member will likely "hear" different confessions in Turner's language.
64. Quashie, *The Sovereignty of Quiet*, 45.
65. Turner, *The Confessions of Nat Turner*, 8–9.
66. Turner, *The Confessions of Nat Turner*, 18.
67. Brooks, *Troubling Confessions*, 19.
68. Brooks, *Troubling Confessions*, 2.
69. Tomlins, *In the Matter of Nat Turner*, 119.
70. Turner, *The Confessions of Nat Turner*, 21.
71. See Brophy, "The Nat Turner Trials,"; also Tragle, *The Southampton Slave Revolt of 1831*.
72. Dayan, *The Law Is a White Dog*, 12. Dayan offers a complex and rich accounting of law's propensity to engage unwelcome subjects in violent legal rituals that put pressure on our understanding of the human, and of "civilization." Chapter 2 of that book, "Civil Death," deals with "how law materializes dispossession," 40.
73. Turner, *The Confessions of Nat Turner*, 8–9.
74. Shipherd, Plumb, and Peck, *History of the Oberlin-Wellington Rescue*, 1–3.
75. Guthrie, "The Oberlin-Wellington Rescue Case, 1859," 85–97. It is not clear why there was such a disparity in the two men's sentences; one possibility that I cannot confirm is that

Langston's relatively high public profile and his post-conviction oration contributed to his reduced penalties.

76. "Fugitive Slave Act 1850," *The Avalon Project: Documents in Law, History, and Diplomacy*, Yale Law School Lillian Goldman Law Library, accessed May 19, 2024, https://avalon.law.yale.edu/19th_century/fugitive.asp.

77. "Fugitive Slave Act 1850," *The Avalon Project*.

78. "Fugitive Slave Act 1850," *The Avalon Project*.

79. Langston, "Charles Langston's Speech at the Cuyahoga Courthouse."

80. Lubet, "The Oberlin Fugitive Slave Rescue."

81. See Lubet, "The Oberlin Fugitive Slave Rescue."

82. "What Is an Allocution Statement?" American Bar Association, November 20, 2018, www.americanbar.org/groups/public_education/publications/teaching-legal-docs/what-is-an-allocution-statement-/.

83. Langston, "Charles Langston's Speech at the Cuyahoga County Courthouse."

84. Langston, "Charles Langston's Speech at the Cuyahoga County Courthouse."

85. Langston, "Charles Langston's Speech at the Cuyahoga County Courthouse."

86. Langston, "Charles Langston's Speech at the Cuyahoga County Courthouse."

87. Langston, "Charles Langston's Speech at the Cuyahoga County Courthouse."

88. Langston, "Charles Langston's Speech at the Cuyahoga County Courthouse."

89. Harney and Moten, *The Undercommons*, 26.

90. Langston, "Charles Langston's Speech at the Cuyahoga County Courthouse."

91. Langston, "Charles Langston's Speech at the Cuyahoga County Courthouse."

92. Best, *The Fugitive's Properties*, 211.

93. Best, *The Fugitive's Properties*, 211 (internal citation omitted).

94. Langston, "Charles Langston's Speech at the Cuyahoga County Courthouse."

95. Langston, "Charles Langston's Speech at the Cuyahoga County Courthouse."

96. Pinto, *Infamous Bodies*, 100.

97. Jacobs, *Incidents in the Life of a Slave Girl*, 27.

98. Yellin, "Written by Herself," 479–86.

99. Foster, "Resisting *Incidents*," 59.

100. Foreman, *Activist Sentiments*, 19.

101. Davis, "Reflections on the Black Woman's Role in the Community of Slaves," 87.

102. Foreman, *Activist Sentiments*, 22.

103. Jacobs, *Incidents in the Life of a Slave Girl*, 57.

104. Hine, "Rape and the Inner Lives of Black Women," 912–20.

105. Hine, "Rape and the Inner Lives of Black Women," 912.

106. Hine, "Rape and the Inner Lives of Black Women," 914.

107. Hine, "Rape and the Inner Lives of Black Women," 915.

108. Jacobs, *Incidents in the Life of a Slave Girl*, 36.

109. Jacobs, *Incidents in the Life of a Slave Girl*, 49.

110. Jacobs, *Incidents in the Life of a Slave Girl*, 49.

111. Owens, *Consent in the Presence of Force*, 14–15, uses the phrase "fantasy of consent" to describe the ways that Black women, including Jacobs, were made vulnerable to sexual abuse due to the legal impossibility of their rape and the impossibility of exercising nonconsent.

112. Jacobs, *Incidents in the Life of a Slave Girl*, 49.

113. In discussing Jacobs's treatment of sexual abuse of men, Foreman writes that Jacobs uses "language that characteristically reveals as it also conceals." *Activist Sentiments*, 22.

114. Jacobs, *Incidents in the Life of a Slave Girl*, 50–51.

115. Turner, *The Confessions of Nat Turner*, 8–9.

116. Quashie, *The Sovereignty of Quiet*, 22.

117. Roach, "Black Sex in the Quiet," 137.

118. When describing events within the text, I refer to Jacobs as Linda, the name she chose to write under and the name of the persona in the text. When referring to the author, I refer to her as Jacobs, reminding myself and my readers that these levels of separation and persona are obtained even at the level of naming. Linda both is and is not Harriet Jacobs; she is a version of her, or perhaps a "re-presentation" of Jacobs's life events, to use Saidiya Hartman's formulation of "critical fabulation." Hartman, "Venus in Two Acts," 16.

119. Jacobs, *Incidents in the Life of a Slave Girl*, 51.

120. Jacobs, *Incidents in the Life of a Slave Girl*, 51.

121. Jacobs, *Incidents in the Life of a Slave Girl*, 52.

122. Foreman, *Activist Sentiments*, 25–26.

123. Foreman, *Activist Sentiments*, 26.

124. Foreman, *Activist Sentiments*, 27.

125. Jacobs, *Incidents in the Life of a Slave Girl*, 155.

126. Jacobs, *Incidents in the Life of a Slave Girl*, 156.

127. Foreman traces the numerous possibilities for Ellen's paternity, observing that the text, through its series of silences and mystifications on this point, leaves open the possibility that Flint was actually the father of one or more of Linda's children. It is worth noting that regardless of whether Flint or Sands is Ellen's biological father, this moment of confession nevertheless verifies Ellen's reappropriation of her ancestry and family.

128. Quashie, *The Sovereignty of Quiet*, 70.

129. Here I am thinking as well with Marisa Fuente's work in *Dispossessed Lives*, which thinks through the limitations on enslaved women's capacity to literally "reproduce" freedom by assigning their children slave status, regardless of paternity.

Chapter Three

1. The Wachowskis, dirs., *The Matrix*.
2. McKittrick, *Demonic Grounds*, 40.
3. *North Carolina v. Mann*, 13 NC 263 (North Carolina 1830).
4. Perry, *Vexy Thing*, 50.
5. McKittrick, *Demonic Grounds*, 44.
6. Dorsett and McVeigh, *Jurisdiction*, 39.
7. For a deeper discussion of "court week," see Welch, *Black Litigants in the Antebellum South*.
8. For a discussion of sovereign jurisdiction in the context of transatlantic adjudications of slave ship captures, see Richards, "The Adjudication of Slave Ship Captures," 836–67.
9. *Pennoyer v. Neff*, 95 US 714 (1878).
10. *International Shoe Co. v. Washington*, 326 US 310 (1945).
11. Dorsett and McVeigh, *Jurisdiction*, 11.
12. See McMillan, *Embodied Avatars*.

13. Jacobs, *Incidents in the Life of a Slave Girl*, 9.
14. Emily Owens also notes Jacobs's engagement with law as a site of possible protection. See *Consent in the Presence of Force*, 60.
15. Jacobs, *Incidents in the Life of a Slave Girl*, 27.
16. Jacobs, *Incidents in the Life of a Slave Girl*, 27.
17. Hartman, *Scenes of Subjection*, 109.
18. Holloway, *Legal Fictions*, 89. See also Owens, *Consent in the Presence of Force*, 25.
19. See Foreman, *Activist Sentiments*, 27.
20. Pinto, *Infamous Bodies*, 182–83.
21. Pinto, *Infamous Bodies*, 177.
22. Jacobs, *Incidents in the Life of a Slave Girl*, 100.
23. McKittrick, *Demonic Grounds*, 43.
24. Pinto, *Infamous Bodies*, 183.
25. Spillers, "Mama's Baby, Papa's Maybe," 67.
26. Perry, *Vexy Thing*, 21.
27. In her monograph on transamerican sentimentalism, Maria Windell has theorized Jacobs and her brother as rehearsing a "black hemispheric imaginary... [that] think[s] beyond the North-South geography that dominated discussions about slavery." This formulation offers yet another possibility for reading Jacobs's jurisdictional imagination. *Transamerican Sentimentalism*, 136.
28. Jacobs, *Incidents in the Life of a Slave Girl*, 111.
29. Jacobs, *Incidents in the Life of a Slave Girl*, 165.
30. Pinto, *Infamous Bodies*, 24.
31. Best, *The Fugitive's Properties*, 211.
32. Best, *The Fugitive's Properties*, 225.
33. Jacobs, *Incidents in the Life of a Slave Girl*, 42.
34. Berlant, *The Queen of America Goes to Washington City*, 223.
35. Jacobs, *Incidents in the Life of a Slave Girl*, 41–42.
36. Jacobs, *Incidents in the Life of a Slave Girl*, 133.
37. See Roberts, *Freedom as Marronage*.
38. Roberts, *Freedom as Marronage*, 4.
39. Pinto, *Infamous Bodies*, 100.
40. Jacobs, *Incidents in the Life of a Slave Girl*, 42.
41. Jacobs, *Incidents in the Life of a Slave Girl*, 42. Note the resonance here from Russwurm and Cornish's opening move in *Freedom's Journal*, where their desire to "plead their own cause" is also expressed as a wish. See Russwurm and Cornish, "To Our Patrons."
42. McMillan, *Embodied Avatars*, 12.
43. Williams, *Narrative of James Williams*; citations refer to 2013 edition.
44. See *Slatter v. Holton*, La. Parish Ct. for the Parish and City of New Orleans (May 10, 1839). Reprinted in Williams, *Narrative of James Williams*, Appendix E.
45. Santamarina, "Fugitive Slave, Fugitive Novelist," 24–46.
46. McMillan, *Embodied Avatars*, 65. Here McMillan refers specifically to Ellen and William Craft, coauthors of the 1860 freedom narrative *Running a Thousand Miles for Freedom*, but this formulation of artful embodiment applies as productively to Williams/Thornton/Wilkins.

47. Again, I have assembled this timeline thanks in great measure to Hank Trent's incredible archival research from his 2013 edition of *Narrative of James Williams*. I offer this overview in a pseudo-linear summary here for purposes of basic framing and legibility, although I am quite adamant about resisting the temptation to attempt to wrestle this complicated collection of personae into a unified linear narrative.

48. For a full account of this public debate, see DeLombard's analysis in *Slavery on Trial*.

49. Best, *The Fugitive's Properties*, 87.

50. Affidavit of Caleb Tate, October 16, 1835. Reprinted in Williams, *Narrative of James Williams*, Appendix D.

51. *Slatter v. Holton*, 19 La. 39 (1841).

52. *Slatter v. Holton*, La. Parish Ct. for the Parish and City of New Orleans (May 10, 1839). Reprinted in Williams, *Narrative of James Williams*, Appendix E.

53. *Slatter v. Holton*, 19 La. 39 (1841). Reprinted in Wiliams, *Narrative of James Williams*, Appendix E.

54. *Slatter v. Holton*, 19 La. 39 (1841). Reprinted in Wiliams, *Narrative of James Williams*, Appendix E.

55. Statement of William M'Bride, January 11, 1839, Docket no. 2894, *Slatter v. Holton*, 19 La. 39 (1841). Reprinted in Williams, *Narrative of James Williams*, Appendix E.

56. "Fifty Dollars Reward," *Alabama Intelligencer and State Rights Expositor* (Tuscaloosa, AL), August 29, 1835.

57. McMillan, *Embodied Avatars*, 9. For a fuller discussion on the dimensions of racialized performances and performative self-actualization, see Brooks, *Bodies in Dissent*.

58. Fuentes, *Dispossessed Lives*, 17.

59. Statement of Ulysses Spalding, June 15, 1838, Docket no. 2894, *Slatter v. Holton*, 19 La. 39 (1841). Reprinted in Williams, *Narrative of James Williams*, Appendix E.

60. Roberts, *Freedom as Marronage*, 4.

61. See Daniel Sharfstein's work in *The Invisible Line* for a fuller history of passing in the nineteenth and twentieth centuries.

62. *Slatter v. Holton*, La. Parish Ct. for the Parish and City of New Orleans (May 10, 1839). Reprinted in Williams, *Narrative of James Williams*, Appendix E.

63. Williams, *Narrative of James Williams*, 26–27.

64. Williams, *Narrative of James Williams*, 3.

65. Daniel 3:24–30.

66. Daniel 3:24–25.

67. Affidavit of Caleb Tate, June 1, 1836. Reprinted in Williams, *Narrative of James Williams*, Appendix D.

68. See Gayatri Spivak, "Translator's Preface," xvii.

69. Warren, *Ontological Terror*, 5.

Chapter Four

An earlier version of this chapter appeared as an article in *MELUS*. Thank you to Gary Totten, the readers, and the editorial staff at *MELUS*. See Barter, "Encrypted Citations."

1. Holloway, *Legal Fictions*, 6.

2. Though published for the first time in 2002, the novel was probably written in the 1850s. For a deeper examination of the author's biography and literary history, see Hecimovich, *The Life and Times of Hannah Crafts*.

3. *Roe v. Wade*, 410 U.S. 113 (1973); *Dobbs v. Jackson Women's Health Organization*, 597 U.S. 215 (2022).

4. *Scott v. Sandford*, 60 U.S. 393 (1857).

5. Stern, "Legal and Literary Fictions," 314, 323, 322.

6. Thank you to Moorland-Spingarn Research Center, Jeannine DeLombard, Kristin Moriah, R. J. Boutelle, and especially Simon Stern for reviewing this document and discussing with me.

7. Mary Ann Shadd Cary, "Brief, Resolved That Too Much Importance," *Articles, Editorials, Reports*, Mary Ann Shadd Cary Collection, Howard University (2020). Accessed September 10, 2024. https://dh.howard.edu/cgi/viewcontent.cgi?article=1001&context=mscary_articles.

8. Fuentes, *Dispossessed Lives*, 1.

9. See, for instance, Gates and Robbins, *In Search of Hannah Crafts*.

10. Julie Bosman, "Professor Says He Has Solved a Mystery Over a Slave's Novel," *New York Times*, September 18, 2013, http://nytimes.com/2013/09/19/books/professor-says-he-has-solved-a-mystery-over-a-slaves-novel.html. I continue to refer to her according to the name she assigned herself in *The Bondwoman's Narrative*, "Hannah Crafts." See also Hecimovich, *The Life and Times of Hannah Crafts*.

11. For example, Daniel Hack, in *Reaping Something New*, situates *The Bondwoman's Narrative* within a broader practice of transatlantic rewriting, focusing on Crafts's work as a reimagining of Charles Dickens's *Bleak House* (1852). Likewise, Abigail Heiniger, in *Jane Eyre's Fairytale Legacy*, has considered the relationship between *The Bondwoman's Narrative* and Charlotte Brontë's *Jane Eyre* (1847). Likewise, in "Literary Graftings," Rebecca Soares offers another example of work that positions *The Bondwoman's Narrative* within a transatlantic literary network.

12. Chakkalakal, *Novel Bondage*, 108.

13. Crafts, *The Bondwoman's Narrative*, 3, 1.

14. Crafts, *The Bondwoman's Narrative*, 5–6.

15. A number of slave narratives, such as *Narrative of the Life of Frederick Douglass, an American Slave* (1845), were written without an amanuensis. The lack of amanuensis here does not disqualify this text from inclusion in the genre, although the presence of an amanuensis would make that classification more likely.

16. See Goddu, *Selling Antislavery*, for a discussion of the antislavery movement's embrace of corporate culture in disseminating and publicizing its own products. As Goddu argues, antislavery societies appropriated slave narratives as part of their corporate branding and publicity.

17. See Pacquet, *Caribbean Autobiography*, 38.

18. McKoy, *The History of the Carolina Twins*, 13.

19. See, for example, Hecimovich, *The Life and Times of Hannah Crafts*.

20. For a discussion of the novel's use of gothic themes, see Marshall, *The Transatlantic Gothic Novel and the Law*.

21. In *The Life and Times of Hannah Crafts*, Gregg Hecimovich verifies a number of the plot points, people, and events referenced in the text.

22. Accepting Douglass's *Narrative* as the quintessential text from the slave narrative genre is not without its own, gendered, limitations. The narrative/novel hybrid style is not entirely without precedent when considering a text such as Harriet Jacobs's *Incidents in the Life of a Slave Girl*. Given that Jacobs's text was not published until 1861, and estimates suggest that *The Bondwoman's Narrative* was written during the mid-1850s. Hannah Crafts likely did not have the benefit of reading Harriet Jacobs's text while writing her own. Note that Hecimovich, in *The Life and Times of Hannah Crafts*, also observes the influence of *Uncle Tom's Cabin* on *The Bondwoman's Narrative*.

23. Crafts, *The Bondwoman's Narrative*, 237–38.

24. Aljoe, *Creole Testimonies*, 21.

25. Hartman, "Venus in Two Acts," 12.

26. Aljoe, *Creole Testimonies*, 21, 13.

27. Hartman, "Venus in Two Acts," 12.

28. Hartman "Venus in Two Acts," 11.

29. Brown, "Speech by William Wells Brown," 339.

30. Crafts, *The Bondwoman's Narrative*, 44.

31. Crafts, *The Bondwoman's Narrative*, 149.

32. Crafts, *The Bondwoman's Narrative*, 152.

33. Acting on information first asserted by Dorothy Porter, the manuscript's previous owner, Gates confirmed this identification in the introduction to the 2002 edition of *The Bondwoman's Narrative*, xlii–lvi. In *The Life and Times of Hannah Crafts*, Gregg Hecimovich makes the same claim.

34. See, for example, "The Case of Colonel Wheeler's Slaves. Decision of Judge Kane," *The National Era* (Washington, DC), October 18, 1855; "The Wheeler Slave Case. Passmore Williamson Committed for Contempt," *Frederick Douglass's Paper* (Rochester, NY), August 3, 1855.

35. Crafts, *The Bondwoman's Narrative*, 149.

36. For a detailed discussion of Jane Johnson's biography and life after her escape, see Hecimovich, *The Life and Times of Hannah Crafts*.

37. *United States ex rel. Wheeler v. Williamson*, 28 F. Cas. 682 (E.D. Pa. 1855); *United States ex rel. Wheeler v. Williamson*, 28 F. Cas. 686 (E.D. Pa. 1855). Hereafter, citations to the former appear as "*U.S. v. Williamson* [Cas. 682]," whereas citations to the latter appear as "*U.S. v. Williamson* [Cas. 686]."

38. *U.S. v. Williamson* [Cas. 682], 686.

39. Lapsansky, "The Liberation of Jane Johnson." The Pennsylvania Supreme Court affirmed Judge Kane's decision in September 1855; Judge Kane finally relented and freed Williamson in November 1855, following months of motions and arguments.

40. *Narrative of Facts in the Case of Passmore Williamson*, 13, 15–16. William Still and a handful of African American codefendants faced charges for riot, assault, and battery, among other things (16).

41. *Prigg v. Pennsylvania*, 41 US 539 (1842).

42. DeLombard, *Slavery on Trial*, 7.

194 Notes to Chapter Four

43. See, for example, "The Case of Colonel Wheeler's Slaves. Decision of Judge Kane," *The National Era* (Washington, DC), October 18, 1855; "The Wheeler Slave Case. Passmore Williamson Committed for Contempt," *Frederick Douglass's Paper* (Rochester, NY), August 3, 1855.

44. Today, court decisions are typically "reported" by courts in official "case reporters." The use of case reporters began at different times in different jurisdictions. Pennsylvania, where the Johnson litigations occurred, presents an example of how case reporting varied among different courts. For instance, the Passmore Williamson litigation took place in federal court, in the Eastern District of Pennsylvania. As a federal court case, the proceedings of the Williamson litigation were reported in *Federal Cases*, a publication covering cases as early as 1779. However, the Still trial took place in the Philadelphia Court of Quarter Sessions, a local Pennsylvania court. Case reporters for Pennsylvania district and county reports did not begin publishing official reporters until decades later. Therefore, the Still trial materials are not part of an official reporter, and this project looks instead to accounts of the Still litigation from newspapers and other archival sources from 1855.

45. *U.S. v. Williamson* [Cas. 686], 687.

46. Here, we might identify a point of comparison with Carla L. Peterson's theorization of Sojourner Truth's carte de visite as a textual extension of herself that both suggested and subverted commodification. See *"Doers of the Word,"* 24–55. The textual forms of erasure and substitution in Jane Johnson's X are also reminiscent of the strikethrough in relation to Williams/Thornton/Wilkins in chapter 3.

47. In fact, and owing most likely to a fear of recapture, Johnson submitted the affidavit through an appearance of her two attorneys, Joseph B. Townsend and John M. Read. See *Case of Passmore Williamson*, 164.

48. *U.S. v. Williamson* [Cas. 686], 687.

49. Hartman, *Scenes of Subjection*, 109.

50. Ironically, the appearance of the name "Jane" by itself in the novel in no way disguises Johnson's identity from a reader who has read any of the newspaper coverage of Johnson.

51. *U.S. v. Williamson* [Cas. 686], 694.

52. *U.S. v. Williamson* [Cas. 686], 694.

53. *U.S. v. Williamson* [Cas. 686], 687.

54. *Narrative of Facts in the Case of Passmore Williamson*, 16, 14. Although the legal record of the Still trial is somewhat muddy, there are several accounts of Johnson's appearance and testimony, all of which substantially corroborate each other. Still devotes an entire section of *The Underground Railroad* (1872) to the Johnson escape and subsequent trials. His account of her appearance at the trial contains a lengthy reproduction of her testimony. See Still, *The Underground Railroad*, 94–95. What is unusual about Still's account, however, is an indication at the conclusion of Johnson's testimony that she signed her mark (95). This may be best explained by this prefatory comment by Still: "Substantially, her testimony on this occasion, was in keeping with the subjoined affidavit, which was as follows" (94). This remark suggests that Johnson may have submitted an affidavit in addition to her oral testimony, or it may refer simply to the affidavit she submitted in the Williamson litigation. Johnson's in-court appearance at the Still trial took place on August 29, 1855, whereas she submitted her written affidavit in the Williamson litigation in October 1855.

55. Still, *The Underground Railroad*, 94.

56. *Narrative of Facts in the Case of Passmore Williamson*, 14.

57. Still, *The Underground Railroad*, 94.

58. Crafts, *The Bondwoman's Narrative*, 5.

59. Still, *The Underground Railroad*, 94.

60. *Narrative of Facts in the Case of Passmore Williamson*, 14.

61. *Narrative of Facts in the Case of Passmore Williamson*, 15. Johnson's testimony here appears to use a strategy of negative proofs, where she employs a double negative in her first sentence and then alternates sentence construction between positive and negative verbs.

62. Note the resonances here with Turner's and Langston's use of "confession" in chapter 2 to offer affirmative defenses rather than to admit guilt.

63. Still, *The Underground Railroad*, 94.

64. Crafts, *The Bondwoman's Narrative*, 149. In *The Bondwoman's Narrative*, Mrs. Wheeler dictates a letter to the man who has inherited Hannah following the slave trader's untimely death. In that letter, which Hannah is forced to transcribe, Mrs. Wheeler describes her as "very homely, and what was worse a bigot in religion; that [she] wept and shuddered at the idea of being transferred to his family" (153). These assertions, all of which are patently untrue, make Hannah deeply uncomfortable; Mrs. Wheeler employs these machinations as a means of securing a lower purchase price.

65. Crafts, *The Bondwoman's Narrative*, 150–51.

66. Hartman, "Venus in Two Acts," 11.

67. Still, *The Underground Railroad*, 94.

68. "Wheeler Slave Case: Opening of the Defence," *The Daily Times* (Philadelphia), August 31, 1855, from the private collection of John Gordan.

69. Crafts, *The Bondwoman's Narrative*, 151.

70. Crafts, *The Bondwoman's Narrative*, 153.

71. Crafts, *The Bondwoman's Narrative*, 176.

72. Crafts, *The Bondwoman's Narrative*, 177–78.

73. This moment also recalls the case of Margaret Garner, the enslaved woman who in 1856 killed her own baby rather than surrender her daughter to an enslaver. Depending on when Crafts penned this part of the novel, it is possible that she would have heard about this case.

74. Still, *The Underground Railroad*, 95.

75. Crafts, *The Bondwoman's Narrative*, 178. It is manifestly unclear *who* the narrator is in this moment. I read the passage as though it proceeds from the novel's main narrator, Hannah; while Lizzy could plausibly be the narrator in this section, the diction and style hew more closely to the literary personality of Hannah. In the 2002 edition of the novel, Gates inserts a double quotation mark in brackets at the conclusion of this passage, presumably considering it part of Lizzy's narration. In the context of the chapter, however, it makes little sense for this interruption to occur within Lizzy's storytelling. First, the preceding chapter concludes with Hannah and Lizzy congregating behind stacked lumber to "be effectually screened from observation" (171). The two women settle in so that Lizzy may relate this story to Hannah alone. It makes little sense for Lizzy to conclude her story by addressing the President, senators, and religious ministers. It is far more plausible, on the other hand, to read this final section as Hannah's commentary on the story she has just heard.

76. Crafts, *The Bondwoman's Narrative*, 178.
77. Crafts, *The Bondwoman's Narrative*, 178.
78. Crafts, *The Bondwoman's Narrative*, 201.

Coda

1. John Russwurm and Samuel Cornish ("The Editors"), "To Our Patrons," *Freedom's Journal* (New York), March 16, 1827.
2. One obvious counterexample here is Jennifer Nash's provocation to let go of intersectionality in order to think beyond defensiveness. *Black Feminism Reimagined*, 3.
3. Goffe, "Stolen Life, Stolen Time," 110.
4. Goffe, "Stolen Life, Stolen Time," 112–14.
5. Mann, "Black Insecurity at the End of the World," 14.
6. Mann, "Pessimistic Futurism," 62.
7. Mann, "Pessimistic Futurism," 64.
8. Goffe, "Stolen Life, Stolen Time," 110.
9. Goffe, "Stolen Life, Stolen Time," 112.
10. Goffe, "Stolen Life, Stolen Time," 127.
11. Kwartang, "The Sankofa Bird and Reflection," 60.
12. Dery, "Black to the Future," 180. Note that Nnedi Okorafor coined the distinct term "africanfuturism" in 2019 to refer specifically to work that is "specifically and more directly rooted in African culture, history, mythology, and point-of-view as it then branches into the Black Diaspora and [that] does not privilege or center the West." Okorafor, "Africanfuturism Defined," October 2019, Nnedi's Wahala Zone Blog, http://nnedi.blogspot.com/2019/10/africanfuturism-defined.html.
13. Womack, *Afrofuturism*, 100–101.
14. Capers, "Afrofuturism, Critical Race Theory, and Policing in the Year 2044," 14.
15. Capers, "Afrofuturism, Critical Race Theory, and Policing in the Year 2044," 16.
16. There is a similar issue that arises in gender studies when discussing performances of trans identity in the nineteenth century; this specific language around gender identity was not then available for nineteenth-century subjects to claim, and while there is no doubt that queer and trans people have existed for as long as people have existed, there is a potential violence in applying that categorical identifier to people who would not have had access to that language for it. In *Black on Both Sides*, C. Riley Snorton attends to this problem of language both by discussing "transness," a term that modifies rather than fixes, and by thinking about Black transness in particular as a "movement with no clear origin and no point of arrival" (2).
17. Capers, "Afrofuturism, Critical Race Theory, and Policing in the Year 2044," 7.
18. Ross, *Slavery, Surveillance, and Genre*, 102.
19. Rusert, *Fugitive Science*, 153.
20. Harris and Carbado, "Loot or Find? Fact or Frame," 91.
21. Harris and Carbado, "Loot or Find? Fact or Frame," 90.
22. Harris and Carbado, "Loot or Find? Fact or Frame," 97.
23. Cover, "Nomos and Narrative," 4–5.
24. Adebisi, "Black/African Science Fiction," 27 (citing Carl Death, "Climate Fiction").

25. Lorde, "The Master's Tools Will Never Dismantle the Master's House," 110–13.
26. See Porter, "Africana Legal Studies," 249–322.
27. Porter, "Africana Legal Studies," 273.
28. Porter, "Africana Legal Studies," 276.
29. Nash, *Black Feminism Reimagined*, 113–14.
30. See Mann, "Black Insecurity at the End of the World"; and Browne, *Dark Matters*.
31. Sharpe, *In the Wake*, 68–101.
32. McKoy, *The History of the Carolina Twins*; Morrison, *Beloved*; Brodber, *Louisiana*; and Okorafor, "Hello, Moto."
33. Owens, *Consent in the Presence of Force*, 25.
34. Owens, *Consent in the Presence of Force*, 19.
35. de la Fuente and Gross, *Becoming Free, Becoming Black*, 4.
36. Combahee River Collective, *The Combahee River Collective Statement*.
37. Roberts, *Freedom as Marronage*.
38. Porter, "Africana Legal Studies," 286.
39. Porter, "Africana Legal Studies," 287–304.
40. Williams, *The Alchemy of Race and Rights*, 164. Notice also the resonance with Laura Edwards's assertion that, specifically in the case of nineteenth-century North Carolina, "rights did not always promote equality." "The Forgotten Legal World of Thomas Ruffin," 860.
41. Williams, *The Alchemy of Race and Rights*, 165.
42. Nash, *Black Feminism Reimagined*, 125.
43. Hannah Murdock, "This River Was Just Granted Legal Personhood: Here's Why," *Deseret News* (Salt Lake City, UT), August 8, 2023.
44. Quashie, *Black Aliveness*, 1.

Bibliography

Primary Sources

ARCHIVES

Philadelphia
   Library Company of Philadelphia
Washington, DC
   Howard University
      Mary Ann Shadd Cary Collection

PERIODICALS

ABA Journal (Chicago)
Alabama Intelligencer and State Rights Expositor (Tuscaloosa, AL)
Colored American (New York)
Daily Times (Philadelphia)
Deseret News (Salt Lake City)
Douglass' Monthly (Rochester, NY)
Emancipator (New York)
Frederick Douglass' Paper (Rochester, NY)
Freedom's Journal (New York)
Liberator (Boston)
National Era (Washington, DC)
New York Times
North Star (Rochester, NY)
Provincial Freeman (Chatham, Canada West)
Statesman & Patriot (Milledgeville, GA)
Washington City Paper (Washington, DC)

BOOKS AND OTHER PUBLISHED SOURCES

Blackstone, William. *Commentaries on the Laws of England in Four Books*. Oxford, UK: Printed at the Clarendon Press, 1765–69. http://avalon.law.yale.edu/18th_century/blackstone_bk4ch23.asp.

Brodber, Erna. *Louisiana*. Jackson: University Press of Mississippi, 1994.

Brontë, Charlotte. *Jane Eyre*. 1847. New York: Penguin, 2006.

Brown, William Wells. *Clotel; or, the President's Daughter: A Narrative of Slave Life in the United States*. London: Partridge and Oakey, 1853. Reprinted with introduction by M. Giulia Fabi. New York: Penguin Classics, 2003.

———. "Speech by William Wells Brown Delivered at the City Assembly Rooms, New York, New York, 8 May 1856." In *The United States, 1847–1858*, edited by C. Peter Ripley and Roy E. Finkenbine, 339–45. Vol. 4 of *The Black Abolitionist Papers*. Chapel Hill: University of North Carolina Press, 2015.

Butler, Octavia. *Dawn*. New York: Warner, 1987.

Case of Passmore Williamson: Report of the Proceedings on the Writ of Habeas Corpus, Issued by the Hon. John K. Kane, Judge of the District Court of the United States for the Eastern District of Pennsylvania, in the Case of the United States of America ex rel. John H. Wheeler vs. Passmore Williamson, Including the Several Opinions Delivered, and the Arguments of

Counsel. Philadelphia: Uriah Hunt and Son, 1856. Library of Congress. Accessed September 10, 2024. https://loc.gov/item/44018349/.
Combahee River Collective. *Combahee River Collective Statement.* 1977. https://americanstudies.yale.edu/sites/default/files/files/Keyword%20Coalition_Readings.pdf.
Craft, Ellen, and William Craft. *Running a Thousand Miles for Freedom, or, the Escape of William and Ellen Craft from Slavery.* London: William Tweedie, 1860. https://docsouth.unc.edu/neh/craft/craft.html.
Crafts, Hannah. *The Bondwoman's Narrative.* Edited by Henry Louis Gates Jr. New York: Grand Central Publishing, 2002.
Cugoano, Ottobah. *Narrative of the Enslavement of Ottobah Cugoano, a Native of Africa: Published by Himself, in the Year 1787.* London: Hatchard and Co., 1825.
Delany, Martin R. *Blake, or the Huts of America.* First published 1859–1862. Edited by Jerome McGann. Cambridge, MA: Harvard University Press, 2017.
Dickens, Charles. *Bleak House.* 1852. Reprint, London: Penguin Books, 2003.
Douglass, Frederick. *Narrative of the Life of Frederick Douglass, an American Slave.* Boston: Anti-Slavery Office, 1845.
Equiano, Olaudah. *The Interesting Narrative of Olaudah Equiano, or Gustavus Vassa, the African.* London: The Author, 1789.
Jacobs, Harriet. *Incidents in the Life of a Slave Girl.* 2nd ed. Edited by Frances Smith Foster and Richard Yarborough. New York: W. W. Norton and Company, 2019. First published 1861 by the author (Boston).
Jefferson, Thomas. *Notes on the State of Virginia.* Philadelphia: Pritchard and Hall, 1787.
Langston, Charles. "Charles Langston's Speech at the Cuyahoga Courthouse." May 12, 1859. *The Oberlin-Wellington 150th Anniversary, 1858–2008.* Electronic Oberlin Group, Oberlin College. 2008. https://www2.oberlin.edu/external/EOG/Oberlin-Wellington_Rescue/c._langston_speech.htm.
Lapsansky, Phil. "The Liberation of Jane Johnson." *The Library Company of Philadelphia.* Accessed September 10, 2024. http://librarycompany.org/JaneJohnson/.
Law & Order. Created by Dick Wolf. Wolf Entertainment Universal Television, 1990–2010; 2021–22.
McKoy, Millie-Christine. *The History of the Carolina Twins: "Told in Their Own Peculiar Way" by "One of Them."* Buffalo, NY: Buffalo Courier Printing House, 18—?. Documenting the American South. University of North Carolina Library, University of North Carolina at Chapel Hill. Accessed September 10, 2024. https://docsouth.unc.edu/neh/millie-christine/millie-christine.html.
Minutes of the State Convention of Coloured Citizens of Pennsylvania, Convened at Harrisburg, December 13th and 14th, 1848. Philadelphia: Merrihew and Thompson, 1849. https://omeka.coloredconventions.org/items/show/241.
Morrison, Toni. *Beloved.* New York: Vintage Books, 1987.
Narrative of Facts in the Case of Passmore Williamson. Philadelphia: Pennsylvania Anti-Slavery Society, 1855. Library of Congress African American Pamphlets Collection. Accessed December 19, 2020. www.loc.gov/item/10034487/.
Okorafor, Nnedi. "Hello, Moto." 2011. www.tor.com/2011/11/02/hello-moto/.
Powell, Thomas W. *The Law of Appellate Proceedings: In Relation to Review, Error, Appeal, and Other Reliefs Upon Final Judgments.* Philadelphia: T & J. W. Johnson, 1873.

Prince, Mary. *The History of Mary Prince, a West Indian Slave. Related by Herself.* London: F. Westley and A. H. Davis, 1831.

Purvis, Robert, et al. *Appeal of Forty Thousand Citizens, Threatened with Disfranchisement, to the People of Pennsylvania.* Philadelphia: Merrihew and Gunn, 1838.

Ripley, C. Peter, ed. *The United States, 1847–1858.* Vol. 4 of *The Black Abolitionist Papers.* Chapel Hill: University of North Carolina Press, 2015.

S. "Theresa, _____ a Haytien Tale." 1828. Reprinted and edited by Frances Smith Foster in "Forgotten Manuscripts: How Do You Solve a Problem Like Theresa?" *African American Review* 40, no. 4 (2006): 639–45.

Séjour, Victor. "The Mulatto." 1837. Translated by Philip Barnard, 1995. In *Norton Anthology of African American Literature, Vol. 1*, edited by Henry Louis Gates Jr., Valerie Smith, et al., 298–309. New York: W. W. Norton, 2014.

Shepherd, Samuel, and William Waller Hening. *The Statutes at Large of Virginia, From October Session 1792, to December Session 1806, Inclusive, In Three Volumes (New Series) Being a Continuation of Hening.* Richmond, VA: S. Shepherd, 1835.

Smith, Venture. *A Narrative of the Life and Adventures of Venture, a Native of Africa: But Resident Above Sixty Years in the United States of America.* New London, CT: C. Holt, 1798.

Still, William. *The Underground Railroad: A Record of Facts, Authentic Narratives, Letters, &c., Narrating the Hardships, Hairbreadth Escapes and Death Struggles of the Slaves in Their Efforts for Freedom.* Philadelphia: Porter and Coates, 1872.

Stowe, Harriet Beecher. *Uncle Tom's Cabin or, Life Among the Lowly.* Boston: John P. Jewett & Company, 1852. Edited with introduction by Ann Douglas. New York: Penguin, 1986.

Styron, William. *The Confessions of Nat Turner.* New York: Vintage International, 1967.

Tragle, Henry Irving, ed. *The Southampton Slave Revolt of 1831: A Compilation of Source Material.* Amherst: University of Massachusetts Press, 1971.

Turner, Nat. *The Confessions of Nat Turner.* Edited by Thomas Ruffin Gray. Baltimore: Lucas & Deaver, 1831.

The Wachowskis, dirs., *The Matrix.* Warner Brothers, 1999.

Walker, David. *Walker's Appeal, in Four Articles; Together with a Preamble, to the Coloured Citizens of the World, But in Particular, and Very Expressly, to Those of the United States of America. Written in Boston, State of Massachusetts, September 28, 1829.* 1830. 3rd ed. In *David Walker's Appeal to the Coloured Citizens of the World*, edited by Peter P. Hinks. University Park: Pennsylvania State University Press, 2000.

Williams, James. *Narrative of James Williams, an American Slave, Who Was for Several Years a Driver on a Cotton Plantation in Alabama.* Edited by Hank Trent. Baton Rouge: Louisiana State University Press, 2013. First published 1838 by American Anti-Slavery Society (New York).

Secondary Sources

Adebisi, Foluke. "Black/African Science Fiction and the Quest for Racial Justice Through Legal Knowledge: How Can We Unsettle Euro-modern Time and Temprorality in Our Teaching?" *Law, Technology and Humans* 4, no. 2 (2022): 24–37.

Akinyela, Makungu M. "Battling the Serpent: Nat Turner, Africanized Christianity, and a Black Ethos." *Journal of Black Studies* 33, no. 3 (2003): 255–80.

Albanese, Mary Grace. "Caribbean Visions: Revolutionary Mysticism in 'Theresa: A Haytien Tale.'" *ESQ: A Journal of Nineteenth-Century American Literature and Culture* 62, no. 4 (2016): 569–609.

Aljoe, Nicole N. *Creole Testimonies: Slave Narratives from the British West Indies, 1709–1838*. New York: Palgrave MacMillan, 2012.

Andrews, William L., ed. *African American Autobiography: A Collection of Critical Essays*. Englewood Cliffs, NJ: Prentice Hall, 1993.

Andrews, William L. *To Tell a Free Story: The First Century of Afro-American Autobiography, 1760–1865*. Urbana: University of Illinois Press, 1986.

Anker, Elizabeth S., and Bernadette Meyler, eds. *New Directions in Law and Literature*. Oxford, UK: Oxford University Press, 2017.

Apap, Chris. "'Let No Man of Us Budge One Step': David Walker and the Rhetoric of African American Emplacement." *Early American Literature* 46, no. 2 (2011): 319–50.

Barrett, Lindon. "Self-Knowledge, Law, and African American Autobiography: Lucy A. Delaney's *From the Darkness Cometh the Light*." In *Conditions of the Present: Selected Essays*, edited by Janet Neary, 139–64. Durham, NC: Duke University Press, 2018.

Barter, Faith. "Encrypted Citations: *The Bondwoman's Narrative* and the Case of Jane Johnson." *MELUS* 46, no. 1 (2021): 51–74.

Berlant Lauren. *The Queen of America Goes to Washington City: Essays on Sex and Citizenship*. Durham, NC: Duke University Press, 1997.

Best, Stephen M. *The Fugitive's Properties: Law and the Poetics of Possession*. Chicago: University of Chicago Press, 2004.

Bhabha, Homi. *The Location of Culture*. New York: Routledge, 1994.

Bilder, Mary Sarah. "The Origin of the Appeal in America." *Hastings Law Journal* 48, no. 5 (1997): 913–68.

Brooks, Daphne. *Bodies in Dissent: Spectacular Performances of Race and Freedom, 1850–1910*. Durham, NC: Duke University Press, 2006.

Brooks, Peter. *Troubling Confessions: Speaking Guilt in Law and Literature*. Chicago: University of Chicago Press, 2000.

Brophy, Alfred. "The Nat Turner Trials." *North Carolina Law Review* 91, no. 5 (2013): 1817–80.

Brown, Christopher Michael. "Seditious Prose: Patriots and Traitors in the African American Literary Tradition." *Law and Literature* 24, no. 2 (2012): 174–212.

Browne, Simone. *Dark Matters: On the Surveillance of Blackness*. Durham, NC: Duke University Press, 2015.

Bryen, Ari Z. *Violence in Roman Egypt: A Study in Legal Interpretation*. Philadelphia: University of Pennsylvania Press, 2013.

Capers, I. Bennett. "Afrofuturism, Critical Race Theory, and Policing in the Year 2044." *New York University Law Review* 94, no. 1 (2019): 1–60.

Carby, Hazel V. *Reconstructing Womanhood: The Emergence of the Afro-American Woman Novelist*. New York: Oxford University Press, 1987.

Chakkalakal, Tess. *Novel Bondage: Slavery, Marriage, and Freedom in Nineteenth-Century America*. Champaign: University of Illinois Press, 2011.

Cover, Robert. *Justice Accused: Antislavery and the Judicial Process*. New Haven, CT: Yale University Press, 1975.

———. "Nomos and Narrative." *Harvard Law Review* 97, no. 4 (1983–84): 4–68.

———. "Violence and the Word." *Yale Law Journal* 95 (1985–86): 1601–29.

Crenshaw, Kimberlé. "Demarginalizing the Intersection of Race and Sex: A Black Feminist Critique of Antidiscrimination Doctrine, Feminist Theory and Antiracist Politics." *University of Chicago Legal Forum* 1989, no. 1 (1989): 139–67.

Davis, Angela. "Reflections on the Black Woman's Role in the Community of Slaves." *Massachusetts Review* 13, no. 1/2 (1971): 81–100.

Davis, Charles T., and Henry Louis Gates Jr., eds. *The Slave's Narrative*. New York: Oxford University Press, 1985.

Dayan, Colin. *The Law Is a White Dog: How Legal Rituals Make and Unmake Persons*. Princeton, NJ: Princeton University Press, 2011.

Death, Carl. "Climate Fiction, Climate Theory: Decolonising Imaginations of Global Futures." *Millennium: Journal of International Studies* 50, no. 2 (2022): 430–55.

de la Fuente, Alejandro, and Ariela J. Gross. *Becoming Free, Becoming Black: Race, Freedom, and Law in Cuba, Virginia, and Louisiana*. Cambridge, UK: Cambridge University Press, 2020.

DeLombard, Jeannine. *In the Shadow of the Gallows: Race, Crime, and American Civic Identity*. Philadelphia: University of Pennsylvania Press, 2012.

———. *Slavery on Trial: Law, Abolitionism, and Print Culture*. Chapel Hill: University of North Carolina Press, 2007.

Derrida, Jacques. *Of Grammatology*. Corrected ed. Translated by Gaytri Chakravorty Spivak. Baltimore, MD: Johns Hopkins University Press, 1976.

Dery, Mark. "Black to the Future: Interviews with Samuel R. Delany, Greg Tate, and Tricia Rose." In *Flame Wars: The Discourse of Cyberculture*, edited by Mark Dery, 179–222. Durham, NC: Duke University Press, 1994.

De Stefano, Jason. "*Persona Ficta*: Frederick Douglass." *ELH* 85, no. 3 (2018): 775–800.

Dinius, Marcy. "'Look!! Look!! At This!!!!': The Radical Typography of David Walker's *Appeal*." *PMLA* 126, no. 1 (2011): 55–72.

Dorsett, Shaunnagh, and Shaun McVeigh. *Jurisdiction*. New York: Routledge, 2012.

Edwards, Laura F. "The Forgotten Legal World of Thomas Ruffin: The Power of Presentism in the History of Slave Law." *North Carolina Law Review* 87, no. 3 (2009): 855–900.

———. *The People and Their Peace: Legal Culture and the Transformation of Inequality in the Post-Revolutionary South*. Chapel Hill: University of North Carolina Press, 2009.

Foreman, P. Gabrielle. *Activist Sentiments: Reading Black Women in the Nineteenth Century*. Urbana: University of Illinois Press, 2009.

Foster, Frances Smith. "Resisting *Incidents*." In *Harriet Jacobs and Incidents in the Life of a Slave Girl: New Critical Essays*, edited by Deborah M. Garfield and Rafia Zafar, 57–75. New York: Cambridge University Press, 1996.

Fuentes, Marisa J. *Dispossessed Lives: Enslaved Women, Violence, and the Archive*. Philadelphia: University of Pennsylvania Press, 2016.

Gardner, Eric. *Unexpected Places: Relocating Nineteenth-Century African American Literature*. Jackson: University Press of Mississippi, 2009.

Gates, Henry Louis, Jr., and Hollis Robbins, eds. *In Search of Hannah Crafts: Critical Essays on The Bondwoman's Narrative.* New York: Basic Civitas Books, 2004.

Glymph, Thavolia. "'She Wears the Flag of Our Country': Women, Nation, and War." *The Journal of the Civil War Era* 12, no. 3 (2022): 305–20.

Goddu, Teresa. *Gothic America: Narrative, History, and Nation.* New York: Columbia University Press, 1997.

———. *Selling Antislavery: Abolition and Mass Media in Antebellum America.* Philadelphia: University of Pennsylvania Press, 2020.

Goffe, Tao Leigh. "Stolen Life, Stolen Time: Black Temporality, Speculation, and Racial Capitalism." *The South Atlantic Quarterly* 121, no. 1 (2022): 109–30.

Guthrie, Warren. "The Oberlin-Wellington Rescue Case, 1859." In *Antislavery and Disunion, 1858–1861: Studies in the Rhetoric of Compromise and Conflict,* edited by J. Jeffery Auer, 85–97. New York: Harper & Row Publishers, 1963.

Hack, Daniel. *Reaping Something New: African American Transformations of Victorian Literature.* Princeton, NJ: Princeton University Press, 2016.

Harney, Stefano, and Fred Moten. *The Undercommons: Fugitive Planning & Black Study.* Brooklyn, NY: Autonomedia, 2013.

Harris, Cheryl I., and Devon W. Carbado. "Loot or Find: Fact or Frame?" In *After the Storm: Black Intellectuals Explore the Meaning of Hurricane Katrina,* edited by David Dante Troutt, 87–110. New York: New Press, 2006.

Hartman, Saidiya V. *Scenes of Subjection: Terror, Slavery, and Self-Making in Nineteenth-Century America.* New York: Oxford University Press, 1997.

———. "Venus in Two Acts." *small axe* 26 (2008): 1–14.

Hartog, Hendrik. "Pigs and Positivism." *Wisconsin Law Review* 1985 (1985): 899–935.

Hecimovich, Gregg. *The Life and Times of Hannah Crafts: The True Story of The Bondwoman's Narrative.* New York: Ecco, 2023.

Heiniger, Abigail. *Jane Eyre's Fairytale Legacy at Home and Abroad: Constructions and Deconstructions of National Identity.* New York: Routledge, 2016.

Hine, Darlene Clark. "Rape and the Inner Lives of Black Women in the Middle West: Preliminary Thoughts on the Culture of Dissemblance." *Signs: Journal of Women in Culture and Society* 14, no. 4 (1989): 912–20.

Hinks, Peter. *To Awaken My Afflicted Brethren: David Walker and the Problem of Antebellum Slave Resistance.* University Park: Pennsylvania State University Press, 1996.

Hinks, Peter P., ed. *David Walker's Appeal to the Coloured Citizens of the World.* University Park: Pennsylvania State University Press, 2000.

Hoeflich, M. H. *Legal Publishing in Antebellum America.* New York: Cambridge University Press, 2010.

Holloway, Karla FC. *Legal Fictions: Constituting Race, Composing Literature.* Durham, NC: Duke University Press, 2014.

Hubbard, Dolan. "David Walker's *Appeal* and the American Puritan Jeremiadic Tradition." *Centennial Review* 30, no. 3 (1986): 331–46.

Hyde, Carrie. *Civic Longing: The Speculative Origins of U.S. Citizenship.* Cambridge, MA: Harvard University Press, 2018.

Jones, Martha S. *Birthright Citizens: A History of Race and Rights in Antebellum America.* Cambridge, UK: Cambridge University Press, 2018.

Kennington, Kelly M. *In the Shadow of Dred Scott: St. Louis Freedom Suits and the Legal Culture of Slavery in Antebellum America*. Athens: University of Georgia Press, 2017.

Kwartang, Appiah K. "The Sankofa Bird and Reflection." *Journal of Applied Christian Leadership* 10, no. 1 (2018): 60–69.

Lamming, George. *Sovereignty of the Imagination: Conversations III*. St. Martin, Caribbean: House of Nehesi Publishers, 2009.

Levine, Caroline. *Forms: Whole, Rhythm, Hierarchy, Network*. Princeton, NJ: Princeton University Press, 2015.

Lorde, Audre. "The Master's Tools Will Never Dismantle the Master's House." In *Sister Outsider: Essays & Speeches by Audre Lorde*, 110–13. 1984. Reprint, New York: Ten Speed Press, 2007.

Lubet, Steven. "The Oberlin Fugitive Slave Rescue: A Victory for the Higher Law." *Northwestern University School of Law Scholarly Commons, Faculty Working Papers*, paper 22, 2011. http://scholarlycommons.law.northwestern.edu/facultyworkingpapers/22.

Mann, Justin. "Black Insecurity at the End of the World." *MELUS* 46, no. 3 (2021): 1–21.

———. "Figuring Black Lives." *American Quarterly* 74, no. 3 (2022): 635–40.

———. "Pessimistic Futurism: Survival and Reproduction in Octavia Butler's *Dawn*." *Feminist Theory* 19, no. 1 (2018): 61–76.

Marshall, Bridget M. *The Transatlantic Gothic Novel and the Law, 1790–1860*. Farnham, UK: Ashgate Publishing, 2011.

M'Baye, Babacar. "Radical and Nationalist Resistance in David Walker's and Frederick Douglass's Antislavery Narratives." In *Critical Insights: The Literature of Protest*, edited by Kimberly Drake, 113–43. New York: Salem Press, 2013.

McBride, Dwight A. *Impossible Witnesses: Truth, Abolitionism, and Slave Testimony*. New York: New York University Press, 2001.

McDowell, Deborah E. "In the First Place: Making Frederick Douglass and the Afro-American Narrative Tradition." In *African American Autobiography: A Collection of Critical Essays*, edited by William L. Andrews, 36–58. Englewood Cliffs, NJ: Prentice Hall, 1993.

McKittrick, Katherine. *Demonic Grounds: Black Women and the Cartographies of Struggle*. Minneapolis: University of Minnesota Press, 2006.

McMillan, Uri. *Embodied Avatars: Genealogies of Black Feminist Art and Performance*. New York: New York University Press, 2015.

Mitchell, Koritha. *From Slave Cabins to the White House: Homemade Citizenship in African American Culture*. Urbana: University of Illinois Press, 2020.

Moody, Joycelyn. *Sentimental Confessions: Spiritual Narratives of Nineteenth-Century African American Women*. Athens: University of Georgia Press, 2001.

Nash, Jennifer C. *Black Feminism Reimagined: After Intersectionality*. Durham, NC: Duke University Press, 2019.

Nyong'o, Tavia. *The Amalgamation Waltz: Race, Performance, and the Ruses of Memory*. Minneapolis: University of Minnesota Press, 2009.

———. "Race, Reenactment, and the 'Natural Born Citizen.'" In *Unsettled States: Nineteenth-Century American Literary Studies*, edited by Dana Luciano and Ivy G. Wilson, 76–102. New York: New York University Press, 2014.

Owens, Emily A. *Consent in the Presence of Force: Sexual Violence and Black Women's Survival in Antebellum New Orleans*. Chapel Hill: University of North Carolina Press, 2023.

Pacquet, Sandra Pouchet. *Caribbean Autobiography: Cultural Identity and Self-Representation*. Madison: University of Wisconsin Press, 2002.

Pelletier, Kevin. *Apocalyptic Sentimentalism: Love and Fear in US Antebellum Literature*. Athens: University of Georgia Press, 2015.

Penningroth, Dylan C. "African American Divorce in Virginia and Washington, D.C., 1865–1930." *Journal of Family History* 33, no. 1 (2008): 21–35.

———. "Law as Redemption: A Historical Comparison of the Ways Marginalized People Use Courts." *Law & Social Inquiry* 40, no. 3 (Summer 2015): 793–96.

Perry, Imani. *Vexy Thing: On Gender and Liberation*. Durham, NC: Duke University Press, 2018.

Peterson, Carla L. *"Doers of the Word": African-American Women Speakers & Writers in the North (1830–1880)*. New York: Oxford University Press, 1995.

Philip, M. NourbeSe. *Zong!* Toronto: Mercury Press, 2008.

Pinto, Samantha. *Infamous Bodies: Early Black Women's Celebrity and the Afterlives of Rights*. Durham, NC: Duke University Press, 2020.

Polley, Diana Hope. *Echoes of Emerson: Rethinking Realism in Twain, James, Wharton, and Cather*. Tuscaloosa: University of Alabama Press, 2017.

Porter, Angi. "Africana Legal Studies: A New Theoretical Approach to Law & Protocol." *Michigan Journal of Race and Law* 27 (2022): 249–322.

Quashie, Kevin. *Black Aliveness, or a Poetics of Being*. Durham, NC: Duke University Press, 2021.

———. *The Sovereignty of Quiet: Beyond Resistance in Black Culture*. New Brunswick, NJ: Rutgers University Press, 2012.

Reichman, Ravit. "Law's Affective Thickets." In *New Directions in Law and Literature*, edited by Elizabeth S. Anker and Bernadette Meyler, 109–22. New York: Oxford University Press, 2017.

Richards, Jake Subryan. "The Adjudication of Slave Ship Captures, Coercive Intervention, and Value Exchange in Comparative Atlantic Perspective, ca. 1839–1870." *Comparative Studies in Society & History* 62, no. 4 (2020): 836–67.

Roach, Shoniqua. "Black Sex in the Quiet." *differences* 30, no. 1 (2019): 126–47.

———. "(Re)turning to 'Rape and the Inner Lives of Black Women': A Black Feminist Forum on the Culture of Dissemblance." *Signs: Journal of Women in Culture and Society* 45, no. 3 (2020): 515–19.

Roane, J. T. "Plotting the Black Commons." *Souls: A Critical Journal of Black Politics, Culture, and Society* 20, no. 3 (2018): 239–66.

Roberts, Neil. *Freedom as Marronage*. Chicago: University of Chicago Press, 2015.

Ross, Kelly. *Slavery, Surveillance, and Genre in Antebellum United States Literature*. New York: Oxford University Press, 2022.

Ross, Rosetta E. *Witnessing & Testifying: Black Women, Religion, and Civil Rights*. Minneapolis, MN: Fortress Press, 2003.

Rusert, Britt. *Fugitive Science: Empiricism and Freedom in Early African American Culture*. New York: New York University Press, 2017.

Samuels, Shirley. "Introduction." In *The Culture of Sentiment: Race, Gender, and Sentimentality in Nineteenth-Century America*, 3–8. New York: Oxford University Press, 1992.

Sandler, Matt. *The Black Romantic Revolution: Abolitionist Poets at the End of Slavery*. New York: Verso Books, 2020.
Santamarina, Xiomara. "Fugitive Slave, Fugitive Novelist: The *Narrative of James Williams* (1838)." *American Literary History* 31, no. 1 (2019): 24–46.
Sharfstein, Daniel. *The Invisible Line: A Secret History of Race in America*. New York: Penguin Press, 2011.
Sharpe, Christina. *In the Wake: On Blackness and Being*. Durham, NC: Duke University Press, 2016.
Shipherd, Jacob R., Ralph Plumb, and Henry E. Peck. *History of the Oberlin-Wellington Rescue*. Boston: J. P. Jewett and Co., 1859.
Simard, Justin. "Slavery's Legalism: Lawyers and the Commercial Routine of Slavery." *Law & History Review* 37, no. 2 (2019): 571–603.
Sinche, Bryan. *Published by the Author: Self-Publication in Nineteenth-Century African American Literature*. Chapel Hill: University of North Carolina Press, 2024.
Smith, Caleb. *The Oracle and the Curse: A Poetics of Justice from the Revolution to the Civil War*. Cambridge, MA: Harvard University Press, 2013.
Smith, Valerie. *Self-Discovery and Authority in Afro-American Narrative*. Cambridge, MA: Harvard University Press, 1987.
Snorton, C. Riley. *Black on Both Sides: A Racial History of Trans Identity*. Minneapolis: University of Minnesota Press, 2017.
Soares, Rebecca. "Literary Graftings: Hannah Crafts's *The Bondwoman's Narrative* and the Nineteenth-Century Transatlantic Reader." *Victorian Periodicals Review* 44, no. 1 (2011): 1–23.
Spillers, Hortense J. "Mama's Baby, Papa's Maybe: An American Grammar Book." *Diacritics* 17, no. 2 (1987): 64–81.
Spires, Derrick R. *The Practice of Citizenship: Black Politics and Print Culture in the Early United States*. Philadelphia: University of Pennsylvania Press, 2019.
Spivak, Gayatri. "Translator's Preface." In Jacques Derrida, *Of Grammatology*, by Jacques Derrida, ix–lxxxviii. Corrected ed. Translated by Gaytri Chakravorty Spivak. Baltimore: Johns Hopkins University Press, 1976.
Stern, Simon. "Legal and Literary Fictions." In *New Directions in Law and Literature*, edited by Elizabeth S. Anker and Bernadette Meyler, 313–26. New York: Oxford University Press, 2017.
Sulzener, Brittany. "Night of Death, Morning of Rebirth: Maria W. Stewart's Apocalyptic Futures." *Nineteenth-Century Contexts* 41, no. 5 (2019): 623–30.
Sundquist, Eric J. *To Wake the Nations: Race in the Making of American Literature*. Cambridge, MA: Belknap Press of Harvard University Press, 1993.
Swank, Drew A. "The Pro Se Phenomenon." *Brigham Young University Journal of Public Law* 19, no. 2 (2005): 373–86.
Thomas, George C., III, and Richard A. Leo. *Confessions of Guilt: From Torture to Miranda and Beyond*. New York: Oxford University Press, 2012.
Tomlins, Christopher. *In the Matter of Nat Turner: A Speculative History*. Princeton, NJ: Princeton University Press, 2020.

Trent, Hank, ed. *Narrative of James Williams, an American Slave, Who Was for Several Years a Driver on a Cotton Plantation in Alabama*. Baton Rouge: Louisiana State University Press, 2013.

Warren, Calvin. *Ontological Terror: Blackness, Nihilism, and Emancipation*. Durham, NC: Duke University Press, 2018.

Welch, Kimberly M. *Black Litigants in the Antebellum South*. Chapel Hill: University of North Carolina Press, 2018.

Williams, Patricia J. *The Alchemy of Race and Rights: Diary of a Law Professor*. Cambridge, MA: Harvard University Press, 1991.

Windell, Maria A. *Transamerican Sentimentalism and Nineteenth-Century US Literary History*. New York: Oxford University Press, 2020.

Womack, Ytasha L. *Afrofuturism: The World of Black Sci-Fi and Fantasy Culture*. Chicago: Lawrence Hill Books, 2013.

Yellin, Jean Fagan. "Written by Herself: Harriet Jacobs' Slave Narrative." *American Literature* 53, no. 3 (1981): 479–86.

Zuck, Rochelle Raineri. *Divided Sovereignties: Race, Nationhood, and Citizenship in Nineteenth-Century America*. Athens: University of Georgia Press, 2016.

Index

abolitionism: abolitionist press, 153; American Anti-Slavery Society (AASS), 125; and appeal genre, 39; Passmore Williamson's imprisonment, 152–53, 156; white abolitionist mediation of freedom narratives, 3, 131, 146. *See also* antislavery movement; Black abolitionism; white racial attitudes
Adebisi, Foluke, 172–73, 174–75
advocacy. *See* pro se representation
African American Autobiography (Andrews), 7
African American literary studies, 7
African American literary tradition, 7, 31, 70–71, 167, 172. *See also* Black literary tradition
African spiritual traditions, 82–83; sankofa bird, 170
Afrofuturism, 38, 170–71, 176
Afrolegalism, 174–76
Akinyela, Makungu M., 82–83
Albanese, Mary Grace, 65–66
The Alchemy of Race and Rights (Williams), 30, 176–77
Aljoe, Nicole, 9, 11, 148
allocution statements, 74, 91
alternative histories, 47, 50, 168, 171; in *The Bondwoman's Narrative* (Crafts), 20, 37; and confession, 95; contrasted with retelling, 168; *Incidents in the Life of a Slave Girl* (Jacobs), 100, 119–22, 145
American Anti-Slavery Society (AASS), 125
Amistad revolt, 39–40, 183n7
Andrews, William, 7, 70
anti-colonialism, 168; Haitian Revolution, 28, 33, 36, 58, 63, 65–66, 169
anti-literacy laws, 5, 21, 46, 120

antislavery movement, 39, 125, 192n16; *Selling Antislavery* (Goddu), 183n8, 192n16. *See also* abolitionism
Anzaldúa, Gloria, 73
apocalypse, language of, 55–57, 63
Apocalyptic Sentimentalism (Pelletier), 55–56
appeal, 39–66; in abolitionist context, 39, 41; *Appeal to the Coloured Citizens of the World* (Walker), 47–56; "Appeal to the Friends of Liberty," 39–40; as check on abuse, 63; English common law, basis in, 44–45; history of, 44–46, 48; and judicial review, 42–44; legal definitions, 42, 46–47; as literary form, 44, 66; literary genre vs. legal form, 40, 42–43; in "The Mulatto" (Séjour), 58–64; Old Testament frameworks, 56–57; private appeals, 46; rhetorical frameworks, 39–41; and rights, seeking and protecting, 59; "sublime appeal," 48; temporal orientations, 168–69; in "Theresa, _____ a Haytien Tale" (S.), 64–66
Appeal to the Coloured Citizens of the World (Walker), 6, 28, 33, 41, 47–57, 160; adversarial components, 53–54; on citizenship, 49–50; distribution of, 49; form and purpose, 51–53; language, use of, 49; as petitionary appeal, 48–49; prophetic discourse, 55–56; retrospective framework, 50–51
"Appeal to the Friends of Liberty," *The Colored American* (newspaper), 39–40
authenticity of Black texts, 8, 9–10, 79, 125, 144, 146, 153
authorial identities: authorship, 122–23; and self-fragmentation, 123, 127–28; unmasking of Hannah Crafts, 144–45

author's methodology: chapter summaries, 32–38; on legal frameworks, 20–21, 24–25, 29–30, 31–32; on testimony, 15; on worldmaking, 26

autobiography: fictional, 122–23; as genre, 9–10; linked to law, 10–11; and self-publishing, 146. *See also* freedom narratives

avatars, embodied, 124, 128; Uri McMillan, 14, 112, 122, 124, 128

Barrett, Lindon, 9–10, 30
Beloved (Morrison), 175
Berlant, Lauren, 120
Best, Stephen, 94, 126
Bhabha, Homi, 54
Bilder, Mary Sarah, 44
Black abolitionism: Black testimony and freedom narratives, 5; *Douglass' Monthly* (abolitionist newspaper), 69; David Walker, 5, 28, 33, 41, 47–57, 120, 160, 164, 165. *See also* Cornish, Samuel; Douglass, Frederick; *Freedom's Journal* (newspaper); Russwurm, John
Black feminism, 9, 26, 174; Carby, Hazel, 7; Combahee River Collective, 175; Fuentes, Marisa, 5, 14, 128, 143, 148, 189n129; Hine, Darlene Clark, 96, 98; McDowell, Deborah, 7, 9; Nash, Jennifer, 3–4, 26, 174, 177; Owens, Emily, 14, 22, 41, 43, 70, 74, 109, 175; Perry, Imani, 21, 73–74, 108, 116–17; Pinto, Samantha, 72, 73–74, 96, 114, 116, 119, 121; Roach, Shoniqua, 101; Spillers, Hortense, 73, 116–17, 151. *See also* Quashie, Kevin
Black legal participation: advocacy, 13, 15–26; Black litigants, 22–23, 70; *Black Litigants in the Antebellum South* (Welch), 22, 23, 24, 70; *Consent in the Presence of Force* (Owens), 74; erasure of, 109; improvisational elements, 23–24, 43; "Law as Redemption" (Penningroth), 23; legal knowledge, 12–13, 21, 41, 174–76; legal status in antebellum period, 46–47, 110; and moral authority, 34; and narrative, use of, 24, 27; as shield and refuge, 44; and survival, 46–47, 70; women's participation, 14, 22, 43, 74, 175. *See also* Black testimony; freedom suits

Black literary tradition: Afrofuturism, 38, 170–71, 176; diasporic discourses, 50–51; as disruptive of white genres, 10, 13, 34, 63, 75, 77, 112; jeremiad tradition, 48; short fiction, early works, 58; storytelling traditions, 170; witnessing in religious practice, 2–3. *See also* African American literary tradition

Black nationalism, 54–55
Black print culture, 7, 10, 24, 31–32, 55–56, 69, 76–77, 88, 164; Colored Conventions Movement, 24; *Douglass' Monthly* (abolitionist newspaper), 69; *Provincial Freeman* (newspaper), 69; David Walker (*Appeal*), 5, 28, 33, 41, 47–57, 120, 160, 164, 165. See also *The Colored American* (newspaper); *Freedom's Journal* (newspaper)
Black's Law Dictionary, 46
Blackstone, William, 44–46
Black Studies curricula, 7
Black testimony, 2–15; as genre, 13; as legal object, 11; limitations of, in white-controlled zones, 11–12, 21–22; as opposition to negative stereotypes, 6; against whites in court, 10
Blake, or the Huts of America (Delany), 61, 171
Bleak House (Dickens), 146
The Bondwoman's Narrative (Crafts), 20, 37, 52, 124, 195n64, 195n75; and abolitionism, 145–46; critical fabulation, 159–61; encryption in, 143–52; intertextuality with legal records, 136, 137; Jane Johnson's authorship and authentication, 154–55; law as framing device, 166; legal language, 161–62, 165
Book of Daniel (Old Testament), 132–33
Boston, Uria, 19

Brodber, Erna, 175
Brooks, Peter, 85
Brown, Christopher Michael, 61
Brown, William Wells, 149
Browne, Simone, 174–75
Bushnell, Simeon, 88
Butler, Octavia, 168

Caldwell, Elias B., 52–53
Capers, Bennett, 171
Capitol, US, burning of, 37, 52, 95, 160, 168
Carbado, Devon, 16, 172
Carby, Hazel, 7
Caribbean region: "alternative selves" (Fuentes), 128. *See also* Fuentes, Marisa; archives of slavery, 14, 143
Carlos, John, 54–55
Case of Passmore Williamson, 156
Chakkalakal, Tess, 145
Child, Lydia Maria, 80
Christian traditions: confession, spiritual context of, 82–83; conversion narratives, 68; Eucharist, 66; and prayer, 55; and prophetic discourse, 55–56
citation: encrypted citation, 142–43; encryption in *The Bondwoman's Narrative*, 143–52; and precedent, 141. *See also* precedent
citizen-outlaw framework, 93, 95, 103
citizenship, 24; good citizenship and Fugitive Slave Act, 89; and natural law, 93; and sovereignty, 75; Spires on, 49–50. *See also* personhood
Clay, Henry, 52
Clotel (Brown), 149
Cobb, Jeremiah, 86–87
colonization, 52–53; colonial discourse, 54; colonial violence, 172–73, 174; legal proceedings in colonial period, 44, 45
The Colored American (newspaper), 19; "Appeal to the Friends of Liberty," 39–40; prophetic discourse, 56
Colored Conventions Movement, 24
Combahee River Collective, 175

Commentaries on the Laws of England (Blackstone), 44–46, 57
Compromise of 1850, 110
confession, 67–104; admissibility of in court, 69, 75–76; allocution statements, 74, 91; and Black worldmaking, 104; coerced or false, 69–70, 76–77; *The Confessions of Nat Turner* (Gray, ed.), 77–88; contrasted with admission, 81–82; criminal confessions, 68; and "critical fabulation," 77–78; forms of literary confession, 72–73; as genre, 169; guilt decoupled from disclosure, 84; *Incidents in the Life of a Slave Girl* (Jacobs), 96–104; Langston and Oberlin-Wellington rescue, 88–96; legal form and literary possibility, 71–72; as narrative, 75–76; out-of-court confession, 74–76, 88; as performance, 96; power of, 67–68; prison confession, 70; suspicion of, 68–69; "truth" of, 97
Confessions of Guilt (Thomas & Leo), 76
The Confessions of Nat Turner (Gray, ed.), 34, 77–88; confession vs. admission, 81–82; guilt decoupled from disclosure, 84; quiet vs. public confession, 84–85; spiritual frameworks, 82–83
The Confessions of Nat Turner (Styron), 77–78
Consent in the Presence of Force (Owens), 74
consent: Hartman's constructions of, 14, 73–74, 113–14, 154–55; and nonconsent, 114–15. *See also* sovereignty
contract law, 114; and sovereignty, 73
Cornish, Samuel, 2, 4–5, 167; Black testimony, calls for, 6, 12, 19, 23, 26; first column, *Freedom's Journal*, 28; on pleadings, 16–17, 30
counterfactual imaginations, 28, 64–65, 94–95, 119–22, 167–68
Cover, Robert, 27, 30, 59, 172
Craft, Ellen, 9, 149
Craft, William, 9, 149
Crafts, Hannah, 9, 20, 37, 136. See also *The Bondwoman's Narrative* (Crafts)

Crenshaw, Kimberlé, 12
Creole Testimonies (Aljoe), 148
critical fabulation, 20, 77, 148–49, 159
critical legal studies, 176
critical race theory, 172
cruelty, language of, 22
Cugoano, Ottobah, 6
Cult of True Womanhood, 99
"cultural vestibularity," 116–17
Cuyahoga County courthouse speech (Langston), 34, 72

Davis, Angela, 97
Davis, Charles, 6, 180n26
Dawn (Butler), 168
Dayan, Colin, 27, 30, 87, 187n72
Declaration of Independence, 92–93, 165, 168
de la Fuente, Alejandro, 175
Delaney, Lucy, 30
Delany, Martin, 61, 83, 171
DeLombard, Jeannine, 10, 21, 70–71, 79, 153
democracy, false mythology of, 3
Derrida, Jacques, 134
Dery, Mark, 170–71
de Stefano, Jason, 19–20
Dickens, Charles, 146
Dimock, Wai Chee, 21
Dispossessed Lives (Fuentes), 143, 189n129
dissemblance, 72, 96, 98
Dobbs v. Jackson Women's Health Organization, 138
Documenting the American South, 6
Dorsett, Shaunnagh, 108–9, 111, 115
Douglass, Frederick, 3, 6, 8; Constitutional interpretations, 19–20, 29–30; *The North Star* editorial, 29
Douglass' Monthly (abolitionist newspaper), 69
Dred Scott decision, 138–39, 141
Du Bois, W. E. B., 170

Edwards, Laura, 22, 23, 70, 109
emancipation, 62; Jane Johnson, 137; Oberlin-Wellington Rescue, 88; self-emancipated persons, 88–89, 90, 145, 152–53. *See also* fugitives; Jacobs, Harriet; Williams/Thornton/Wilkins persona
encoding vs. encryption, 37
encrypted citation, 142–43; encryption in *The Bondwoman's Narrative*, 143–52; in legal histories, 36–37
enslaved persons: erasure of, 130–31, 133–34; as fugitives, 89–90; heritability of, 5; surveillance of, 97–98, 157. *See also* emancipation
equality, false mythology of, 3
Equiano, Olaudah, 6
erasure: of Black legal records, 109, 126, 130–31; strikethrough as, 134, 140, 194n46; "under-erasure," 133–34
Ezekiel (Old Testament), 56, 57, 78, 164

fiction: boundary and nonfiction, 8–9; and legal interpretation, 20; science fiction, 173
Foreman, P. Gabrielle, 97, 100, 101, 102, 114
form, theory of, 14
forma pauperis status, 18
Foster, Frances Smith, 97
Fourteenth Amendment, 139, 179n14
Freedom as Marronage (Roberts), 60–61
freedom narratives: and authenticity, 9–10, 153–54; and Black pain, 3–4; and Black testimony, 137; critical treatment of, 9; documentary importance, 6–7; features of genre, 7–8; gothic influence on, 7–8; growth and influence, 5–7; "The History of the Carolina Twins" (McKoy), 146, 175; limitations of, 3–4, 145; self-authorship vs. white scribes, 158–60, 192n15; sentimental frames, 7–9; and slave narratives, terminology, 179n13; testimony as form, 2; white abolitionist mediation of, 3. *See also The Bondwoman's Narrative* (Crafts); *Incidents in the Life of a Slave Girl* (Jacobs), *Narrative of James Williams*

Freedom's Journal (newspaper), 1, 5–6, 12, 15, 19, 26, 28, 167; Blackstone, references to, 44; "Theresa, ____ a Haytien Tale" (S.), 33, 64–66; David Walker's *Appeal*, 47
freedom suits, 17–18, 22; Dred Scott decision, 138–39, 141; Lucy Delaney, 30
Fuentes, Marisa, 5, 14, 128, 143, 148, 189n129
fugitives from slavery, 60–61, 121; legal status, 126, 155–56; litigation surrounding, 152–53; Northern vs. Southern spaces, 118; "passing," 129; slave patrols, 109. *See also* emancipation
"fugitive science", 171–72
Fugitive Slave Act (1793), 153
Fugitive Slave Act (1850), 34, 72, 88, 89–90, 93–94, 108, 137, 153, 179n14; in *Incidents in the Life of a Slave Girl*, 112; and jurisdiction, 111
futurity: apocalyptic frameworks, 56–57; and Black storytelling, 170, 177; in Haiti, 63, 66; through retrospection, 31, 50, 140. *See also* Afrofuturism; retrospective futurism

gallows literature, 70–71, 79
Gardner, Eric, 9
Garner, Margaret, 195n73
Garnet, Henry Highland, 48
Gates, Henry Louis, Jr., 6, 143–44, 146, 180n26
gender roles. *See* women's roles
gender studies, 196n16
"geographic domination," 107, 109
geography. *See* space/geography
Glymph, Thavolia, 43, 109
Goddu, Teresa, 7, 80, 180n30
Goffe, Tao Leigh, 168–69, 170
gothic tropes and themes, 7–8, 55, 146, 180n30
Gray, Thomas Ruffin, 77, 78–81, 87–88, 164, 187n63
Great Dismal Swamp, 121. *See also* marronage
Gregson v. Gilbert, 31

Gresh, Joel, 69
Gross, Ariela, 175

Haitian Revolution, 28, 33, 36, 58, 63, 65–66, 169
Harney, Stefano, 93
Harris, Cheryl, 16, 172
Hartman, Saidiya V., 3, 12, 14, 62, 73–74, 109, 113–14, 143, 154–55; critical fabulation, 20, 77, 148–49, 159
Hartog, Hendrik, 22, 109
Hecimovich, Gregg, 136, 144
"Hello, Moto" (Okorafor), 175
Hine, Darlene Clark, 96, 98
history: and Afrofuturism, 171–72; alternative vs. retelling, 168
The History of Mary Prince (Prince), 80
The History of the Carolina Twins (McKoy), 146, 175
Hoeflich, M. H., 25, 109
Holloway, Karla, 3, 32, 38, 114, 136
Hurricane Katrina, 172
Hyde, Carrie, 24

Impossible Witnesses (McBride), 11
incarceration, mass, 18–19
Incidents in the Life of a Slave Girl (Jacobs), 5, 34, 35, 72, 80, 96–104, 155; confession, strategic use of, 100–101; counterfactual imaginations, 119–22; Fugitive Slave Act (1850), 112; grandmother and absolution, 101–2; jurisdictional thinking, 117–19; Linda Brent narrator/character, 112, 189n118; links to Turner's confession, 96–98; love, disappointed, 98–99; and sovereignty, 74
insurrection, white fear of, 97–98, 132
interiority, 133, 148
International Shoe Company v. Washington, 110
intersectionality, 21, 26, 78, 150, 161, 174
intertextuality, 9, 136, 146. *See also* citation
In the Shadow of the Gallows (DeLombard), 70

Jacobs, Harriet, 5, 8, 28–29, 34–36, 96–104; and authenticity, 9; and confession, 71, 72, 74, 75, 96–104; and jurisdiction, 105, 111–15, 117–22, 132; loophole of retreat, 61, 112–13, 115–17; on protection of law, 44; strategic disclosure, 142; trans readings of, 9

Jacobs, John S., 8

Jefferson, Thomas, 47, 48

Johnson, Jane, 20, 37, 52, 148–49, 150–51; legal documents, 142–43, 152–58; testimonial records, 136–37

Jones, Martha, 24

judicial review: appeal as, 42–43; colonial vs. modern, 44; as disassembly, 53, 58–59; pleas for, 53

Judiciary Act (1789), 16–17

jurisdiction, 105–35; *Incidents in the Life of a Slave Girl* (Jacobs), 112–22; jurisdictional misdirection, 117–19; and "loopholes of retreat," 115–17; in *The Matrix* (film), 105–7; in *Narrative of James Williams* (Williams), 122–34; personal, 110–11; plantation jurisdiction, 107–8; temporal orientations, 169; territorial, 108–9; worldmaking and imagined alternatives, 119–22

Justice Accused (Cover), 59

Kane, John, 152, 154, 155–56

Kennington, Kelly, 22

Kimber, Emmor, 125

kinship and marriage, 104, 113, 169

Kwartang, Appiah, 170

Lamming, George, 73

Langston, Charles Henry, 34, 72, 75, 88–96, 164; post-conviction statement, 90–91

language; of apocalypse, 55–56; meaning-making of legal language, 25, 30; use of pronouns, 51; vocative direct address, 51. *See also* worldbuilding/worldmaking

law: and autobiography, 10–11; common law tradition, 138–42; Constitutionality, 94; contract law, 114; "court week" proceedings, 109; Eurocentric vs. African, 174; Euro-modern law, 172–73; framing of narratives, 16; and freedom, 174, 175; law schools vs. apprenticeship, 25, 40; legal precedent and authority, 136–38; legal spaces as white spaces, 12; local customs, 109; natural law, 92, 93; in Old South, 23; pleadings, 15–17, 91; positive law, 34, 73, 83, 92; and protection of fugitive slaves, 118–19; "shadow of law," 96; stare decisis, 139; temporal capacities, 169–70, 172; textual nature of legal culture, 25; tort law, 45; US judicial system, 17; and victims, 45; and worldmaking, 172–73, 174, 177

legal forms, 13–15; appeal, 32, 33; citation to precedent, 32, 36–37; confession, 32, 33–35; jurisdiction, 32, 35–36

Leo, Richard, 76

Levine, Caroline, 14

The Liberator, 47; apocalyptic language, 56–57

The Life and Times of Hannah Crafts (Hecimovich), 136

Lincoln, Abraham, 44

literacy: anti-literacy laws, 5, 21, 46, 120

Locke, John, 73

"loophole of retreat," 112–13, 115–17

Lorde, Audre, 174

Louisiana (Brodber), 175

L'Ouverture, Toussaint, 64–65, 168

Lubet, Steven, 91

lynching, 69

Mann, Justin, 28, 55, 56, 168–69, 170, 174–75

Māori nation, New Zealand, 177

marriage, 21, 100, 113

marronage, 60–61, 121, 129, 175

Marshall, Bridget, 144

The Matrix (film), 105–7

M'Baye, Babacar, 52

McBride, Dwight, 11–12

McBride, William, 127

McDowell, Deborah, 7, 9

McKittrick, Katherine, 9, 107–8, 109, 116
McKoy twins (Millie-Christine), 146, 175
McMillan, Uri, 14, 112, 122, 124, 128
McVeigh, Shaun, 108–9, 111, 115
Meshach (Old Testament character), 132–33
Miranda v. Arizona, 75
Mitchell, Koritha, 24
Moody, Joycelyn, 8, 68, 70
Morrison, Toni, 175
Moten, Fred, 93
"The Mulatto" (Séjour), 33, 41, 58–64, 171

Narrative of Facts in the Case of Passmore Williamson, 156, 194n54, 195n61
Narrative of James Williams, an American Slave (Williams), 35, 105, 111, 122–35; novel, reframed as, 133–34; questioning and critiques, 125–26, 131–32
Narrative of the Life of Frederick Douglass (Douglass), 6, 147, 192n15, 193n22
Nash, Jennifer, 3–4, 26, 174, 177
The National Era (abolitionist newspaper), 69
National Intelligencer (Washington, DC newspaper), 52
New Zealand, 177
nonfiction: and fiction, 8–9, 20, 96, 142, 170; freedom narratives as, 9–10
North Carolina v. Mann, 108
The North Star (abolitionist newspaper), 29, 69–70
Notes on the State of Virginia (Jefferson), 48
Nyong'o, Tavia, 10, 48, 51

Oberlin, Ohio, 88
Oberlin-Wellington Rescue, 88
Okorafor, Nnedi, 175, 196n12
Olympics (1968 Mexico City), 54–55
opportunism, 80–81
"outlaw": citizen-outlaw framework, 88, 93, 95–96, 103, 164; figure of, 75, 95. *See also* fugitives

Owens, Emily, 14, 22, 41, 43, 70, 74, 109, 175
Oxford English Dictionary, 46

Pacquet, Sandra, 146
Pan-Africanism, 55
Parker, James, 78
partus sequitur ventrem, 5
"passing" for fugitives from slavery, 129, 150
Pelletier, Kevin, 55–56
Penningroth, Dylan, 22, 23–24, 41, 109
Pennoyer v. Neff, 110
Perry, Imani, 21, 73–74, 108, 116–17
personae, creation of, 111–12, 123, 124–28, 130, 134. *See also* authorial identities
personhood: language of, 3, 113; legal, 18, 20, 27, 91–92, 151, 161; production of, 14, 126, 128–29, 177. *See also* citizenship
Peterson, Carla L., 194n46
Philip, M. NourbeSe, 30–31, 66
Pinto, Samantha, 72, 73–74, 96, 114, 116, 119, 121
plantation abuse, 68
pleadings, 15–16, 18, 49; *Appeal to the Coloured Citizens of the World* (Walker), 53–55; and confession, 75; Jacobs's, 99, 101; Langston's, 91; rules of, 12, 23
Polley, Diana, 7
Porter, Angi, 174, 176
poverty, 18
Powell, Thomas Watkins, 42–43
The Practice of Citizenship (Spires), 24
prayer, 55
precedent, 136–66; in *The Bondwoman's Narrative* (Crafts), 143–52; and citation, 141; common law traditions, 138–42; and encrypted citation, 142–43; Jane Johnson's testimony, 153–66; and judicial stability, 139–40; judicial teleology, 140; legal precedent and authority, 136–38; as narrative, 136; temporal orientations, 169–70
Price, John, 88, 92, 93–94
Prigg v. Pennsylvania, 152–53
Prince, Mary, 6, 146

Pringle, Thomas, 80
prison confession, 68, 70; gallows literature, 70–71, 79. See also *The Confessions of Nat Turner* (Gray, ed.)
privacy, 148; "loophole of retreat," 115–17. See also quiet
prophetic discourse, 55–56, 82
pro se representation, 1–2, 21, 30, 50, 181n63; Douglass and, 20; *forma pauperis* status, 18; and gap in legal resources, 19; rights to, 16–17; Turner and, 81–82
Provincial Freeman (newspaper), 69
pseudonymous identities. See authorial identities
"publicness," 4–5. See also Quashie, Kevin

Quarles, Ralph, 93
Quashie, Kevin, 54–55, 73, 78, 84–85, 96, 101, 103, 148, 177; "publicness," 4–5
The Queen of America Goes to Washington City (Berlant), 120
quiet, 78, 84–85, 101; "publicness" contrasted with, 4–5; sovereignty of, 54–55. See also privacy

racism: anti-Black legal theories, 110; anti-Black oppression and confession, 67–68; stereotypes and criminality, 70; systemic, 93
Reconstructing Womanhood (Carby), 7
Reichman, Ravit, 12
retrospective frameworks, 2, 50–51, 63, 71, 81, 88, 140, 167
retrospective futurism, 2, 66, 71, 88, 137, 140, 167
revolution: American vs. Black, 93
Revue des Colonies (French abolitionist journal), 58, 61
rights: as framework, 39–40, 72–73, 176–77; to legal appeal, 44; property rights of enslavers, 17, 89, 108, 153; in public sphere, 24, 114–15. See also citizenship
Roach, Shoniqua, 101
Roane, J. T., 83
Roberts, Neil, 60–61, 121, 129, 175

Roe v. Wade, 138
Ross, Kelly, 171
Ross, Rosetta, 3
Running a Thousand Miles for Freedom (Craft), 149
Rusert, Britt, 171–72
Russwurm, John, 2, 4–5, 167; and Black testimony, 6, 19, 23, 26; first column *Freedom's Journal*, 12, 28; on pleadings, 16–17, 30

Saint-Domingue, Haiti, 58, 64. See also Haitian Revolution
Samuels, Shirley, 8
Sandler, Matt, 55
sankofa bird, 170
Santamarina, Xiomara, 124, 131, 133
Scenes of Subjection (Hartman), 113–14
science fiction, 173
Scott v. Sandford (Dred Scott decision), 138–39, 141, 179n14
"scriptive" texts, 51–52
Séjour, Victor, 8, 28, 33, 41, 169; "The Mulatto," 58–64
Self-Discovery and Authority in Afro-American Narrative (Smith), 7
sentimentalism, 8; in appeal genre, 39
sexual abuse and trauma, 34–35, 43, 107; *Incidents in the Life of a Slave Girl* (Jacobs), 34–35, 98–99, 113, 115; "The Mulatto" (Séjour), 33, 41, 58–64, 171
sexual violence, 113, 188n111; "The Mulatto" (Séjour), 58–64
Shadd Cary, Mary Ann, 37, 141–42
"shadow of law," 75, 96, 113–14, 115, 117
Shadrach (Old Testament character), 132–33
Sharpe, Christina, 175
Simard, Justin, 14
Slatter v. Holton, 126–27, 129, 130
slave narratives. See freedom narratives
slavery: autobiographical knowledge, theft of, 157; bureaucracy of, 5; Caribbean archives, 14; as chattel, 31, 66, 163–64; Compromise of 1850, 110; misinforma-

tion concerning, 6; and nation-state, 164–65; plantation abuse, 68; plantation jurisdiction, 107–8; slave codes, 21–22; slave patrols, 109; "slavery on trial," 10–11; slave states vs. free states, 109–10; surveillance of enslaved people, 97, 157–58. *See also* Fugitive Slave Act (1850)

The Slave's Narrative (Davis & Gates), 180n26

Smith, Caleb, 79

Smith, Tommie, 54–55

Smith, Valerie, 7

Smith, Venture, 6

Snorton, C. Riley, 9

Sojourner Truth, 194n46

Southampton Rebellion (1831), 34, 72, 75, 78, 109. *See also* Turner, Nat

sovereignty: Black, 33–34, 35, 36, 66; Black women's, 74, 114–15, 119; confession as expression of, 72–73; countersovereignty, 86; as legal form, 73; overview, 36; personal, 75; placebound, 120; of quiet, 54; sexual, 34–35, 75, 101, 111; shifting constructions of, 74; spiritual, 34, 68, 74–75, 81, 82–83, 87–88, 104, 142; and "territory," 108–9, 116, 120

The Sovereignty of Quiet (Quashie), 73

The Sovereignty of the Imagination (Lamming), 73

space and geography: confessional space, 83, 87–88; of enslavement, 35, 105, 108; of freedom, 60–61, 62, 66, 72, 83, 95, 96, 121, 171, 175; and "loophole of retreat," 115–17; Katherine McKittrick, 9, 107–8, 109, 116; North-South, 118, 190n27; and political authority, 107; testimony in public space, 2, 11; white legal spaces, 12, 34

speculative fiction, 28, 142, 168, 170–72

Spillers, Hortense, 73, 116–17, 151

Spires, Derrick, 24, 43, 48, 49–50

spiritual sovereignty, 34, 68, 74–75, 81, 82–83, 87–88, 104, 142

Spivak, Gayatri, 73, 134

stare decisis, 139

Statesman & Patriot, 47

stereotypes, anti-Black, 6, 10

Stern, Simon, 141

Stewart, Maria, 48, 56

Still, William, 152, 157, 158

Stowe, Harriet Beecher, 147

Styron, William, 77–78

"subjunctive rhetoric," 119. *See also* counterfactual imaginations

"sublime appeal," 48

Sulzener, Brittany, 56

Sundquist, Eric, 79, 83

Swank, Drew, 17

Tappan, Lewis, 39, 125

technoculture, 170–71

"territory," 108–9

testimonios, 9

testimony: and abolitionism, 5; Black feminist, 4; calls for, 2; cruelty, language of, 22; as documentation, 2; in emancipation proceedings, 137; Jane Johnson in *The Bondwoman's Narrative*, 155; political urgency of, 4–5; religious significance of, 2–3

"Theresa, _____ a Haytien Tale" (S.), 42, 64–66, 168, 169, 171

Thomas, George, 76

time and temporality: and appeal, 63, 65–66, 67; and confession, 103; fluidity of law, 13, 32, 33, 50, 58; and precedent, 137, 140; worldmaking, 27–28, 67, 168–70

Tomlins, Christopher, 78, 79, 81, 82, 86

torture and extorted confession, 69–70

To Tell a Free Story (Andrews), 7

The Transatlantic Gothic Novel and the Law (Marshall), 144

Trent, Hank, 122–23, 124, 126

Trezvant, James, 78

Turner, Nat, 8, 77–88; execution of, 86–87; insurrectionary revelation, 142; and prophetic discourse, 56; and sovereignty, 75. *See also* *The Confessions of Nat Turner* (Gray, ed.)

Uncle Tom's Cabin (Stowe), 147

"under-erasure," 133–34. *See also* erasure

"unexpected places" (Gardner), 9
United States: Capitol, burning of, 37, 52, 95, 160, 168; Constitution, 19–20, 29–30; equity, fictions of, 57; false mythologies, 3; freedom suits, 17–18; legal system, 25, 45; myth of civilized status, 164–65; Supreme Court, 52; white racialization of US identity, 55

vigilantism, 61
violence: Black violence and criminal liability, 54; plantation abuse, 68; slavery, and legal mechanisms, 22–23; and vengeance, 59; against women, 113

Walker, David, 5, 28, 33, 41, 47–57, 120, 160, 164, 165
Warren, Calvin, 134
wealth gap, 18–19
Welch, Kimberly, 22, 23–24, 27, 41, 70, 109
Wheatley, Phillis, 97
Wheeler, John Hill, 144, 151–52, 154–56, 157–58, 161
Wheeler, Mrs., 150–51, 155, 159–60, 161–62
white Christianity, 83, 132
white nationalism, 55, 93
white racial innocence, 51–52
white saviorism, 80–81
white supremacy, 48, 54, 130, 175, 177
white women readers, 99–100

Whittier, John Greenleaf, 125
Wilkins, Shadrach, 123–24
Williams, James, 9, 35–36. *See also* Williams/Thornton/Wilkins persona
Williams, Patricia, 25, 30–31, 66, 176–77
"Williams, James," 122–35
Williamson, Passmore, 152–53, 156, 194n44, 194n54
Williams/Thornton/Wilkins persona, 111–12, 122–35
Willson, Judge, 91–92
Windell, Maria, 8
witnessing. *See* testimony
Womack, Ytasha, 171
women's roles: abolitionist expectations of Black women, 97; Caribbean women fugitivity, 128; Cult of True Womanhood, 99; sentimentalism, 8; sexual abuse, 43–44; sexual purity, 99–100; and sovereignty, 114–15; and white paternity, 102–4; white women readers, 99–100
Word Magic (meaning-making language), 25, 30–31, 66
worldbuilding and worldmaking: Black, 55, 57, 72, 95, 100, 102, 104, 142–43, 177; legal language, 25, 26–32, 49, 66, 70, 172; textual and language, 30, 94, 119

Yellin, Jean Fagan, 96

Zong! (Philip), 31, 66

www.ingramcontent.com/pod-product-compliance
Lightning Source LLC
Chambersburg PA
CBHW020022270225
22642CB00002B/7